To Sandra

Lets Learn
together how
to make quality
real

Ed Baker

# UNIONS, MANAGEMENT, AND QUALITY

## Opportunities for Innovation and Excellence

# UNIONS, MANAGEMENT, AND QUALITY
## Opportunities for Innovation and Excellence

*Edited by*
*Edward Cohen-Rosenthal*
*with assistance from Frank J. Wayno, Jr.*

*Co-published with the Association for Quality and Participation*

**IRWIN**
Professional Publishing

Chicago • Bogotá • Boston • Buenos Aires • Caracas
London • Madrid • Mexico City • Sydney • Toronto

Senior sponsoring editor: Cynthia A. Zigmund
Project editor: Susan Trentacosti
Production manager: Laurie Kersch
Designer: Mercedes Santos
Art manager: Kim Meriwether
Compositor: E.T. Lowe Publishing Co.
Typeface: 11/13 Times Roman
Printer: Book Press, Inc.

**Library of Congress Cataloging-in-Publication Data**

Unions, management, and quality : opportunities for innovation and
 excellence / Edward Cohen-Rosenthal, editor.
    p.  cm.
    "Co-published with the Association for Quality and Participation."
    Includes index.
    ISBN 0-7863-0157-0
    1. Industrial relations—United States—Case studies. 2. Quality
control—United States—Case studies. 3. Trade-unions—United
States—Case studies. 4. Technological innovations—Economic
aspects—United States—Case studies. 5. Excellence—Case studies.
I. Cohen-Rosenthal, Edward. II. Association for Quality and
Participation.
HD8072.5.U52   1995
331'.0973—dc20                       94–27614

*Printed in the United States of America*
1  2  3  4  5  6  7  8  9  0  BP  1  0  9  8  7  6  5  4

# Preface

*Unions, Management, and Quality* explores for the first time the extraordinary positive possibilities of joint action on quality improvement. In large measure, this book is designed for managers in unionized workplaces who want insight on how to proceed with joint quality efforts. Two groups of managers will be interested. The largest group will probably be managers perplexed about how to get the union on board in quality efforts. Well-intentioned efforts don't seem to go fast enough, far enough, or have the breadth of support that it seems quality efforts should have. This book can provide insight into how other companies have adjusted their programs to get enthusiastic union support. Some managers reading this will be staring at the prospects of starting a quality program and wondering ahead of time how to engage the union in this activity. They need not make the initial mistake of going it alone from which the first group is recovering. They can find the benefits of joint commitment and action.

Trade unionists will also find this volume of great interest. Union leaders speak out on what it has meant to them—both the positive results but also the great difficulties they needed to overcome. It speaks from the union voice in most places of the book. This is deliberate. There is little need for another book where managers talk to managers about quality— what managers need is a clear articulation of the union voice, so that they can judge for themselves clearly what should be done—not simply what other managers wish were the case. And unionists insecure in their role in quality need a confirmation that their role can be front and center; that quality can be rooted in union values; and that the union can emerge as a strengthened partner.

We do not take a view in this book that quality is an unabashed wonder. Quality has its wonderful traits, but it also has its limitations and misapplications as well. A frank and honest review of the field, this book neither fears quality initiatives as some in the extreme wings of labor have done, nor fauns over it like many sycophantic business publications. Broad thinking, expansive involvement, determined implementation and honest measurement and feedback take different faces in different organizations. There is no magic wand or one miraculous approach that will make quality work.

Writing this book was an exercise in collaboration. Some of the best cases and thinkers about this subject were selected and invited to participate. In September of 1993, almost all of the contributors to this book attended a session at Cornell University where the initial drafts and ideas were discussed. It provided a window into the possibilities of union involvement in quality action that had not been discussed before. Testimony to quality programs had from time to time included recognition of union counterparts. Product quality had been in the agenda of numerous labor-management conferences. But this was the first time that the joint union-management approach to quality had been the sole focus of discussion.

There was much in common but also many voices were heard about what should be done and how it should be accomplished. The first questions at the writing conference were who are our customers for this book, and what do they need to know? The unanimous decision was that readers need to hear accurately the voices of those who have struggled with these issues. This will imply greater diversity in how the story is told as well as accepting differences in what was done. Good points and successes need to be told, but so do the concerns, problems, and detours. Your organization may just be setting out on a quality path and these lessons can help you design a process with greater likelihood of success. Or you may have begun unilaterally like most companies in America and be looking for new ways to broaden the process to include union involvement. The cases in this book provide a set of benchmarks for those seeking to engage in quality improvement. They did many things well but also learned from their stumbles along the way.

I want to address up-front the questions of the tone and tenor of this book. It unabashedly presents a view of the affirmative possibilities of joint quality efforts, not because there aren't examples of failed programs in unionized organizations—indeed there are many—but because our interest is in promoting the best quality programs there can be. We, the contributors to this book, focus more on living benchmarks than cadavers. The American labor movement had also recently stepped up its support for new work systems that are based on true partnership. In February of 1994, the AFL-CIO Executive Council called for a new workplace that improves working lives, productivity and quality through new working arrangements. Now more than ever, labor and management have come to realize the importance of quality as a means to insure competitiveness and employment security in a global marketplace. We hope that this book can contribute to the rethinking of American labor-management relations and catalyze new action that will be beneficial not only for unions and employers but also the customers of their organizations.

We recognize that there are many managers and some workers who have deeply felt philosophical differences with unionization. They assert with conviction that employee empowerment, especially of individuals, is important and the union acts as a limiting and/or divisive factor. Rather than seeing the union as leader of change, it is viewed as a guardian of the past and a protector of shirkers. While this may be true some of the time, assuming this ahead of time practically guarantees it all of the time. Our effort is to find a more positive prescription, where the union is invited or challenged—indeed where the union also challenges management—to higher-quality performance. Our analysis is simple: hostile unions can undermine even sincere quality efforts and partnered unions can enhance even the best quality efforts.

But the purpose in putting together this book is not to argue the political argument of whether unions are good or bad. While there can be many good nonunion companies and many poor union companies, I believe, on the whole, union status can be a positive contributor to quality. Assuredly, a union is not necessarily a barrier to high quality. But to stop there is a great mistake. Excellent industrial relations can be one factor that helps make quality efforts spread faster and take stronger root in an organization. When the union is truly a partner, the magnitude of commitment, ideas, and results is expanded.

Section I provides an overview of quality and unions. The first chapter lays out a general framework for thinking about quality and unions and sets out principles for successful joint efforts. Chapter Two takes a look at the history of unions and quality. Ordinarily, history is one of the chapters skipped over. But there is a fascinating set of themes illustrated. It is also true that one of the blind spots of current quality efforts is understanding its historical context. Frank Wayno in Chapter Three on quality workplaces discusses the philosophical roots of total quality; paints a picture of what a TQ workplace looks like; and presents some implementation guidelines. The next chapter on quality unions by Art Shostak, author of *Robust Unionism,* and I take an unprecedented look at how unions should become quality organizations as part of being quality partners.

Section II offers six cases of joint quality action. Each of these is written with the union representative in the setting taking the lead in writing the case. These are very diverse. Half the cases are jointly written with the management counterparts. Some tell it as a story, some as a personal witness to what happened, some as a journalistic review, some as an in-depth case study. Two exemplary manufacturing cases are represented by an extensive review of the United Automobile Workers and General Motors in their jointly led Quality Network and another, an insightful look into the partnership process at Corning, Incorporated with the American Flint Glass Workers Union. Two communications examples are provided. The Communications Workers of America and U S WEST have broken new ground especially in terms of developing nonlinear systems redesign in service operations and the union has applied many quality and participation principles to revitalizing the union. The Graphic Arts Communications International Union is the only North American union with a formal resolution endorsing total quality management. In the public sector, Robert Tobias, president of the National Treasury Employees Union provides an insightful review of the context and operation of one of the most successful quality initiatives in the public sector—their joint effort to create a total quality organization with the Internal Revenue Service. The National Council of Field Labor Locals affiliated with the American Federation of Government Employees describes joint employee involvement and quality improvement activities that use minimal bureaucracy and maximum labor-management leadership. Contributors worked from a common outline. Each contribution provides a background on their situation, a description of their joint quality activities with a focus on the union role and an analysis of the effect of quality on the union and labor relations. Even with this common skeleton there is much variation in how it is fleshed out.

Section III provides a variety of perspectives on quality and unions. Cynthia Burton of ECR Associates applies the principles of quality to the labor relations function—a critical niche in the organization usually unconsidered as part of quality alignment. Sally Klingel of Cornell University wrestles with the dilemmas and challenges affecting unions. With a wry look at the issues, she honestly discusses the concerns that unions have and how they might address them. These are based on a series of seminars she has conducted with local labor leadership on high-performance work systems. Ernest Savoie, director of employee development for the Ford Motor Company and past president of the Industrial Relations Research Association, understands how to work with unions and how to build an envied quality system. He provides a witty and wise managerial view of quality and unions that helps inform managers on what to expect and what to do. The diversity of views in this book means that the opinions expressed in each of the chapters reflect the views of the authors themselves and may not be precisely those of other contributors or the editor.

I want to thank my colleagues at Programs for Employment and Workplace Systems (PEWS) at Cornell University in Ithaca, New York, for their support of this activity and participation in the discussions that took place. Special appreciation is due to Frank Wayno who took time out of a pressing set of demands to help during the initial editing of the book and provided many clarifying suggestions to the authors. I also want to express my appreciation to Ellen, Janna, Mollie, and Jacob for too many nights and holidays huddled with manuscripts and editing pencils. Todd Cain, a graduate student at the School of Industrial and Labor Relations, was very helpful in doggedly researching the history session, helping with the arrangements for the writing conference and working with the manuscript. The input of Donovan King of the American Federation of State County and Municipal Employees (AFSCME), Melena Barkman of the United Steel Workers of America, and Carl Proper of the International Ladies Garment Workers Union was also very valuable. They contributed to the discussion at the writing conference and while their cases do not appear in this volume, the spirit of the activities in those unions is represented.

The editors of the quality series for Irwin Professional Publishing deserve great credit for their determined interest in unions and quality. This was despite delay in getting manuscripts and the nettlesome difficulties in working with so many contributors. In particular Jean Geracie stayed on top of the preparation of this book from the beginning. The Association for Quality and Participation, which is cosponsoring this book, has also been a principled and principal supporter of joint union-management quality efforts. But it was the contributors who gave this book life. They have demonstrated that joint quality action is worth pursuing and—beyond being merely possible—is desirable. They have shown that new ideas and new commitment can come when labor and management work together in the quality way.

**Edward Cohen-Rosenthal**

# A Note on the Authors

***Jim Armshaw*** is a career manager, internal consultant, trainer, and member of the U.S. Department of Labor (DOL) Training Academy and Reinvention Office. He was the department's coordinator for employee participation and for Employee Involvement and Quality Improvement (EIQI). Under Jim's guidance, in cooperation with AFGE Local 12, the headquarters QWL effort was expanded to include TQM. Jim also served as the lead management official in the design and implementation of EIQI and its union-management pair network. Jim codeveloped the Serving Our Customer (SOC) exercise. For three years, Jim was a member of the National Mediation Board staff, and spent 10 years in airline labor-management relations. He holds a bachelor's degree in economics from the State University of New York and a master's degree in labor studies from the University of Massachusetts.

***Lawrence Bankowski*** has served as national president since 1989 of the American Flint Glass Workers Union, based in Toledo, Ohio. His career with the AFGWU began as a mold maker for the Ohio Permanent Mold Company in Toledo where he served in various union capacities in Local Union 65. He was elected a member of the National Executive Board in 1964 and subsequently was elected national representative in 1973. Larry was elected national assistant secretary in 1975.

He is one of the principals of the Labor Industry Coalition on International Trade (LICIT). He is on the Board of Trustees of the Nickel Solution, a joint labor-management venture to promote the sale of glass containers. Larry is also a member of the Labor Advisory Committee for Trade Negotiations and Trade Policy, U.S. Department of Labor, and the Advisory Board of the Northwest Ohio Center for Labor-Management Cooperation.

***Kevin Boyle*** is an organizational development consultant and member of the Communications Workers Local 7906. Kevin began his consulting career as facilitator for the Communications Workers of America (CWA) in joint Employee Involvement with U S WEST Communications. He began his work and union career as a lineman and shop steward in the union, serving later as local vice president, local president, Executive Board member, and in 1989 was elected to the union's bargaining committee with U S WEST Communications.

As a consultant, he uses a systematic approach to developing high performing work organizations and effective union locals. Specializing in a labor-management approach to whole systems change, he now works with a variety of other unions and organizations committed to transforming their organizations.

*Cynthia Burton* is president of ECR Associates in Foster, Virginia, specializing in the development of union-management cooperation in a wide range of industries. She is a consultant to private and public organizations, unions, government agencies, and nonprofit organizations, with which she works to improve their organizational effectiveness. Before joining ECR Associates in 1980, she was program associate at the Maryland Center for Productivity and Quality of Working Life, and coordinator of Strongforce, Inc., a Washington, D.C., economic development organization. She began her career in management at a major international company. In addition to publications in union-management cooperation, Cynthia is coauthor of a book on women and economic development and a workbook on equal education for women. Cynthia holds a bachelor's degree from Western Michigan University.

*Edward Cohen-Rosenthal*'s career has been marked by a commitment to building innovative union-management partnerships. He is currently on the faculty of the Cornell University School of Industrial and Labor Relations as a senior extension associate in Programs for Employment and Workplace Systems (PEWS), director of the Work and Environment Initiative, and labor director of the Institute for Collective Bargaining.

He has consulted extensively to unions, companies, and government agencies around the world on union-management relations and participatory systems. His international experience spans the globe including Asia, Australia, Eastern and Western Europe, Scandinavia, Central America, and the Caribbean.

Previously, Ed was assistant to the president of the International Union of Bricklayers and Allied Craftsmen (AFL-CIO) and associate director of the American Center for Quality of Work Life. He was a faculty member at the Rutgers Labor Education Center and coordinated the Trade Union Seminar on Alternative Working Patterns in Europe. In 1979, Ed founded ECR Associates, a consulting firm specializing in participation in unionized workplaces.

He is coauthor with Cynthia Burton of *Mutual Gains: A Guide to Union-Management Cooperation,* second edition (ILR Press, 1993), and numerous other articles on union-management cooperation and workplace learning. He holds a master's degree in education from the Harvard Graduate School of Education and a bachelor's degree from Rutgers College.

*Herald Grandstaff* has served as managing editor of the Graphic Communications International Union's newspaper the *GraphiCommunicator* and GCIU information department director since July 1988. He has worked in newspaper journalism since 1966 and in labor journalism since 1979, serving as a reporter for the *United Mine Workers Journal* and the GCIU and providing editorial services for the Plasterers and Cement Masons, the Iron Workers, and the Operating Engineers International unions. He graduated from the College of the Dayton Art Institute and attended Wittenburg and Ohio Universities. In 1964 and 1965, Herald worked at a nonunion factory as a chipper, hand grinder, and a finisher of cast iron piano plates.

*Hank Jonas* is a senior organization consultant with Corning Incorporated, headquartered in Corning, New York. He is responsible for organization development activities in conjunction with managing cultural change within Corning, as well as for managing employee attitude surveys within the company. Prior to joining Corning, Hank was an independent consultant specializing in organization development and employee involvement strategies in a variety of Fortune 100 companies. From 1987 through 1989, Hank was a faculty member in the organizational behavior department at Case Western Reserve University in Cleveland, Ohio, where he received his Ph.D. in 1987.

*Susan C. Pisha* has worked in Communications Workers of America District 7 since 1976, serving most recently as district vice president. Sue also worked as an operator for Pacific Northwestern Bell for 14 years. She has been very active within the Oregon State AFL-CIO, in many community activities, and in political campaigns. Sue served one term in the Oregon House of Representatives.

**Ernest J. Savoie** is the director of the Employee Development Office, Ford Motor Company. In this capacity, he is responsible for planning, designing, and installing a wide range of human resource development programs for Ford hourly and salaried employees, represented and non-represented, worldwide. He is key architect of new programs and processes in the areas of joint labor-management processes, participative management, management education, employee involvement, employee education and training, employee assistance and employee communications. He is coeditor of two books and has been published widely in professional journals. He was president of the Industrial Relations Research Association in 1992. He was a member of the Advisory Panel for the Office of Technology Assessment's study of Worker Training, and of the Training Subcouncil of the Competitiveness Policy Council.

**Mario Scarselletta** is a doctoral student in the organizational behavior department at the New York State School of Industrial and Labor Relations. His research and teaching interests include the sociology of work and occupations; organizational ethnography; work practice and skill; systems of labor participation in management; organizational leadership and decision making; and organizations as political systems. His Ph.D. thesis is a participant-observation study of four high-performance/high-involvement factories within Corning, Incorporated.

**Arthur B. Shostak** is a professor of sociology at Drexel University, Philadelphia, Pennsylvania, and an adjunct professor in the Antioch College Degree Program at the AFL-CIO George Meany Center for Labor Studies, Silver Spring, Maryland. He earned his bachelor's degree from the Industrial and Labor Relations School of Cornell University in 1958 and his Ph.D. from Princeton University in 1961. His 15 books include *Robust Unionism* (1991), *The Air Controllers Controversy* (1980), *Blue-Collar Life* (1968), and *Blue-Collar World* (1964). He has served as an educator, speaker, and/or consultant for AFSCME, Air Line Pilots, Graphic Communications International Union, Electrical Workers, PATCO, Transportation Communications International Union, Steelworkers, and other unions.

**Robert M. Tobias** is the national president of the National Treasury Employees Union, which represents over 155,000 employees in more than 20 federal agencies and focuses on the interests of white-collar employees outside the Department of Defense. He was elected to this position in 1983 while serving as general counsel to the union. He taught at the George Washington National School of Law where he received a J.D. and has a bachelor's degree and MBA from the University of Michigan.

**Bruce A. Waltuck** recently completed a term as vice president of the National Council of Field Labor Locals (American Federation of Government Employees, AFL-CIO). He spent the four years as the Council's national coordinator for Employee Involvement and Quality Improvement (EIQI). With Jim Armshaw, Bruce coauthored the joint NCFLL-USDOL EIQI system. He has developed computer-based hypertext training and total quality policy guides, and is currently designing a comprehensive software system to track individual and team participation in TQM. In September 1993, Bruce was selected to deliver 22 lectures throughout Brazil on quality improvement and reinventing government. Bruce holds a bachelor's degree in economics from Syracuse.

**Frank J. Wayno, Jr.** is executive director of Cornell's Center for Manufacturing Enterprise (CME) and a senior associate of Programs for Employment and Workplace Systems (PEWS), an applied research and consulting group in the School of Industrial and Labor Relations. He is a specialist in organizational design, development, and change; competency-based management education; small group dynamics; and cross-cultural work behavior. He holds a Ph.D. in sociology from Princeton University and a bachelor's degree in engineering physics from Cornell.

Frank came to Cornell from industry, where he was a founding partner of Powers, Wayno and Associates, a consulting firm that specializes in improving the effectiveness of organizations through participative design strategies and the effectiveness of individual managers through competency-based behavioral education programs. In that capacity, he has worked with organizations of all sizes and from all sectors of the economy. Prior to that, he was a corporate officer at Merrill Lynch and Company charged with advising senior management on organizational restructuring, and has been a project engineer in the defense industry.

*Thomas L. Weekley,* was appointed in 1990 as assistant director in the UAW General Motors department and assistant director of the UAW/General Motors Quality Network. He joined UAW Local 122 as a tool and die apprentice in 1965 at the Chrysler stamping plant in Twinsburg, Ohio. In 1970, after completing his apprenticeship, he became a member of UAW Local 1714 after hiring in as a tool and die journeyman at the GM Fisher Body plant in Lordstown, Ohio. He served as a shop committeeman, district committeeman, and bargaining committee chairman of the Local and held various other positions, including that of chairman of GM Subcouncil 3.

Tom was appointed to the skilled trades department staff in 1978, as an international representative and has published articles and technical papers on new technological developments. In 1981, he was appointed coordinator of the UAW skilled trades department and in February 1985, he became assistant director.

An ordained minister with the Assemblies of God, Tom has attended Ohio State University and Youngstown State University, and has studied at numerous technical and labor schools. In 1981, he received a bachelor's degree from Baptist Christian College in Shreveport, Louisiana. In 1990, he received a master's degree from Central Michigan University in the science of administration. In 1993, he received his Ph.D. in management and labor relations. His dissertation is titled, "Total Quality from a Joint Management and Labor Perspective."

*Jay C. Wilber* has served as executive director of the UAW/General Motors Quality Network since 1990. He began his career with General Motors Corporation in 1965 as an hourly production employee with Chevrolet Motor Division's Flint Engine plant. From 1965 to 1968, he was enrolled in a tool maker apprentice program and successfully attained journeyman status. In 1972, he became a labor relation representative, and five years later was promoted to supervisor, labor relations.

In 1978, Jay was named senior staff assistant on the GM industrial relations staff at corporate headquarters in Detroit. While there, he served in several different capacities, including responsibilities for UAW-GM contract negotiations in 1979, 1982, 1984, 1990, and 1993. He has served as chairperson for several negotiating committees and has written extensive contract provisions.

In 1985, Jay was named director of labor relations for GM of Canada headquartered in Oshawa, Ontario, working with the car and truck assembly operations. He was a chief spokesman for General Motors during the creation of the first CAW-GM Master Agreement negotiated following the split between the UAW and their Canadian members. Jay assisted in negotiating the first GM Joint Venture Agreement with Suzuki, Inc. for GM of Canada creating CAMI, the most productive automotive assembly facility in North America. In 1993, he was named director of human resource management for the Automotive Components Group—Worldwide, headquartered in Troy, Michigan.

Jay holds a bachelor's degree in business administration from the University of Michigan. He also has completed the University of Toronto's advanced program in human resource management and is a certified personnel manager (CPM).

# Contents

# List of Figures

# I

# OVERVIEW OF QUALITY AND UNIONS

## Chapter One

# Thinking about Quality and Unions
## An Introduction

**Edward Cohen-Rosenthal**
*Programs for Employment and Workplace Systems*
*Cornell University*

In today's marketplace, quality is no longer a question mark. It is the price of entry into the market. You can't get to the starting line without excellent quality performance. And that demand-for-quality level continues to ratchet up. Today's customers want it all: price, service, and quality. You can't pick one niche anymore. Given the pressures on public service and taxpayer anger at value, quality is rapidly becoming a fundamental requirement for public agencies as well.

For managers charged with leading their organizations, the search for more effective ways to insure competitiveness in a quality-demanding world is never ending. They must relentlessly seek out ways to use every resource effectively. As managers at Saturn, US WEST, Corning, Cadillac, Xerox, and others have learned, the union can be a competitive resource that can lead to market success. Despite protestations to the contrary, in unionized organizations, managers have no choice but to work with the unions representing their employees if they want to be truly successful in a quality effort. Not to do so risks partial engagement of employees, misaligned functions, and barriers to change. True engagement leads to positive energy, synergy, and opportunity.

Union leadership faces no less of a certain choice. For unions today, demanding quality is not a question but a prerequisite for employment security. Bargaining partners who slip in the quality competition will soon be handing out pink slips. Union membership is clear; they want to work in quality workplaces that produce quality products. They want their unions to stand up proudly for quality; not to shy away out of paranoia about management's intentions or malfeasance. When management wavers on quality, the union ought to be resolved to ensure that the products are first rate and the work environment and rewards are, too.

Although it has become increasingly clear that union involvement is a key part of a quality strategy, discussion of this issue has been strangely absent. The quality gurus such as Juran, Deming, and Crosby have collectively ignored the union role. Look in the table of contents for practically every book on quality and it is impossible to find any significant treatment of the union role. Indeed, if you flip to the index, there is barely a mention of unions. In many cases, their correct assumption that management must exercise leadership in this area has also been interpreted to mean the union does not have a leadership role in this arena at all. There is no doubt that managers must lead quality efforts and step up to the task of creating an organizational culture that ensures quality performance. They must also doggedly guarantee that quality commitment is translated into quality action and quality results. But as we will see in this book, accomplishing these objectives requires not sidestepping unions, but engaging them.

In well-meaning haste to implement a quality focus, some managers have charged ahead without the broad involvement it takes to build support for quality. Often the union was an overlooked member of the family left at the train station. Usually such impetuous quality deployment also left lots of other people and groups standing behind, feeling both confused and abandoned. Rather than hurrying up and waiting—anxious to finally achieve high quality—it is better to do it right the first time, or at least to take corrective action to get all the necessary participants engaged.

The union can be a valuable and valued partner in a quality effort. When the Malcolm Baldrige Awards for quality excellence were presented, prominent among the winners were Xerox, which partnered with the Amalgamated Clothing and Textile Workers; Cadillac, which worked with the United Auto Workers; and American Transtech, which cooperated with the Communications Workers, among other examples of union-management quality excellence. Given that unions represent about 12 percent of the private-sector work force and less than 5 percent of all workplaces, this is an impressive showing. It isn't that managers in nonunion facilities cannot have fine quality programs—for there are many examples—but in unionized work organizations, reaching excellence is impossible without partnering with the union.

As this book will illustrate, achieving sustained excellence is not possible when the union is shut out of the process. Indeed, if the union is a half-hearted bystander, it diminishes the possibilities for quality improvement. Success in a unionized workplace is not getting labor to let management do what it wants, but labor working *with* management to do what is best. True engagement is far more than getting the union to sign a manifesto that world-class quality is important—all too prevalent an approach in many union workplaces—and then expecting that this lovely document will suddenly unleash the high commitment and energy of union members. It is not about getting out of the way, but about getting on board— not just as a passenger, but as one of the engineers of the process.

There is a growing body of evidence that shows that unionization and good industrial relations can be positive contributors to productivity growth and quality improvement.[1] High-quality competitors from other countries often have higher levels of unionization than in the United States. The much-vaunted Japanese have a very high level of unionization in their export trade sector, as do the Germans, and both are known for their high quality. Given less flexibility around wage rates, unionization can often encourage management to seek differentiation in the market on quality rather than price. This impetus to quality as a market driver occurs whether the union consciously pursues a quality strategy or not. In essence, unionization is a market force that drives the quality focus. Similarly, less turnover in unionized locations can lead to higher skills and lower turnover costs, which in turn can positively affect quality. Of course, this can also lead to problems of potential rigidity when the market demands a very rapid turnover in skills or job assignments. The challenge for managers is to tap into these economic forces for the benefit of the company and its stakeholders.

One of the wonderful aspects of the quality movement has been to focus organizations on the importance of customers and stakeholder partnerships. These two principles alone should create the incentive to involve the union as a respected and substantial partner in quality efforts.

---

[1]Lawrence Mishel and Paula Voos, *Unions and Economic Competitiveness* (Armonk, NY: M.E. Sharpe, 1992).

Legendary customer service comes from a two-pronged approach—external customer connection and a strong chain of internal customers. Alignment with customers in the marketplace, or in the public sector with the community, makes perfect sense. Understanding customer requirements and meeting or exceeding them is a fundamental tenet of quality management. The development of partnerships with the customer, where you exchange information and provide feedback to each other, is also part of the process. It moves from a strict supplier relationship, where goods and services are thrown over the transom, to one where there is a blending between provider and customer that seeks to add value to each party. But to meet those goals requires a work force committed and able to deliver on this promise and possibility. Internal customers are an equally critical variable in the quality process. Some such as Hal Rosenbluth, a highly successful travel industry businessman, argue that the customer comes second to the employee in quality processes.[2] Regardless of who comes where in the pecking order, the simple observation remains that employees are a vital part of the process. The chain of customers within an organization is the linkage that makes superb quality and customer service possible. The union is a critical part of this equation. It cannot be left out of the discussion and follow-up actions on internal customer satisfaction and capability. First, improving service in a fundamental way often involves new responsibilities and new working arrangements, and by law the union must be consulted. You cannot talk about new responsibilities and empowerment of employees without addressing the power and responsibility of the union. Like it or not, the union must be consulted when its members' jobs will be affected.

But there is a far more important reason. Union involvement can produce both commitment and ideas from the work force on how to increase customer service. Union members frequently have the most direct contact with customers. They often produce the products and directly serve the customers. They are on the receiving end of customer feedback—good and bad. They see the frustrations and unmet needs of the current customer base. However, the union role can be even more expansive than customer satisfaction. They also have a vested interest in an expanding and satisfied customer base. Without a growing customer connection and revenue, there is less chance for increased wages, benefits, and career

---

[2]Hal F. Rosenbluth, *The Customer Comes Second* (New York: Morrow, 1992).

advancement. When customers abandon the company, job security is at risk. Indeed, the union interest may be even stronger than those of more mobile managers. Given their strong connection to customer satisfaction, unions and their members can add value to a broad strategy of connection with external customers and can help in rethinking the customer satisfaction systems that comprise the organization.

The principle of stakeholder alliances is also a powerful reason for union involvement. From a managerial perspective, unions can either be a drag on the performance of quality efforts, with constant carping about the allegedly true intent of quality programs, or they can be a great asset that helps create and spread quality processes that make a real difference in the organization. Partnership approaches—as opposed to those that are mandated—recognize that managers can help conceptualize and steer but do not, cannot, and should not control the entire process. Other partners add value and give dimension to a quality process. The union can be such a partner. In many ways, the issue is in management's lap—either play a lone ranger role, or develop a partnership with the union(s) representing employees in the organization just as would be done with other vital stakeholders.

Working with the union is the right thing to do in a quality effort because it flows from basic quality principles. But it is the practical approach as well. In the early days of quality's national prominence, there was an assumption that quality was such an unassailable and understandable goal that it would sweep up organizations and would automatically work. Clear statements from top management of their commitment to quality and a cascading deployment of quality principles that were modeled through management's ranks were expected to transform organizations permanently. Hallelujahs would be heard from the workplace that quality—finally—is number one. Nice theory—but the reality was far different. Many employees experienced a quality focus as the program of the month. When push came to shove, in too many places quality still got shoved aside for production. Organizational politics within management interfered. Union resistance was frosty. Estimates of the failures of total quality management implementations range as high as 80 percent. Many total quality management (TQM) programs became objects of ridicule— labeled *totally quality mess* and other less kind assertions. Raising the banner of empowerment lifted many expectations that employees would truly make decisions. Sometimes they did; often they did not. Like Plato's shadow in the cave, the reality of quality didn't approximate the ideal notion preached from corporate platforms and regaled in the business press.

The naive assumption that management alone could make quality work without the active partnership of the work force ran up against the shoals of reality. Indeed, in many cases in the 1980s, quality processes were intended to supersede or eliminate previous joint union-management quality of work life (QWL) efforts. The conflict between earlier worker participation efforts and the new quality movement was nasty, brutal, and short. Derided as soft and squishy approaches to organizational change, joint QWL processes in organizations like General Motors and AT&T were bypassed in favor of the management-driven, hard-data-rooted quality efforts. In very few of the joint union-management quality processes described in this book and elsewhere was there an up-front involvement of the union. Usually there was a phase in which management tried to go it alone. Two kinds of circumstances forced change. One was the failure of quality processes to diffuse throughout an organization when quality was implemented unilaterally and from on high. Rarely was there a problem in finding a few examples of successful unilateral quality initiatives, especially among quality action teams. It just didn't spread well. There was a deception of exception. The quality circles phenomenon in the United States in the early 1980s fell prey to the same problems of outstanding individual team success stories followed by organizational disappointment at how slowly circles spread and how little they really impacted the organization.

In other cases, unions pounded on the doors and demanded in—sometimes having to use legal means to assert their legitimate role in dealing with mandatory subjects for bargaining. The recent *Electromation* and *DuPont* decisions by the National Labor Relations Board[3] have chastened many organizations as to the legality of expansive unilateral quality or involvement efforts. So long as quality dealt solely with the work process, a unilateral approach was possible. But when it began to deal with the hard issues of systems alignment, compensation, job duties and responsibilities, and employment levels, there was no way to continue to exclude unions. When quality just meant learning statistical process control (SPC)

---

[3]*Electromation Inc.*, 309 NLRB 163, 142 LRRM 1001 (1993); and *El Dupont de Nemours &Co.*, 311 NLRB 88, 143 LRRM 1121, corrected at 143 LRRM 1268 (1992).

and making charts of machines, it was fairly easy. But when the truly significant work of system change was started, union involvement was unavoidable. In cases where unions were resisted as partners in the process, agreements around significant changes in work became much more labored and difficult. Frequently, they resulted in compromises that diminished the possibilities of new quality work systems.

Chapter 2 discusses the history of quality and unions in some detail. But there is an important general historical lesson that informs current practice. The rise of scientific management and the birth of industrial engineering as a profession serves as a parallel to the issues being discussed in today's quality movement. Frederick Winslow Taylor, founder of scientific management, emerged from a society entranced by science. His belief was that objective science applied to the workplace would reveal objective and irrefutable truths about how work should be done. He attempted to take questions of work organization out of the political realm of management or trade unions. In his view, managers were behind the times, beholden to internal managerial politics, prone to favoritism and slow to change. Unions were denizens of the past, stubbornly holding onto outmoded craft practices and obstacles to industrial progress. Fervent belief and praise of Taylorism as the salvation of American industry filled the lecture halls and publications of the day. While Taylor's impact then and now was profound, he ran into exceptional resistance. Taylorism, despite its internal logic and fervor of its supporters, remained a series of highly touted exceptions. Most managers didn't change, and most unionists resisted its introduction in their workplace, seeking ways to foil the time-study man.

After his death, the Taylor Society, based on eye-opening experiments in the application of new work methods in Cleveland involving the International Ladies Garment Workers Union and in joint efforts in other locations, developed an alliance with the labor movement to press for scientific management. Their belief was that the combination of science and due process would be an unbeatable combination. They saw joining forces as a better route than continued confrontation. Unilateral management-driven approaches were less effective, they said, than seeking common purpose with employees through their unions. The results were not only greater compliance and easier implementation, but also better standards.

The analogy to today's quality movement is clear. Admittedly there are important differences between Taylorism and TQM in approach, but the parallel. is in the diffusion strategy, not protestations of a superior and unassailable logic. A decade ago when quality became a national rage, its promoters believed that they had found a rational system for reform of American industry that stood outside of traditional workplace politics, sullied by misdirected managers and irrelevant unions. The quality workplace was to be one that resulted in fulfillment for customers and employees, while leading to better bottom-line performance. The fervency of testimony to quality and the degree that quality became the overarching and preeminent value would determine the degree of success. The world had changed and quality was king. Unfortunately, the variance within the definitions of quality by TQM proponents led to confusion about what quality is and how it can be accomplished. A workplace science dedicated to controlling variance and measuring against standards was weakened by a panoply of processes that few could clearly define and meaningfully measure. Companies looking for instant changes lost patience when transformation took time. Unions looked at failures and held them up as excuses to not get involved.

We are now entering a more mature stage of quality improvement. Now we recognize that in many markets and in many companies, quality is not the only or even the most essential element to market success. Important? Absolutely. But it takes its place among market position, capital access, technological base, environmental concerns, and other similar market drivers. Still, an increasing number of companies are confronting the need to dramatically elevate quality in importance and performance. A growing global marketplace makes this unavoidable. We recognize that there is no one magic wand that will cure all business ills. Instead we have come to understand that it is the systematic examination of the entire organization—*all* of its systems and *each* of their component parts in a determined and continuous search for improvements—that leads to quality. We know that quality is not simply meeting current customer specifications, but anticipating customers' needs and working together with them to meet new needs and reach new opportunities. We now appreciate that there are indeed complex organizational dynamics at work that must be taken into account when attempting a comprehensive cultural transformation of an organization. It is not as simple as it looks on a flow chart. Everyone must be on board or else support for quality is eroded. The link to business performance and work life that is measurable and positive is not an end, but a platform. Properly conceived, quality can become a trademark of an excellent organization. Today's quality concept is both a deeper and more sober understanding of quality which views it less as a theology and more as an embedded strategy.

## CRITICAL COMPONENTS OF QUALITY PROGRAMS IN UNIONIZED WORKPLACES

### *1. Clear and Commonly Shared Concept of Quality by Both Management and the Union*

What you can see affects what you can get. The more narrow the scope of union-management quality vision, the less management and the union can accomplish individually and together. Sometimes, perspective is limited to better inspection processes on current technology and work procedures. It can devolve into checking compliance to assure that workers do as they were told. In other settings, it can expand to systematic and continuous assessments of both current and future customer requirements and an openness to rethinking how work is done—to using quality creatively to invigorate organizations.

The development of a commonly shared quality vision is one step in articulating shared understanding. A common quality credo, that in motivating and ringing ways sends the message of quality commitment, helps an organization focus and dedicate itself to the quality challenge. This vision must place the customer as the central focus of all activities, with a commitment to continuous and systemic improvement. It must also seek to open all parts of the organization to a data-rooted examination of ways that work can be done better—and still better. It should speak to the notion of quality infusing all parts of the organization and providing the measuring rod for all activities. And it must recognize that quality of the product or service is only one facet of quality, while quality of life for employees—union-represented and not—is a necessary concomitant facet. These new organizational expectations, both at the goal and practical operational level, must be communicated and discussed with all members of the organization. Questions need to be raised and answered. Contradictions need to be confronted and resolved.

It is best if the commitment comes from the top of the management and union organizations and is shared and amplified at all levels. Top-level sanction can't guarantee success—but lack of it guarantees tremendous obstacles. A clear understanding of quality includes an understanding of how it will be implemented throughout the organization and the union. A joint declaration of administrative responsibility is one way to make the quality commitment clearer. As a quality commitment engages an organization at all levels, it must take on further definition for all those who work in the organization, so that they understand what quality means and how they can contribute. Each organizational unit must define for itself how it demonstrates quality focus, not only in statements, but in daily behaviors and performance.

The union can play a key role in this process. Since it has a long-term concern for seeing employees collect pensions from their employer, it must constantly check to see if quality strategies build for the long term and not just satisfy current pressures. Long-term focus includes raising issues of employment security, anticipating new skills and employment transitions, and providing a means to adjust to new circumstances while preserving quality jobs. Since local unions are rooted in their communities, they should insist that a quality vision also incorporate community and social responsibility such as environmental integrity and community involvement. Many managers will share these concerns, but the union has a particular obligation to raise them. The union can also serve as a bridge between management transitions, so that quality doesn't fade with the newest fad or when new managers assume responsibility, but remains an enduring organizational cornerstone.

In excellent programs, union and management together develop an understanding of the need for quality. They articulate the organization's quality goals as a joint journey. Everyone is clear on their part in the quality mission. And each side holds the other's feet to the fire when they tire of the effort it takes.

### 2. Common Passionate Commitment to the Highest-Quality Results

A quality effort must make a real difference. Customers should see it. Employees should experience it. Managers should be able to monitor it. Union leaders should be able to run for office on it. When stirring quality statements and well-thought-out quality action plans don't seem to be reflected in actuality, each party must constructively confront the other to ask why and what will be done. And when they are getting positive results, each party still has the obligation to ask what can be done better still.

Senior management wants to point to improvements in quality when speaking to stockholders and key customers. Middle managers should be noting quality accomplishments in performance reviews. Union leaders want to point with pride to accomplishments in their election campaigns. To be able to do so requires that leaders insist on important outcomes of a joint quality process, support those who help make that possible, and model quality principles in their own work. This does not happen by happenstance. It occurs because of intense effort by everyone involved. Launching a quality effort is easy—seeing it through to quality results is the hard part.

Lukewarm or halfhearted attempts to improve quality don't cut the mustard. Nor does testing the other party without looking for constructive engagement. In some cases, the fact that the union and its members are fed up with poor quality, poor service, or pushing the product out the door is the impetus for quality. They tell management that *management* should do something about it. Not surprisingly, the result is managerial defensiveness, not a joint attack on the quality problem. Sometimes managers, eager to begin a quality process, slide a statement of commitment to world-class quality under the noses of the union and ask them to sign it. Like motherhood and apple pie, there is little in the document that the union can disagree with and it usually signs the paper. But there is little commitment behind the signature. Managers subsequently get frustrated with the union because it signed an agreement, but seems to do little to make it happen. It is a case of commitment mismatch. You cannot have half-quality performance. Both management and the union need to be strongly committed and concretely demonstrate that commitment in every way possible.

A successful quality effort will lead to an empowered, enabled work organization that will be successful in the marketplace. It should also lead to an empowered, effective union. Both organizations must feel they are better because of the quality effort. It should improve the internal processes of employers *and* unions, lead to more satisfied customers *and* union members, and promote a better public image for *both* organizations. The results will lead to pride and performance.

### 3. Public Display of Common Purpose for Quality Achievement

Saying publicly that you are committed to the highest-quality products and services provides a variety of important benefits. Public broadcasting allows less "wiggle" room when quality performance or commitment wanes. It also sends a public message that is well received. The union and management can't keep their quality commitment a secret; it has to be trumpeted.

Public display means being upfront about a quality commitment with one's own constituency, with your counterpart management or union, with customers and, with the larger industrial community. Union leaders need to stand up at union meetings and proudly proclaim their commitment to quality—not to blindly follow management's initiatives, but to support those the union believes wise. Unions should support truly joint quality efforts with the same pride and fervor as a union label. Management leaders should share credit with the union when meeting with other managers, both privately and in public forums. Public commitment includes joint participation in conferences and other programs to share with the broader public what has been accomplished together. It includes jointly meeting with customers to display a united commitment to the customer's satisfaction.

This kind of public display has very profound effects on the customers themselves and deepens commitment within and between the parties. Whether it is a steel company whose customer knows that quality and supply won't suffer when contract negotiations approach; or a buyer in the automotive showroom seeking assurance about American quality; or a taxpayer concerned about public spending: seeing an active and joint effort to improve sends a comforting and welcomed message. That quality message of a strong joint commitment can make a difference in sustaining employment through increased sales and revenue to an employer or budget allocations from a legislature.

### 4. Joint Responsibility for Administration and Training of Quality Efforts

The case of General Motors and the United Automobile Workers provides a superb example of how to grow a joint commitment to quality. The degree that the union is involved in the administration of a process demonstrates its leadership and also commits it to responsibility and accountability for the success of a quality effort. In many programs, the union is left out of the implementation process and/or may be brought in in a pro forma fashion. Superficial involvement in how a process is implemented is often reflected in superficial commitment. Some quality programs add the union to its steering committee as if the union is another managerial function to be included. This approach tends to marginalize the union.

There are various ways joint involvement can be carried out. Current practice runs the gamut from early involvement to information after the fact. The best way—and most unusual—is involvement from the earliest definition of what should be done. The Saturn/UAW example illustrates that an enthusiastic quality focus can be the result of the earliest possible involvement of the union. To design Saturn, a group of 99, two-thirds of whom were union-appointed participants, developed the concept for this very successful high-quality new car. Perhaps the most exciting development in joint quality efforts is described in the GM/UAW case in this book where union participation has been invited in the product design process. Such early involvement of the union allows it to participate in system-level change, thereby expanding the range of options available to both the management and the union about possible adjustments among the work force and in technical systems.

This increases flexibility and reduces the potential for later conflicts. Previous thinking among quality enthusiasts was that the union should be brought in when quality actions were implemented at the shop floor because that was when union members were affected. Little value was attached to having union input earlier. In the Crosby system, employees pointed out quality problems but management was responsible for taking action on them. Such narrow views of union value not only missed opportunities for good ideas earlier in the process, but guaranteed resistance to the limited range of choices when quality initiatives finally appeared. Quality, rather than being a common challenge, was experienced as a management-controlled process that neither demonstrated trust in nor empowered workers. It had an inherently demeaning logic of what was the worker's place in the scheme of things juxtaposed with testimony to the need for employee commitment and empowerment.

Some joint quality efforts have been established with joint administration. This is particularly true in the auto industry. At times these programs supplement management quality efforts, and, in some cases, they provide overall leadership. Joint administration can be defined in many ways, ranging from extensive jointly funded and administered programs, such as those in the auto industry or at Boeing with the International Association of Machinists, to the more common establishment of a joint steering committee that provides oversight for a quality program.

In a number of companies, union-backed hourly workers have been trained as trainers to spread the skills necessary for the success of a program. Union trainers and facilitators have demonstrated excellent training skills. They also are able to reach a broader cross section of the work force than management trainers alone. Management partners, where there is joint training and facilitation, routinely testify to the value their union partners bring and how they work to complement each other.

Joint administration means joint responsibility for designing evaluation and measurement systems that assess how effectively quality processes are implemented and the extent to which these processes actually meet the goals that have been set out for them. Because of the central role that data-driven decisions and measurement processes have in quality improvement strategies, joint responsibility helps in designing effective and fair measurement systems, interpreting their results, and developing workable corrective strategies. These measurement systems target process improvements, and don't fix blame on individual workers.

### 5. Direct Union Involvement with Customers to Increase Customer Awareness and Enhance Customer Responsiveness

If customers are the centerpiece of a quality effort, then both partners need to be connected directly to the customer. When union workers and their representatives are hidden off to the side because of fear of what they might do or say, organizations and customers lose out. When there is a genuine connection between an organization's customers and its union which sends a high-quality message, everyone is a winner. Customers appreciate a quality focus among employees and their union. It gives customers greater confidence in the organization and its product. Ford advertises its joint quality commitment because it helps sell cars, not just because it boosts internal morale.

When employees and their union have greater communication with customers, they have a greater awareness of customer needs. Employees can then suggest ways to improve customer responsiveness. If there are work rules and other union agreements that inhibit effective service, the union is more willing to change practices or find alternative ways to assure that customer satisfaction is maintained. Customer contact and awareness is best done throughout the organization, not just in point-of-contact positions. Some paper companies have sponsored tours of printing facilities so that production workers can see how their product is used.

Increasingly, unions are becoming involved in meetings with investors, especially in employee-owned companies. The same principles that make sense for customers also make sense for investors—demonstration of union commitment strengthens investor confidence, and contact with investors reinforces the need for business success. Indeed, a demonstrable joint commitment to more customers, and hence more revenue, can increase the incentive to invest in the company.

The logic of connection with customers makes sense with end customers both for quality and marketing purposes. But it also has great importance for internal customer alignment. Efforts in union-management quality projects to connect for feedback and seek more effective integration between functions are other ways to breed internal customer alliances and connections. From a union perspective, such internal connections break down barriers between different groups of the membership and increase union solidarity. A customer focus advocated by the union that seeks both internal and external customer satisfaction improves quality of working life while improving product quality. This quality awareness also infuses the union, which becomes more aware of recognizing and resolving membership concerns and interests.

### 6. Awareness of the Need for Alignment of Quality Product Improvement Processes with Quality Labor Relations and Human Resource Policies

The paradigm of quality improvement must suffuse all elements of organizational life. This means identifying ways that industrial relations and human resources can reflect a quality commitment. Not only do these systems provide a vital system for means to meet quality commitments, but they also must in and of themselves reflect quality principles.

Human resource systems that assist in the recruitment, training, compensation, and promotion of personnel are all critical variables in a quality organization. Recruitment policies select into the organization those with a high commitment to quality performance, teamwork, and problem solving. This includes recruitment of those committed to cooperative problem solving and quality action with the union.

At root, the quality challenge facing the employee is like a puzzle facing a puzzle solver. When the organization doesn't perform as well as it could, the puzzle solver twists and turns over possibilities until a solution—or better yet, many solutions—are identified. He doesn't throw up his hands in frustration, but gathers data and tests new ideas until a problem can be resolved. Hence, quality organizations require people who have individual perseverance and a willingness to work with others.

Systematic, high-quality skills development can provide employees with skills training to increase technical competency and understanding of standards and offer education about higher-order reasoning and group dynamics skills. Training systems that build the skills necessary for performance in a quality-oriented organization can also provide skills that help employees to grow as people, family members, and participants in their community. This starts by assuring that all people in the organization—those newly recruited and those currently on the payroll—have the necessary literacy and numeracy skills to take part in the quality data analyses and discussions. This all adds up to a better quality work force.

Career ladders and promotion activities that are based upon clear expectations guarantee that quality performance and commitment will be acknowledged and rewarded. This sends an important message to the organization that quality is valued and supported. Performance appraisals should enhance quality skills and reward participation in joint quality programs. A human resource policy that reinforces quality commitment sends a strong message to both parties. Union members wonder about quality commitment when they see managers and supervisors who push production over quality get promoted. The converse is also true; those who subvert joint commitments must not be allowed to undermine a cooperative quality policy.

Industrial relations practices are also very important in sending a clear message to both organizations. The union wonders why every other system in the organization gets changed but industrial relations is still conducted in the same old manner. In Chapter 11, Cynthia Burton raises a number of these issues. The way organizations conduct collective bargaining and administer contracts is fundamentally important. Contract bargaining that strategically aligns labor relations with quality makes good sense. Contract administration that is data-driven and prevention-oriented, while avoiding punitive focus, can help improve organizational functioning. New partnerships are possible at the first-line level between first-line supervision and union stewards. The willing involvement of the union in a positive manner in the conduct of the business demonstrates respect and honor for the company; a sincere desire by the management to conduct labor relations in a more productive and responsive way demonstrates a parallel consideration and respect for the union.

## 7. Sharing the Recognition and the Reward for Quality Achievements

The results of all of these efforts should be recognizable. Achievements should be recognized and rewarded. This recognition will come in several forms—additional compensation and increased esteem. Letting those inside and outside of a quality effort know about what is planned and what has been done both informs and motivates.

There is a caveat to elaborate publicity campaigns. They must celebrate the substance of quality and quality-related accomplishments, but not inflate or fabricate them. Reaching quality milestones and noteworthy quality achievements ought to be widely known and appreciated. But when these are used to mortar over general problems in a quality effort, public relations lead to cynicism. Leaders of quality efforts understand that any individual sits within a larger system that supports quality activity. Recognition of special and extraordinary effort must not only honor individual achievements, but also acknowledge the people and systems in the employer and union organization that made it possible.

In a union-management effort, both parties must share in the credit for their program. When Ford decided to put a joint logo of the company and the UAW on the sticker of its cars, it sent a powerful message both to consumers and their employees that "Quality Is Job One" is a commitment of both parties, and that both deserve credit for their accomplishments. When there is one-sided or lopsided credit, it can throw the other party way off—or even out of a joint quality program.

Believing that quality has its own inherent motivating force, the issue of compensation was largely overlooked a decade ago. Today, compensation is turning from an afterthought into a driver for quality change. Corporations are investing large amounts of resources in quality improvements in anticipation that there will be bottom-line returns. While the impact may not be immediate, there has to be an ultimate return for these efforts to be sustained. Employees also want to see some returns. There is just so long that buttons, placards, and newsletter pictures can motivate. Employees also want to see continuous improvement in their paychecks that can translate into a better quality of life. One of the more promising avenues to joint financial benefit is gainsharing. Gainsharing programs that place a high value on quality indexes, develop the employee participation and managerial practices that enable employees to affect those measures, and provide returns at a high enough level to be motivating, increase bottom-line return for both companies and employees. The company and the union can negotiate a fair gainsharing program that places a premium on quality. This win-win payoff from quality is a key component for long-term success.

## SUMMARY

This book opens a window to the mutually advantageous possibilities for quality improvement and illustrates some of its pitfalls. We ask here, as you must in your own organization, a few simple questions: Do our customers or our employees deserve anything less than the best quality possible? How can we marshal all stakeholders and all resources in meeting the quality challenge? In a unionized organization, the next question is, how do we draw on the commitment and resources of *both* organizations to have the very best union-management quality initiative?

Quality is an exciting and challenging frontier for union-management cooperation. It can not only provide a way to ensure stockholders a better-run business, but add real value to other stakeholders, including customers and employees. All quality journeys are learning adventures, and employers and unions who have partnered in quality improvement are setting the stage for others who can have an even higher-quality quality process. Each situation and each employer-union pair live within a unique set of circumstances which will require adaptation and innovation. You can draw on the energy, experience, and imagination both parties bring to set new standards and new benchmarks for joint quality accomplishments.

## Chapter Two

# History of Unions and Quality

**Edward Cohen-Rosenthal**
*Programs for Employment and Workplace Systems*
*Cornell University*

Union concern for quality is not a new phenomenon. Since the earliest guild days, unions have placed great importance on the quality of goods their members produced. In the charter of the Boston Guild for the Coopers and Shoemakers granted in 1651, it states "the main object of shoemakers was the suppression of inferior workmen, who damaged the country by 'the occasion of bad ware.'"[1] Unions have always objected to bottom-of-the-barrel quality. "The Long Island coopers petitioned in 1675 for protection against the competition of 'strange coopers' who were inefficient workmen and who made 'defective and insufficient caske.'"[2]

Quality has been an enduring and underlying theme for American unions. At times it has been a front-burner issue, especially in periods of extensive union-management cooperation, and at times it has not been a high priority—but it has always been a part of labor's agenda.

The task for managers is not to convince unions that quality is a goal that unionists should adopt. They already have that goal. History can, however, connect all participants to union values and previous accom-

---

[1] John R. Commons, "American Shoemakers-1648–1895," in *Trade Unions in the United States*, Robert Franklin Hoxie (New York: D. Appleton, 1920), p. 57.

[2] John R. Commons et al, *History of Labour in the United States* (New York: MacMillan, 1921), p. 46.

plishments to serve as a foundation for joint initiatives to improve future quality.

The historical connection of unions to quality takes quality action out of the realm of current fads or simple responses to foreign competition. The kinds of issues discussed below are still themes today as unions and management wrestle with conceptualizing and implementing quality efforts. Yet historical perspective is a sobering antidote to naive approaches to continuous improvement that assume quality improvement is simply drawing an upward slope on a quality control chart. There are peaks and valleys. History helps us recognize that even the best intentions or the newest techniques do not change the necessity for constant attention, hard work, and continuous renewal.

The historical connection has another important dimension. Current economic realities require a rethinking and reinvention of the guild roles that were formerly the province of early industrial organization. Today's quality workplace looks more like the craft and guild system than the factory of Dickens' London smokestacks, Sinclair's packinghouse jungle or Steinbeck's cannery row. Today's advanced workplace is based on high concern for quality, worker autonomy, continuous work-rooted learning, and adaptation to customer requirements. It relies more on the value-added contribution and customer attention characteristic of an early age.

Noted labor historian and theorist, John R. Commons, in tracing the evolution of work, talks about how mass markets and mass-production technologies initially drove out high-quality local production.

> It was the widening of these markets with their lower levels of competition and quality, but without any changes in the instruments of production, that destroyed the primitive identity of master and journeyman cordwainers and split their community of interest into the modern alignment of employer association and trade union. The growth of mass retail markets more dominated by price and availability than quality further eroded the quality connection. In this way, the journeyman has lost control over quality and is forced to adapt his quality to his price.[3]

The development of a mass-market economy supported improved manufacturing methods that could often produce core operations equal or superior to basic units of quality craftsmanship. Hence quality craftsmanship, much to the dismay of the early unions, took a backseat to low-cost,

[3] Ibid., p. 67.

large-scale production of standardized products. In the customer-driven product flexible world of today, quality has reentered the debate as a fundamental issue for dialogue between employers and unions. It calls into question yet again the relationship of workers to their products in a way that seeks high commitment, high performance, and high quality.

This chapter addresses the thematic issues that have motivated union and union-management efforts for quality improvement. Rather than take a chronological view of activities over the last century, the chapter summarizes the underlying issues, motivations, and themes that hold across time.[4] Indeed, we are in the third wave of union-management cooperation. The first was in the early part of the century, when shop committees were formed during World War I, up to the beginning of the Great Depression. The onset of World War II brought a second wave of cooperative activities that swept American industry but fizzled in the 1950s. This chapter draws lessons from these two periods in industrial relations history. A third wave began in the 1980s, starting with the spread of quality circles and evolving into more systemic quality improvement efforts. As this chapter will illustrate, there is little that is new in today's work world. Many concepts that we consider new have roots in these two earlier periods of industrial cooperation.

## HIGH-QUALITY SKILLS AND CRAFTSMANSHIP AS A MEANS FOR HIGHER WAGES AND BETTER CONDITIONS

High-quality skills, especially among skilled trades workers, are the foundation for high wages and craftsmanship. High skill level is presumed to be a win-win for employers and employees. Unions have argued that a downward spiral in wages would ultimately hurt employers. Such a spiral would drive out of an industry the kind of worker that would earn the employer good money through improved performance and enhanced reputation for its products or services.

Philadelphia manufacturers have won a reputation throughout the industry of producing the finest fabric in full fashioned knit goods in any market in the

---

[4]Edward Cohen-Rosenthal and Cynthia E. Burton, *Mutual Gains: A Guide to Union-Management Cooperation* (New York: Praeger, 1987), ch. 4.

country. This is due, I am convinced, very largely to the high percentage of really skilled mechanics employed in the shops in this city and is also due in very great measure to the improved morale of the large majority of workers throughout the union controlled shops in this town. . . . In most cases, the workers are interested in their work, make fewer mistakes due to inattention or carelessness, and when good work is appreciated by the employer take pride in doing their best. This all tends to insure to the employer a fine quality of goods and a minimum of shop trouble.[5]

Asserting that union workers had higher skill levels played a major role in union arguments at the bargaining table for wages higher than those in the nonunion sector. They contended that the higher productivity and higher quality of performance provided an edge to the employer that should be shared with employees. An editorial in the *Shoemakers Journal* in 1905 labeled this issue baldly, "Trade unions have always stood for the highest grade of workmanship. The most skilled, efficient and best workmen are members of the unions of their respective trades. They are more intelligent along higher, broader and more progressive lines than professional nonunionists."[6] In *Justice,* the journal of the Ladies Garment Workers a 1930 editorial asserted: "Cheap labor cannot be good labor, and when cloak manufacturers pay very poorly for labor, they get their money's worth—very poor work. And so there is an old rule, 'The cheaper, the dearer.' And this rule particularly holds good for labor. . . . One can obtain cheap labor only from such as do not know the work well; in other words, from such as enter the trade casually and have no strong interest to remain long in it, since they earn little at it anyhow. Such workers produce not only poor work, but little work."[7]

Indeed, at times union anger at incompetent workmanship among their own ranks was palpable:

There is no gainsaying the fact that a great deal of preventable injury is done the cause of organized labor when an employer can refer to instances where he was compelled to keep a bad workman. . . . Unions should be very chary of going on strike in the interests of an incompetent member. . . . It is incumbent

---

[5]Gustave·Geiges, "Full Fashioned Hosiery Industry," *American Federationist* 34, no. 6 (June 1927), p. 673.

[6]"Union Standards of Workmanship," editorial, *The Shoemaker's Journal* VI, no. 6 (June 1905), p. 25.

[7]"How Cloaks Should be Made," *Justice* 12, no. 10 (May 16, 1930), p. 4.

upon every wage earner intentionally or presently belonging to a labor organization to make every effort to gain the skill the possession of which places the holder in the first rank of craftsmen.[8]

The AF of L Railway Employees Conference in 1928 stated: "There is no denying the fact that our willingness as union employees to play a constructive part in the railway industry has been one of the most effective arguments we could bring to bear in the conferences, negotiations, arbitrations, and other activities which in due time led to improvements in wage income." It was estimated that workers garnered a 25 percent increase in real wages over the five years since the start of cooperative activities on the B&O Railroad at the Glenwood shops outside of Pittsburgh, a program begun at the suggestion of the International Association of Machinists. The rail workers felt that this was in exchange for a long list of benefits for management that included "improved railroad service by bettering safety, decreasing car, locomotive and track defects and failures and so reducing train delays . . . and reduced material expenses through the interest developed on the part of the men in material conservation."[9]

Dorothea de Schweinitz, an analyst of union-management cooperation during World War II, "emphasizes the point that quality of work depends on the active cooperation of workers both as individuals and as part of a group. On the present situation, a union representative in a large textile firm, with no committee, said: 'No one cares about quality—just so they can get by the inspector. They can put a weak spot under a fold but the shirt made from that piece will wear through after a few washings.' Quality will become important in such industries as textiles, electrical parts, etc., as the supply of goods meets demand and where labor organizes all or large sections of an industry. With the level of competition among manufacturers raised through relatively uniform labor costs or rates, the contest for the buyer's good will may be in terms of quality."[10] She outlines a basic union belief that taking wages out of competition through creation of a higher standard of living for all workers in an industry creates the

---

[8]Bernard Rose, "The Union and the Incompetent Workman," *The Paper Makers Journal* III, no. 12 (Nov. 1, 1904), p. 11.

[9]*Report of the AF of L Railways Employee Conference,* 7th Annual Conference, 1928, p. 17.

[10]Dorothea de Schweinitz, *Labor and Management in a Common Enterprise* (Cambridge, MA: Harvard University Press, 1949), p. 159.

basis for quality improvement. The interfirm competitive challenge is then based primarily on quality, not lower wages. Higher wages also create a more affluent work force better able to demand and pay for premium quality goods and services. Hence there is a two-directional argument for wages and quality: good quality work deserves higher wages, and higher wages lead to higher-quality workers and competition based on quality.

## QUALITY AS A MEANS TO ASSURE REASONABLE WORK PACE

The history of industrial organization is a frantic search for new methods of work means that produce more goods at a lower price. When quality can be maintained or enhanced by working smarter—not harder or less safe—then unions have welcomed these changes unless they came with job loss. Indeed, the Luddite allegations that unions are violently antitechnological progress are rarely true. New technology and new work processes can be the basis for negotiation for higher wages and open opportunities to improve working conditions. But union objections have been loud and strong when new methods look like speedups that increase the stress on the worker or toss members onto the street.

Quality has been an ally in the argument for reasonable work pace. Obviously, quality can also be a smokescreen for "soldiering" or an excuse for resistance to change. But a discerning management must recognize the potential validity of union objections to speedup because of its potential impact on quality. These ought not to be dismissed out of hand. High production may make one part of the operation look good, but when it ignores poor quality and increased scrap, it becomes counterproductive and depresses the overall bottom line and reputation of the company.

A good example was found in the following story told by Steelworker activists Clint Golden and Harold Ruttenberg:

> The union representatives on the War Production Committee suggested to the management that if the speed of the particular machine was reduced from 2,000 pieces per 24 hours to 1,600 pieces per 24 hours, its efficiency would be greatly increased. A test was made. Side by side, two identical machines operated for 24 hours, one at a 2,000 piece rate and the other at the 1,600 piece rate, the union suggested. At the end of the 24 hours, the former has given 450

pieces of scrap. The slower machine yielded only seven pieces of scrap. The latter at the slower pace, produced 43 more perfect pieces than the other.[11]

When employers pushed too hard for production over quality, the union screamed foul. Often this was ineffective in changing management behavior. An exception has been in the clothing industry, where union-made garments have been able to retain their high-quality image. For example, the *Shoemakers Journal* in the 1920s lamented, "Manufacturers in all lines are howling 'price' instead of 'quality.' We see this every day in autos, clothing, homes—yes, even in the burial of the dead. With certain exceptions most lines of business are ruled by 'price' instead of 'quality.' One of these exceptions is the work clothing industry, where in the union-made field 'quality' still rules."[12] Objecting to price is a code word for objections to speedup that agressively pushes product out the door to lower unit costs. While the real relationship between price, quality, and marketability is a complex one, unions have reacted viscerally to the push-it-out-the-door approach, thinking that it is often penny wise and pound foolish.

## QUALITY AS AN EMPLOYMENT SECURITY STRATEGY

During the 1920s, many unions began to hire industrial engineers who not only helped in negotiation over fair work standards but also consulted with employers to improve performance. The operating practices of firms where union members work have always run the gamut from excellent to shoddy. The union's broad perspective of an industry helps it to see which business practices are effective and which are not. When management suspends its worry that the union is manipulating the situation just to advance its own interests, then the employer can often benefit from this broad industrial view. The union worries about its members losing work because of poor management practices and thus, in some cases, has systematically worked to improve the managerial practices of their counter-

---

[11]Myron H. Clark, "Organizing a War Production Drive," *American Federationist,* May 3–14, 1942, pp. 3–7.

[12]W.J. Brooks, "The Union Label Campaign," *The Shoemakers Journal* 30, no. 8. (August 1929), p. 6.

part employers. This is largely out of an instinct for self-preservation, but one should not discount the level of pride that union workers have in their industry and the fact that they, too, want it to be the very best possible.

The classic case in this regard occurred in the 1920s in the clothing industry, when union and management came together to define work standards and work organization. Beginning in 1919 in Cleveland, the Ladies Garment Workers Union joined with area employers to improve performance. This activity paved the way for labor's industrial engineers to work with employers in conducting joint research on work practices and establish time studies and piece rates. At Hart, Schaffner and Marx in Chicago, the Clothing Workers Union worked with the company on these issues and created a success story celebrated around the world. "The A. Nash Co., clothing manufacturer of Cincinnati, found that a rapid expansion of production in the middle twenties had caused a deterioration in quality. The Amalgamated Clothing Workers Union was appealed to and it is a matter of record that in a relatively short time the situation was rectified and the firm saved a considerable amount of money."[13]

Unions became enamored with scientific management when the Taylor Society embraced union organization in the late 1920s, after the death of Frederick Winslow Taylor. Taylor himself had little use for unions, which he viewed as often stubborn and obstructionist; then again, Taylor thought most managers were similarly problematic. Scientific management, the beatification of science in the industrial arena, led its early proponents to believe that objective and impartial science would set irrefutable and fair standards for the workplace that would improve both productivity and employee income. This naive belief in charting and eliminating wasted motion as an "objective" solution simply did not work well in practice. It gave way to a new view of workplace change—one that involved labor and management becoming partners in change, jointly conducting research and jointly developing new work methods and standards. Proponents of the new approach recognized that the ideas and commitment of workers were a requirement for even the best-designed industrial engineering proposals to work. Thus, scientific management's proponents switched from an early dismissal of unions to a recognition that they were the only organized group that could broadly connect with workers, maintain the integrity of industrial science's processes, and help magnify the

---

[13]"Management Looks at the Labor Probem,"*Business Week*, September 26, 1942, p. 74.

results of their efforts to bring greater rationality to the workplace. They converged on the notion that for work to be more sensibly accomplished required true attention to due process and stakeholder engagement. Early quality purists and reengineering enthusiasts in the last decade have hit the same wall and many have been forced to come to the same conclusion.

Joint conferences were held between the Taylor Society and the AF of L, including a widely reported 1927 conference held in Philadelphia on the elimination of waste in industry. As evidence of this growing connection, other labor unions built on the earlier clothing industry experience and added industrial engineers to their staff. They helped in the orderly adjustment of wage standards, not only in the skilled trades but also in the early industrial unions. They served two roles: one was to assure that workers were fairly treated and weren't snookered by company-paid time study experts. But they also served a valuable role to help unionized companies compete more effectively on the basis of the best work methods, rather than on cutting wages and benefits. "In cases where the union through its shop representatives and committees has contributed to the improvement of quantity and quality of production as in the clothing industry and the railroad shops of the Baltimore and Ohio, the employer has benefited greatly."[14]

In fact, the AF of L hired engineers to advise its own staff on ways to improve the labor movement. Philip Murray, president of the Congress of Industrial Organizations (CIO) and Morris Cooke, president of the Taylor Society, collaborated on a book, *Organized Labor and Production*, published in 1940, that urged union recognition, new workplace standards, and employee and union participation.[15] These leading figures discussed how a new workplace based on a more secure union role through union recognition and union-shop agreements would free up workers to participate in improvements in performance. These would take place at the workplace, company, and industrial levels.

The following story from the 1930s told by Golden and Ruttenberg underscores the importance that labor put on linking quality to sales and hence to employer survival:

---

[14]Gordon S. Watkins, *Labor Management* (Chicago: AW Shaw Company, 1928), p. 695.

[15]Morris Llewellyn Cooke and Philip Murray, *Organized Labor and Production: Next Steps in Industrial Democracy* (New York: Harper and Brothers Publishers, 1940).

Nick Rondo, who led the picket line during the strike for recognition in the mid-thirties, is the final inspector. Defective water heaters do not get past him. Four years ago when Nick saw a defective unit on its way out of the plant he said to himself, "Let 'er go. She'll come back." Today he knows a lot about the water-heater business that he did not know then. He realizes that only good heaters can sell, that perfect units build and expand a business and that, in the last analysis, he and his fellow workers pay for defective units in the loss of business and the replacement of returned heaters.[16]

## UNION LABEL: QUALITY AS A MARKETING TOOL FOR EMPLOYMENT SECURITY

The union label is a quality marketing tool. It has historically been viewed as a symbol of solidarity among union members and a public symbol for quality. By urging the public to buy on the basis of the union label, unionized companies can benefit and hence be able to afford higher wages and better benefits and working conditions. Today, the ILGWU jingle, "Look for the Union Label," brings to mind instantly the connection between quality and unions. The label was first started in 1869 in San Francisco by carpenters who had won the eight-hour day. Five years later, the cigar makers union marked a union label on cigar boxes to certify that the cigars had been made by "a first class workman." "By 1888, the United Hatters of America could report with satisfaction that they had affixed 95 million individual labels to their wares and by 1898, the label was being used by unions representing ladies garment workers, printers, bakers, harness makers, wood workers, brewers, egg inspectors, barrel makers, and by barbers."[17]

But for the union label to have any meaning, it had to become synonymous with quality. If a union label implied poor quality, then people would not purchase union-made products of any kind. "The Trade Council, composed of leading factors of the cloak jobbers association and of the cloak sub-manufacturer's body, calls upon [employers] to exert every effort to the end that 'quality shall predominate in the manufacture

---

[16]Clint Golden and Harold Ruttenberg, *The Dynamics of Industrial Democracy* (New York: Harper Brothers, 1942), p. 279.

[17]*The Union Label: An Historical Overview, Union Label and Services,* Trade Department, AFL-CIO, 1992, pamphlet.

of cloaks.'" The editorial in the union newspaper goes on to say that "The non-union shop, the chief source of cheap, poorly made up merchandise in the New York market, is proving a boomerang and a menace to the industry. The economy of pennies that the jobbers and the manufacturers sought to introduce in the production of the garment at the expense of workmanship . . . is false economy."[18]

Unionists also felt betrayed when employers used the union label to produce second-class products at top-drawer prices. In the *Typographical Journal* in 1936, F. G. Barrett, a union vice president, railed:

> Many complaints have been received because the quality appears to be lacking in a number of our label goods. . . . It appears manufacturers of label products are taking advantage of the label-buying public. They are in other words selling the union label, but leaving quality out of the product. . . . In discussing this question of quality with many of our members, this has been advanced as constructive criticism in the hope that some way could be found to induce union manufacturers to improve their products.[19]

In the 1920s, a version of just-in-time inventory control and manufacturing processes was being deployed in the hosiery industry. The union saw quality and capability as a marketing tool for employers anxious to accommodate a demanding market.

> The rapid extension of the hand-to-mouth buying system has made quick deliveries imperative in the hosiery business. We urge our members to assist the manufacturers to attract business from unfair shops by enabling them to meet the demands of the market. And in this we have frequently succeeded. The rapid style changes in hosiery, the sudden demand for new colors, for black bottoms and what not all requires quick delivery from the mills. Style changes stimulate business. We seek to assist the industry by making our people receptive to the need for adaptations required in the production of these fancy heels and various novelties.[20]

---

[18]*Justice* IX, no. 31 (August 5, 1927), p. 4.

[19]F.G. Bennett, "Capitalizing on Union Label Goods," *The Typographical Journal* LXXXIX, no. 5 (November 1936), p. 452.

[20]Geiges, "Hosiery Industry," p. 674.

## QUALITY CONSULTATION AS A MEANS TO RECRUIT EMPLOYERS

Quality was seen not only as a way to recruit workers by providing social standing and wage benefits befitting a quality craftsperson, but also as a way to enlist more union employers or contractors. Historically, the building trades have always recruited employers in a top-down fashion by asserting that quality training and craftsmanship will be of benefit to contractors and that union hiring halls reduce employment overhead by retaining access to quality labor.

In the printing trades, unions used to review newspapers from around the country and send back information free of charge to employers as a way to improve quality and to induce employers to value the union.

> [A] rather unique instance of union interest in efficiency and quality production should be noted. This is the Pressmen's Engineering Service, founded in 1922. For many years the President of the organization, Mr. George L. Berry, has been preaching the importance of trade union responsibility for output. Thus in 1914, while testifying before the Industrial Relations Commission, he declared: 'We believe the international printing pressmen and assistants notwithstanding the fact that it is known as a militant union . . . that the success of the printing industry means our success, and we can not expect to be prosperous unless our industry is prosperous.' After the war, Mr. Berry continued to point out to the rank and file the need for cooperation between the union and the employing printers in eliminating waste and guaranteeing quality production.[21]

The Newspaper Engineering Service created by the union examined over 500 daily newspapers, recording all defects in printing or engraving and then sent suggestions on how the papers could be improved back to publishers. Indeed, if the defect wasn't corrected in a few months, the union sent an engineer to the company to discuss the matter. Initially this was funded totally by the union, but the employers found it so valuable they later shared in its expense. William HcHugh, a vice president of the union, said:

---

[21]Jean McKelvey, "Trade Union Interest in Production," (Ph.D. diss., Harvard University, 1933) pp. 249–50.

Not only has it been possible to get better returns for our members in organized shops, but in many that were hitherto unorganized we were able to show the employers, through the fact that we were equipped to reorganize some very inefficient shops in an up-to-date manner, the feasibility of having workers under the control of our union. Creating an engineering service by a labor organization may be a departure from the regular practices of trade unionism, but it has convinced us that it is one of the very best organization methods Labor could devise.[22]

The AF of L Executive Council in 1928 stated: "Good business men can not permanently resist cooperative relations with [a union] that offers results in elimination of industrial wastes, higher quality standards of production, improvements in operating machinery and constructive suggestions based on experience and reflection."[23]

Many union enthusiasts believed that seeing the union's value-added contribution would reduce or eliminate management resistance to union organization. Believing that the sole concern of the manager was higher profitability, they thought telling stories of union-management quality and operational success would create new employer openness to union organization. Unfortunately, the record shows that objective data and excellent case studies were rarely if ever sufficient to remove managerial concerns.

Testimony was solicited by union-management quality and cooperation enthusiasts from managers such as Daniel Willard, president of the B&O Railroad and textile industrialist "Golden Rule" Nash, who told the *Daily News* that the Amalgamated Clothing Workers had improved quality "in a way that could not have been accomplished otherwise without a tremendous expense and perhaps not at all."[24] These leading progressive-era industrialists spoke out at many forums. Many nonunion managers appreciated the progress reported in the union examples, but expected that their copycat efforts would perform as well, if not better. This was equally foolish.

---

[22]William McHugh, "Pressmen's Engineering Service," *American Federationist,* June 1927, p. 676.

[23]AF of L Convention Proceedings, 1928, pp. 42–43.

[24]McKelvey, "Trade Union Interest," pp. 387–88.

## QUALITY AND EFFICIENCY AS AN OBJECT OF INDUSTRIAL ORGANIZATION

In the union literature, there is also a fundamental belief that quality is the right thing to do, not simply an instrumental activity that would help the union preserve its employment base or improve working conditions. Take for example, a resolution submitted to the 1940 Bricklayers convention that proposed: "Whereas it is the desire of the members of this Union to perform a quality of brickwork which will endure forever and be a subject of admiration in ages to come . . . resolved that the shop steward on each job be charged with the duty of seeing to the enforcement of these resolutions pertaining to a better quality of brickwork on all buildings."[25]

The Railway Employees stated in the 1920s:

> For under co-operation the organized railroad employes [sic] through their unions, no less than management, become definitely active in the elimination of wasteful practices, in the conservation of material and time, and the improvement of safety and service. Thus, the second big lesson to be learned from the performance of our co-operative policy to date is that our unions in particular and organized labor in general are capable of being as potent a force making for better industrial performance and so a richer life than any of the other factors composing our society today."[26]

Sterling cases such as the one on the B&O Railroad were admired internationally and were touted in Congressional hearings for setting a standard for union-management cooperation and creating a higher moral plane for labor-capital relations. Regrettably, it was a standard more often studied than emulated.

"Union-management co-operation to reduce costs, eliminate wastes, increase productive efficiency and improve quality represents a practical program that provides workers with effective direct participation in the creative phases of management."[27] So wrote perhaps the most passionate labor voices in this area, Steel Worker Organizing Committee (SWOC) leaders Clint Golden and Harold Ruttenberg. They went on to say:

---

[25]Bricklayers, Masons and Plasterers International Union, *Convention Proceedings,* September 9, 1940. p. 132.

[26]*Report of the AF of L Railways Employee Conference,* p. 20.

[27]Golden and Ruttenberg, *Dynamics,* p. 255.

One of the compelling motives for union membership is the desire of workers to give their personalities dignity and their lives a meaning. They join unions to become something more than a check number that is ordered around as a piece of material is forged. They crave to be recognized as human beings, to be treated with respect, to be given the opportunity to find satisfaction in their daily work through the free play of their inherent creativeness, and to win the praise of their fellow workers and secure personal recognition and advancement for their ideas and ability to think. Collective bargaining, as it is currently practiced, in most productive enterprises, fails to satisfy this motive for union membership except in a limited sense. . . .

Protecting a worker's job, getting him more money and better working conditions and haggling over grievances largely satisfy the economic and social motives for union membership, and the extent to which workers have a voice in these matters partially satisfied their psychological motives for joining unions. But it is not until union-management relations become essentially constructive will workers find full satisfaction for their inherent creative desires; nor will management attain optimum efficiency, because creative participation of workers in making the vital decisions with management is the key to full production.[28]

## QUALITY PURSUIT AS A PATRIOTIC ACT

In reviewing union and industrial history, there is another category of union motivation for quality that doesn't fit neatly into the categories described above. Yet these efforts represent a significant part of the history of union involvement in quality. It is the notion that quality action is a patriotic act, especially when the country is under wartime pressures. Quality is not simply for the union's self-interest or to meet management's goals of profitability and market share. It is, instead, for a higher national interest where those in battle depend on the best products. During both World Wars I and II, organized labor became part of a national consensus to improve production. This involved many activities in addition to quality, including war bond drives and rallies and other production-boosting efforts. During these times, management and labor let down their guard a bit and linked arms to meet a common external threat. This phenomenon can be glibly connected to national crisis temporarily overcom-

---

[28]Ibid., p. 240.

ing innate adversarialism. It can also prompt us to ask: why do we need to rely on national crisis to seek a common cause? Why we can't we cooperate for quality as well in peace time, if not better than when our nation is at war? Can global economic competition lead to a renewed common purpose?

The banner under which this flew in World War I was the call for clean coal. Both John L. Lewis, the legendary labor leader, and William Green, a mineworkers official and later the president of the AF of L, took up these issues. In an article in the *United Mineworkers Journal* in 1919, William Green declared:

> Service in coal production, so essential to the success of our war aims and our armies is a test of loyalty. The kind of service, the quality of coal produced, the volume of production and devotion to duty, are all tests that each associated with the coal industry must meet. The way in which this is met determines their loyalty to our government, and the young manhood of our nation who are defending it with their lives upon the battlefields of Europe. . . . Let all, therefore, engaged in coal production; unite in emphasizing the necessity of mining clean coal. Let there be perfect co-operation between miners and operators in every locality, where coal is mined, in maintaining the quality of coal produced as well as increased production.[29]

He goes on to suggest regular meetings between coal operators and union representatives to achieve these goals. "It is only by the application of joint efforts at the fountain-head, figuratively speaking, where coal is mined, that this happy result can be brought about."[30]

During World War II, there was an extensive use of labor-management committees to improve quality performance. Thousands of joint labor-management committees were established to help during the war effort. A review of the kinds of activities they engaged in looks strikingly familiar to many working on quality improvement today. According to reviews of the practice at that time, the committees worked on many issues including:

> *Conservation, reclamation and salvage.* The efficient use of raw materials and the reworking, recovery or salvage of raw materials and materials in process and tools.

---

[29]William Green, "Clean Coal is Proof of Loyalty," *United Mine Workers Journal* XXIX, no. 17 (September 15, 1918), p. 17

[30]Ibid.

*Design, product.* Changes in parts or in the entire product to facilitate manufacture, or to improve the usability or salability of the product.

*Design, tool.* Changes in machine, tool, jig, or fixture primarily to facilitate manufacture, includes design changes which conserve tool steel or other materials.

*Interprocess relations.* Systems and methods to improve correlation of production processes to facilitate manufacture, including layout of production units and the rearrangements of one or more machines. . . .

*Process change.* The modification of a process, change in sequence of processes, addition or substitution of one process for another to facilitate manufacture, including process study and means of setting production standards.

*Progress charts.* The preparation and use of progress records covering production and quality problems as an aid to cooperation, including discussion and use of statistical control charts for that purpose.

*Quality improvement.* Analysis of causes of poor quality, changes in instructions or inspection to facilitate standard grade production to eliminate unnecessary expenses for inspection and further processing of defective parts, including statistical quality control for executive use. . . .[31]

These activities were not minor factors addressed by the committees. Indeed, analysis showed that quality improvement was a focus of 66 percent of 1,266 committees studied in 1944 and 72 percent of a smaller sample of committees examined in 1947. The research attributed the increase in quality attention in part to increased competition on quality after the war concluded. It also may be that those which proved their worth on quality were more likely to be retained after the war.

When examining the breakdown of topics addressed within each committee, quality was the largest single category. After the Westinghouse Electric Company/United Electrical Workers Union (UE) joint committee categorized 229 of its actions, quality emerged as the major focus. Indeed, researchers have concluded that the committees not only helped organizations that clearly needed improving, but also "increased production and improved quality of output in both large and small business organizations which were reasonably efficient and not functioning in distress situations of high costs and severe competition."[32]

---

[31]De Schweinitz, *Labor and Management,* pp. 41–43.
[32]Ibid., p. 155.

The union played an active and public role in pushing for quality. "Occasionally the business agent or union president took up production problems, as in the case at the Hazard Insulated Wire Division of the Okonite Company where the business agent of the Electrical Workers Union (AF of L) addresses the union meeting under 'Good and Welfare' on the problem of maintaining standards in their high quality product."[33]

De Schweinitz described in detail the role that committees played in quality improvement:

> Although the task of improving quality and reducing rejects is part of the problem of plant efficiency, it is considered separately because there was considerable subcommittee work on this subject whether under the name of the production committee, quality committee, or "scrap" committee. . . .The following illustration shows how a quality committee, a main committee and department committees can work together in this field. . . .
>
> The Quality Improvement Committee consists of three from labor and three from management. . . . Different members of this committee try to sit in on department committee meetings at least once each month in order to stimulate the idea of quality importance, and the fact that better quality means increased production, that increased production means a bigger pay check. . . .
>
> In July 1943, a "Make it Good" campaign was launched by the Quality Improvement Committee, with special posters, and a banner in each department reading, "Make it Good." . . . If rejects are being caused by faulty workmanship, the foreman calls the workman in after the meeting and asks him why. A union representative always sits in on any such questioning. Reports are kept of these interviews and if mistakes continue it is arranged to place that particular worker on a job that he can handle.
>
> The quality committee also stresses to the workers, through department committee meetings, and in the Labor-Management Bulletin, the effect of mixing scrap with good materials, or rejects with inspected parts; the cost of tearing down and scrapping that comes as a result of these practices, the increase in the percentage of scrap resulting from these practices. . . .
>
> Girls from the assembly of parts in this department were taken to other departments to see what the parts were going into, since the committee contended that it was important that each worker know what he, or she, was working on, and the application of the particular parts. The committee also devised better tools and fixtures further to reduce faulty work. . . . Within two and one-half months after the 1943 "Make it Good" campaign was started, the percentage of scrap was reduced to 6 percent from 12.7 percent.[34]

---

[33]Ibid., p. 88.
[34]Ibid., pp. 105–7.

At the end of the war, pent-up issues surfaced. Rather than sublimating power issues for quality concerns, institutional positioning returned to the fore and committees fell apart, both from management's reassertion of control and labor's pique at particular provocations or frustrations.

## CONCLUSION

The above cases demonstrate that quality has been a defining issue for labor since its inception. Rarely was it the dominant theme except during the 1920s, when elimination of waste was a central issue and clearly a way of framing quality joint action. However, the fact that quality was always a part of union debate both inside the union and in the larger society is important to note. Quality was and is a fundamental value of the labor movement both for instrumental and intrinsic reasons.

However, these programs were not without their problems and detractors. They at times did not involve rank and file membership as fully as they should. Crosscurrents of different ideologies from the Wobblies to Communist organizers to traditional syndicalists took aim at these efforts. In some cases, they were able to reverse policies for joint processes. Managers changed and previous relationships and commitments took a turn. Economic challenges such as downturns in the economy, commodity price drops, shifting consumer preferences, and competitive pressures swelled to the fore, sometimes engulfing fragile efforts. In the case of the Cleveland textile case in the early 1920s, they had an idea of jointness but little awareness of how to implement their common commitment jointly and effectively—and that led to discord and disappointment. Raising the shortcomings of previous quality efforts does not demean their importance or even their impact when the key purpose of criticism and analysis is continuous improvement and resolving root problems.

Granted, joint or union-based quality initiatives didn't always last; they didn't always reach their potential; and sometimes huge shifts in markets, politics, or the economy made them irrelevant. But caveats aside, early union and joint quality efforts showed much of what is possible and laid out a conceptual framework that still makes sense today. Joint efforts for quality that drew on the union as an organization were able to produce better products, better jobs, and better consumer value than would have been the case had managers gone it alone. If there is one lesson of history, it is that it repeats itself. If we learn from it, we can make progress. If we don't, then once again in the future unionists and managers will repeat the stories of the past, hoping that they will finally learn how to do it right— if not the first time, then at least the next time.

# Chapter Three

# Quality Workplaces

**Frank J. Wayno, Jr.**
*Programs for Employment and Workplace Systems*
*New York State School of Industrial and Labor Relations*
*Cornell University*

## INTRODUCTION

Since the early 1980s, the American business community has undergone profound change. Gone are the days when American production capacity was the marvel of the world; when the label *Made in America* signified a product of the highest quality and functionality. During the time when American business was "riding the wave," American managers and management methods were universally admired and emulated. That also, is a thing of the past.

Today, America finds itself in a very competitive world indeed. We are still the biggest producer of goods and services in that world. No longer, however, can we delude ourselves into believing we are the best.

To be successful in this new world, American businesses have had to confront many—in fact most—of the basic assumptions that guided operations in the past. In this effort, no value has gone unchallenged, no function has been immune, and no employee has remained untouched. For many businesses, this has meant virtually reinventing themselves.

The lessons of industry have not been lost on other sectors of American economic life. When the rules of the economic game change completely and with startling rapidity, concern for survival shoots to the fore. And when the issue is not the fate of a single company, but the viability of entire industries, the debate over correct responses moves out of the boardroom and into the public domain. The urgency of such debates often leads to new standards for judging organizational effectiveness and wholly new organizational structures and principles of operation. Minds are opened to new possibilities and new ideas diffuse into the culture, even into areas where the need for them is less critical. Thus, we find that the innovations of business are being adopted by government agencies, unions, public schools, universities, the military, and religious institutions, among others.

In this rush to improve organizational performance, one approach has proven to be particularly powerful, has gained widespread attention, and has been pervasively implemented. Known as total quality (TQ), or total quality management (TQM), it in many ways captures the philosophical essence of the "new" organizations we are creating to respond to the changing economic environment.

*Total quality* has been defined in many ways. The Total Quality Forum, a collaborative group of universities and major corporations that promotes both teaching and research about total quality and its application to university operations has a particularly captivating definition. What it lacks in conciseness, it more than makes up for in comprehensiveness.

> Total quality is a people-focused management system that aims at continual increase in customer satisfaction at continually lower real cost. Total quality is a total system approach (not a separate area or program), and an integral part of high-level strategy; it works horizontally across functions and departments, involves all employees, top to bottom, and extends backwards and forwards to include the supply chain and the customer chain. Total quality stresses learning and adaptation to continual change as keys to organizational success.
>
> The foundation of total quality is philosophical: the scientific method. Total quality includes systems, methods, and tools. The systems permit change; the philosophy remains the same. Total quality is anchored in values that stress the dignity of the individual and the power of community action.[1]

It is this broad-based, systemic character that has made total quality a particularly attractive and effective organizational innovation. Total quality is certainly about product/service quality. But it is about much more than that. It involves a striving for excellence in all aspects of an organization's operation, for ever greater alignment with the needs of those who

---

[1] *A Report of The Total Quality Leadership Steering Committee and Working Councils.* (Cincinnati, OH: The Proctor & Gamble Co.) November 1992, p. 1–8.

use an organization's products and services. Such excellence is a fundamental requirement given the ever greater competitive pressures found in a global economy. U.S. Secretary of Labor Robert Reich has put this well: ". . . firms that are surviving and succeeding are shifting form high volume to high value. . . . In the high-value enterprise, profits derive not from scale and volume but from continuous discovery of new linkages between solutions and needs."[2]

Yet despite its ever greater application in business and nonbusiness organizations, total quality remains an elusive goal for many. All too frequently, it is implemented in ways that suggest a basic lack of understanding of both total quality's philosophical roots, systemic character and the subtle dynamics of organizational change. Predictably, such efforts lead only to disillusioned workers and managers, frustrated consumers, and competitive stagnation.

The premise behind this book is that unions can contribute in powerful ways to the success of a total quality implementation. For this to happen, however, both union and management must have the same understanding of the possibilities, subtleties, and complexity of total quality. Both must be reading from the same playbook, or the game will not be won. To that end, the sections that follow provide a broad overview of the principles and systemic elements of total quality; explore some of the internal characteristics of a total quality workplace; and present some key implementation lessons from successful total quality efforts in unionized workplaces.

## TOTAL QUALITY—A CUSTOMER-FOCUSED MANAGEMENT SYSTEM

The need to be concerned about product or service quality is not a new phenomenon. Effective organizations have always defined appropriate quality levels and monitored performance against those goals. What then, is so different about total quality?

To help answer this question, I would like to "unbundle" total quality into some basic philosophical principles and compare them, point by point, to the principles behind more conventional approaches to quality. I

---

[2]Robert B. Reich, *The Work of Nations—Preparing Ourselves for 21st Century Capitalism* (New York: Alfred A. Knopf, 1991), pp. 82, 85.

would then like to show how those principles are fulfilled through an integrated set of actions—a system to assure quality.

There is, I know, some risk to this approach. Total quality has many advocates and their approaches differ, at times markedly. Any effort to suggest fundamentals is likely to run up against someone who would define the principles differently, put them in a different order, or make some other eminently reasonable modification. For those who might react in this way to what follows, I ask forbearance. My goal here is not to lay out the definitive total quality system, but merely to help those who are contemplating a swim at an attractive beach to better appreciate what lies in wait beneath the water's surface.

### *The Big Three of Total Quality Philosophy*

From a philosophical perspective, three principles distinguish total quality from conventional approaches to quality. They are:

- Being customer-focused in all activities.
- Preventing errors.
- Never being satisfied with performance.

Let us explore each of these in turn.

**Being customer-focused.**   Perhaps the aspect of total quality that has received the most publicity is its requirement that all members of an organization develop a customer orientation. Under total quality, the meaning of *quality* in any production activity is derived from the needs/requirements of those who will use the output of that activity—the customer for that activity. To have a customer orientation, then, means that the customer's requirements delineate work outcomes and high-quality performance occurs only when the customer is fully satisfied that those requirements have been met or exceeded.

Several things are noteworthy about this principle. First, under total quality, quality performance is always ultimately defined by someone *outside* the direct production activity. No matter how expert or knowledgeable the producer, the user of the output has the final say. This emphasis on satisfaction inevitably shifts the reference frame for evaluating quality away from the purely objective (conformance to product specifications, product functionality, etc.) and into a realm that also includes expectations and the notion of value. To define these accurately requires producers to interact directly and intensively with the customer. This is all in marked contrast to conventional approaches to quality, where the standards that delineate quality are largely defined by those inside the producing organization, with only filtered input from the consumer.

Second, the notion of being sensitive and responsive to customer requirements extends not just to the ultimate consumer outside the organization, but to those inside the organization who "consume" or somehow use what coworkers produce. Thus, transactions between workers, between units, or between functions must be influenced by a concern for customer satisfaction in a total quality world. Collaboration is emphasized and the internal competitiveness so often found in conventional quality organizations becomes a thing of the past. For many, directing a concern about satisfaction toward *internal* colleagues is a far more difficult challenge than becoming focused on the ultimate external consumer. The habits of the past, in this regard, are very hard to break.

**Preventing errors.** Conventional quality systems have always placed great weight on quality assurance activities. This has been a matter of assigning personnel to inspect the final product or significant components to assure that they meet preset specifications. If they did not, such products were rejected and either had to be reworked or became scrap. This methodology minimizes the chance that a customer, whether external or internal, will receive out-of-tolerance product, but does nothing to actually prevent errors from occurring in the first place. It is a reactive approach that minimizes the visibility of errors, but does not necessarily minimize variability in production processes and unnecessary cost due to errors. It is also an approach that potentially pits workers against each other and gives ultimate responsibility for product quality to a limited number of workers, the inspectors.

Total quality is, in part, a reaction to the inefficiency of such conventional approaches. It is based on the principle that errors must be prevented, not merely detected. This, in part, derives from the belief that the capacity for error resides far less in the individual worker than in the design of the production system. Responsibility for doing things correctly is pushed to those actually doing the work. Workers are given the power and authority to analyze work practices and take action to *prevent* error and the assignment of unnecessary cost to the product or service. This is a *proactive* system that encourages a search for sources of unnecessary cost associated with inappropriate or flawed methods. To that end, it disproves the widely held belief that to improve quality, cost must go up. Under total quality, when higher quality is attained through the elimination of waste or the removal of production constraints, cost goes down.

**Continuous improvement.** The third of the key philosophical principles of total quality deals with the notion of continuous improvement. Under total quality, attaining and then maintaining a given performance level is not sufficient for competitive success. However high our standards might be, we must strive to improve—to, if you will, raise the performance bar.

In part, this principle is reflective of the practical realities of economic life. Those who are exceptional at something and garner market share and customer loyalty become the target, personify the aspirations, of those who seek that stature. Thus, to *maintain* our position, we must get better; to *improve* our position, we must get much better.

The principle of continuous improvement goes beyond the practical, however. Continuous improvement is about excellence, about the never-ending journey toward excellence. It is a philosophical commitment to the attainment of perfection. In that sense, it captures the yearning of each of us to know the unknowable, to strive to be more than we are. It is the manifestation in the production arena of the philosophical position that we best reflect and honor our humanity through our efforts to be more than we are, to grow in our capacities, to accomplish what we have not yet accomplished. Thus performance targets or standards or process definitions are not plateaus of excellence at which we strive to live, as in conventional quality approaches, but merely useful indicators that we are making progress in our efforts to be better. There must be glory in hitting targets, but it is only transitory—the journey toward perfection has no end.

### The System of Total Quality

Customer focus. Prevention of errors. Continuous improvement. These are admirable principles, but asserting them will not be sufficient to improve performance. As noted in the definition presented earlier, *total quality* is a "people-focused management system that aims at continual increase in customer satisfaction at continually lower real cost." What are the key elements to such a management system? There are at minimum four:

- The full involvement of all employees in competitive improvement.
- Quantifiable measures for quality.
- Data collection that includes both output measures *and* process measures.
- Comprehensive data analysis techniques and skills understood by all employees.

**Employee involvement.** "Total quality is a total system approach (not a separate area or program). . . . [It] works horizontally across functions and departments, involves all employees, top to bottom, and extends backwards and forwards to include the supply chain and the customer chain." Total quality can *only* be successful at improving organizational performance if all employees are fully engaged in the quest for ever higher levels of customer satisfaction at ever lower cost.

From a practical perspective, the employee actually doing a given piece of work has the detailed knowledge of actual work practice required to inform efforts to reduce process variance, eliminate sources of waste, and prevent errors. For this reason alone, employee involvement makes sense.

In point of fact, however, such practical considerations are only a small portion of the reason why employee involvement is critical. Total quality seeks to enlist the worker in the pursuit of quality. Yet it has been persuasively argued that most workers have always had a desire to produce a high-quality product or service, to be associated with excellence. The design of work into ever smaller bundles of tasks, following Tayloristic principles, together with managerial control over the work process, has removed from the worker the capacity to truly influence quality in significant ways. Workers are buffered from the customer and often have no understanding of the nature of the whole production process, or of the ultimate product or service.

Employee involvement attempts to reconnect the worker to the essence of his or her work. It requires that all employees be given the responsibility and most critically, the associated authority to "touch" the customer and analyze and make changes to work processes in pursuit of customer needs and organizational efficiency. By empowering workers and providing opportunities for them to come together in small groups to address problems that they themselves have identified, it encourages the spirit of craftsmanship and the pride of ownership that is fundamental both to the dignity and self-worth of workers, and to efforts to create satisfied customers. Thus, employee involvement complements the union's goal that workers not be victimized by the work processes and systems that guide their efforts. But, as we will discuss later, the union must play a significant role in defining and implementing employee involvement.

**The key enablers to management by fact.**  While shifting responsibility and authority for the improvement of work practices and processes to workers is essential to the success of total quality, it alone will not suffice. To give workers such responsibility without also giving them the tools, skills, and supporting systems to fulfill those responsibilities is an empty gesture that will only frustrate and alienate workers and destroy quality improvement hopes. The three remaining system elements—quantifiable measures for quality; process- and outcome-related data collection; data analysis skills and techniques—are important enablers to the worker's participation. They constitute a mini-system that encourages management by fact.

*Quantifiable measures for quality* refers to the need for a system to translate customer requirements into objective criteria that can be measured. Such a system must address the needs of both external *and* internal customers. It helps employees at all levels of organizational life to make tangible the needs of others, to understand the impact of day-to-day work activity on those needs. When combined with a set of standards for each measure, it provides workers with a template to help uncover opportunities for improvement.

This system of measures must address both the significant outcomes of the organization's production efforts *and* the processes used to create those outcomes. Continuous improvement and prevention require that production processes be comprehensively mapped out. Process steps that most impact key output measures must be identified and data collection systems must be created to allow these critical aspects of the process to be monitored on an ongoing basis. The goal in this effort is to minimize process variation. For many in an organization, becoming sensitive to *how* things are accomplished, not just *whether* they are accomplished, involves a significant transformation of consciousness and must be carefully facilitated.

Finally, the existence of appropriate quality-related measures and the systems to collect data pertinent to those measures are meaningless if workers do not have the skills to rigorously analyze that data to assess performance and uncover opportunities for improvement. Such skills include problem solving and the use of basic statistical tools such as control charts, Pareto charts, fishbone diagrams, histograms, runcharts, scatter diagrams, and flow charts. They also include the interpersonal, group dynamics, and conflict resolution skills so necessary if the small employee problem-solving groups essential to total quality are to function properly.

To draw a parallel from the management development field, in the early 1980s research on managerial performance indicated that truly superior performance resulted when managers had command of a small number of highly focused behavioral skills, called *competencies*.[3] One of these competencies was the capacity to accurately assess one's own performance in terms of strength and weakness, articulate that self-assessment, and take action on it to improve. Basically, it is the capacity to look in the mirror and test what we see against the perceptions of others.

In the simplest possible terms, total quality is accurate institutional self-assessment. It is the capacity of an organization, reflected in the day-to-day actions of all its members, to look in the mirror. To identify those things that contribute to or detract from its ability to fully satisfy the needs of key stakeholders. Creating this capacity for accurate self-assessment throughout an organization involves, for most organizations, a fundamental culture change. And that change requires a realignment of behaviors, structures, systems, procedures, and policies throughout the organization to support the desired behavior.

## WHAT IS A TOTAL QUALITY CULTURE?

To this point, I have tried to paint a picture of the philosophical and technical elements of total quality. Such a picture inevitably hints at what life would be like in a total quality organization. For some, however, such hints at the nature of the workplace may not be sufficient. Thus, I would like to explore, a bit more fully, some of the salient cultural and structural characteristics of a total quality organization.

Perhaps the place to start in this enterprise, is to remind ourselves that total quality is a people-focused management system that centers on the

---

[3]Richard E. Boyatzis, *The Competent Manager* (New York: Wiley, 1982).

needs of organizational stakeholders. It is a system of organizational governance that, when it is working successfully, induces employees at all levels of organizational life to act in the best interests of the organization when dealing with both customers and coworkers—to be committed to the organization.

Richard Walton of Harvard University has, over the last 10 years explored the evolution of what he calls the *commitment model* of organizational operation. His research has shown that as pressures for high performance have become more intense, managements have moved away from a control strategy in their dealings with the work force to one that elicits worker commitment to the organization. For our purposes, Walton has done a very nice job delineating some of the key cultural and structural components of a high-commitment organization. Among these are the following:

- Flat organization structures mean fewer layers and large spans of control for managers and supervisors.
- Hierarchical distinctions are not emphasized; influence processes dominate interactions rather than the use of formal power.
- Managers exist to facilitate problem solving; coach employees and create a developmental climate; and help employees to better understand the company's competitive situation and strategic goals.
- Employees not only do their jobs, they redesign their work to improve effectiveness.
- Jobs are broadly defined to address whole tasks; job definitions change with changing conditions.
- Teams/groups are often used as the basic accountable unit.
- Employees are assured that participation will not result in loss of their jobs.
- Priority is given to training and retraining the work force.
- Internal coordination depends far more on shared values, goals, and traditions, rather than formal rules and procedures.
- Business information is shared widely, rather than on a need-to-know basis.
- Individual pay is linked to skills and mastery; variable rewards are used to create equity and reinforce group achievements.
- There is mutuality in labor relations with joint planning and problem solving on an expanded agenda.

- Corporate governance encourages employee participation on a wide range of issues.[4]

The key lesson that this list should convey is that a total quality workplace is one where all cultural components are aligned with the requirements of total quality. Structures, management behavior, job definitions, coordination methods, communication, labor relations, and reward practices are all compatible with the fundamental requirement of total quality: employee commitment. Such cultural characteristics bond employees to the organization by conveying to them that they are valued, trusted partners in a common enterprise. Of particular importance, job guarantees and an open, problem-solving attitude by management encourage employees to take risks; to bring problems to light; and to question themselves, their coworkers, and their bosses. Without such powerful cultural evidence that the organization is committed to them, looking in the mirror will be a rare occurrence indeed.

What should also be clear is that the cultural characteristics of a high-commitment workplace are entirely coincident with basic union values. A diminution of autocratic managerial control; worker participation in the design of work processes; job security; shared values; a common knowledge base; fair and equitable rewards; and continuous education for workers are important goals for unions and necessary requirements for total quality. Successfully implementing total quality, therefore, requires that the creation of these cultural characteristics become the central concern of joint labor-management action.

## IMPLEMENTING TOTAL QUALITY: SOME LESSONS

Many who read this book will be contemplating implementing total quality in their own organization, or cooperating with such an effort in another. To those must go a few words of caution.

Total quality is a powerful system for improving an organization. Its power, however, comes from its comprehensiveness, from its *total system* character. As noted earlier, for the vast majority of organizations, it will

---

[4]Richard E. Walton, "From Control to Commitment in the Workplace," *Harvard Business Review*, March–April 1985, p. 81.

constitute a significant, indeed massive, change in culture. This is not an innovation that can be grafted onto an existing system. All parts of the existing system (structures, procedures, values, behaviors, and so on) must be assessed for compatibility with the principles of total quality. Those that do not support, encourage, and facilitate the behaviors required by total quality must be changed.

Such changes are not to be taken lightly. They will require enormous energy from all in the organization, but especially from those in leadership positions. They will also require steadfastness of purpose and limitless patience. They will take time—a great deal of time. They can be planned, but there will always be unanticipated and often unpleasant consequences that must be dealt with. And these reactions will lead to still other unanticipated consequences, some good, some bad.

In a unionized setting, the key component to successfully creating a total quality culture will be the involvement of the union in the transformational effort. *Total* quality, by definition, touches all aspects of organizational life. Implementing *total* quality, therefore, requires the complete engagement of *all* key stakeholders in the organization.

Unfortunately, this is not always self-evident. Many leaders of business organizations erroneously believe that concern about quality is unique to those in management. As the preceding chapter clearly shows, workers and their unions have, from the earliest days of the guild system, been keenly sensitive to the relationships between product quality, market success, and ultimate job security. Concern about quality is, thus, a shared value that can and should be one of the bases for joint action between labor collectivities and business organizations.

If such joint action is to be mutually productive, however, it must take the proper form. The first issue is a matter of timing. It is quite important that the union be involved from the moment the firm's competitive capabilities become a concern. Union leaders can thus contribute to the development of strategic responses to competitive decline.

This is particularly important when it is concluded that total quality should become the centerpiece of a competitive renewal effort. As noted earlier, employee involvement is a fundamental systemic element to total quality. In unionized settings, the union is the traditional mechanism through which employees influence organizational activity. When the union does not play a role in defining employee involvement-related competitive strategies, the lessons from industry are clear: the union is likely to see such strategies as an intrusion into their historic domain, may define this intrusion as a threat, and may oppose the renewal effort. Thus, early union participation as an equal partner in the planning and analysis phase of a renewal effort built around total quality is a must.

Beyond the issue of timing, however, the joint relationship between union and management must have a certain tenor if total quality is the goal. The issue here is creating the spirit and reality of a true partnership in the implementation of total quality. Such a partnership involves concrete manifestations of respect for and trust of the other party; involves structures and tangible mechanisms to exercise joint control of jointly developed initiatives; involves addressing roadblocks or unanticipated consequences as problems to be solved, not battles to be won. Again the lessons of industry are clear: without equal partnership in a total quality-based renewal effort, return on investment will be marginal or may even hurt the organization.

If the correct bases are touched, however, success can be attained. Transforming an organization, leading it to wrap its collective mind around a new operating philosophy, is the ultimate challenge of organizational leadership. In support of that goal, I offer this transformation checklist[5] derived from the experience of those who have taken up that challenge and succeeded. It is equally relevant to unions seeking to improve themselves and unionized organizations seeking competitive renewal.

### *Transformation Checklist*

**Develop a vision to guide renewal: an internal benchmark.** A clearly articulated vision acts to galvanize the attention of organizational members and becomes a shared aspiration for what the organization can become. In unionized organizations, such a vision should be jointly developed.

**Assign someone to promote and support the vision.** A corporate staff position to oversee its implementation becomes the physical manifestation of senior management's commitment to the con-

---

[5]Frank J. Wayno, Jr., and Carolyn Milkovich, "Quality-Focused Strategic Transformation: Human Resource Lessons from Xerox." (Center for Advanced Human Resource Studies, ILR/Cornell, July 1992, Special Topics in Human Resources Monograph).

cept, a catalyst for action, an ombudsman for participation, an educator about the range of participative activities that could be implemented, and a facilitator of high-level decision making around the concept.

**Use high-level champions to unfreeze the culture.** These are individuals who look critically at the organization, identify what has to be different, and assiduously advocate the new over the old.

**Achieve and sustain union involvement.** In unionized settings, high-level labor-management dialogue in a spirit of openness and shared concern sets a tone within the organization that allows the difficult, painful structural changes in the way work is organized and staffed to be accomplished as expeditiously as possible. The union should participate as an equal partner in both strategy formation and day-to-day oversight of improvement activities.

**Manage the context of change.** This is a matter of helping people who must live with the consequences of a large-scale change understand the reasons why such change is necessary. Openly sharing information about organizational performance is a minimal requirement, if this is to be accomplished.

### Create a cadre of dedicated internal change agents.

- In the early stages of renewal effort, a group of dedicated internal change agents provides visible evidence to employees that the firm intends to function in a different way.
- Change agents with union backgrounds provide a credible communication bridge between the union and management.
- Comanaging change agents create a system of checks and balances that assures that the basic tenets of participation are honored in both spirit and fact.
- The internal change agents are consultants with responsibility for assisting in the continuous evaluation of all aspects of the workplace relevant to the core change dimension. Additionally, they should be responsible for assisting with the implementation of necessary modifications to the firm's production environment. Change agents should be trained in consulting skills and the

dynamics of organizational change to increase their effectiveness when dealing with the higher levels of the firm.

- Change agents will be most successful when they are integrated into the management systems of the organizations—employer and union—to which they are assigned.
- The notion that employees can profitably serve as change agents for a limited period of time and then return to their old job is not realistic.
- Recognize that a cadre of internal change agents shifts day-to-day responsibility for implementation of the vision away from line management.

**Create mechanisms for information sharing, learning and catharsis.** Internal forums for the sharing of information and experience, whether formal or informal, facilitate the flow of innovation throughout the organization. Equally important, they provide a mechanism for emotional catharsis, in which employees attempting to facilitate or manage organizational change can discuss their frustrations and seek solace and support from colleagues.

**Create opportunities for different "world views" to interact.** Exposing influential people to a broader set of criteria for evaluating organizational performance change helps them understand the social and cultural aspects of organizational life and the processes through which organizational change is brought about. It can also change the way employees think about their jobs. Exposure to wholly different perspectives on organizational life challenges fundamental assumptions and opens the door to the possibility of new approaches to doing business.

**Facilitate cultural change through structural change.** Reducing the size of the supervisory work force forces managers to involve their subordinates more fully and pushes decision-making responsibility downward. While such changes do not constitute active philosophical support for the concept of participation, they do put in place operating constraints that make active opposition less likely.

**Create multiple mechanisms for participation.** A range of participative activities allows employees to become involved in a way that is compatible with their values and current skill levels. It also allows for an evolution in the depth of any employee's level of participation.

**Develop a detailed strategy for change using participative methods.** A set of principles and a time-phased plan of action to make those principles come alive help make sense of the disruption of internal patterns of behavior. Developing such a reasoned strategy participatively can make change understandable, thereby reducing uncertainty, and increasing buy-in by key organizational members.

**Recognize that total quality involves a fundamental redesign of managerial work.** Management in this new world is far more a matter of facilitating and coaching than control. Hierarchical systems are not compatible with a quality-based organization. In unions, this means that union leadership may have to go about their tasks in a very different way, or indeed may have a fundamentally different role.

**Provide specific descriptions of desired behavior when roles are redefined.** Specification of role model behaviors allows managers to focus on the factors that lead to advancement. Incrementally defining an ever more specific set of critical behaviors and skills required for promotion provides both an unequivocal message that the firm is committed to a new way of doing business and a template to help managers to understand the implications of that new way of doing business.

**Facilitate behavioral feedback when roles are being redefined.** Develop mechanisms to provide feedback to managers or union leaders about the effectiveness of their management style. These serve as a developmental tool to help managers or union leaders fine-tune their behavior.

**Express strategic concepts in tangible tools.** Clearly defined analytical processes can be very powerful mechanisms to accomplish change. Defining the meaning of quality for employees in terms related to their actual work transforms abstractions like *participation* and *quality* into behaviors that can be seen and learned.

**Rigorous training facilitates cultural change.** Training is a key element to the success of a total quality implementation. Employees must learn new analytical and interactive skills if they are to participate constructively in organizational improvement activities.

**Celebrate success.**  Given the long time period required for cultural renewal, reinforcement activities are critical, or frustration and disillusionment will sidetrack the improvement program. Celebrating success provides a reaffirmation of principles and an opportunity to reenergize.

**Top-down change is required.**  A comprehensive, totally integrated renewal program designed to bring about cultural change must heavily involve those at the very top of the organization. Senior leaders in the employer and/or union are the most influential carriers of the organization's culture.

**Change the infrastructure to support total quality.**  When significant cultural change is desired, all internal systems, structures, procedures, and practices must be evaluated in light of the new cultural characteristics and, where necessary, must be redesigned to be supportive of those new characteristics. In unionized settings, the collective bargaining agreement is not immune to this effort.

**Human resource and labor relations strategy must be an integral part of the overall change strategy.**  The personnel and industrial relations functions must evaluate all human resource management systems and practices to assure their compatibility with new strategic business objectives, and must aggressively alter those not supportive of those objectives.

## Chapter Four

# Quality Unions

**Edward Cohen-Rosenthal**
*Programs for Employment and Workplace Systems*
*Cornell University*

**Arthur Shostak**
*Department of Sociology*
*Drexel University*

The premise of this book is that joint action is the most effective way to conceive, design, and implement quality processes. A company or agency needs to manage itself in a quality manner throughout in order to have a powerful impact on the quality of its products and services. It must walk its talk. For a joint partnership with organized labor to work best the union must *also* configure itself in a quality manner.

This is true at all levels of the union organization: from the local union which may partner with local management in a quality process, to the regional union structures which service the local union, to the international union which may set policy and provide guidance. Our premise in this chapter is that the best quality processes are a result of a combination of a quality employer *and* a quality union. We believe the steady and cumulative improvement of joint action hinges on related improvements in the parties themselves—both employers and unions.

This chapter demonstrates that unions in many places have already taken this challenge and are better off for having done so. While no one particular feature or any set combination of them automatically identifies a national union or a local as a quality organization, the more such features an organization can boast, the closer it gets to earning the *quality* label.

We also believe that a quality union has inherent virtue regardless of whether or not it is participating in a joint process. Union members and society at large are best served when the labor movement aims for the highest standards and the best practices. Even if the reality falls short of the mark, setting sights high is an important goal. A quality union in or outside of a joint process represents its membership well, organizes effectively, and is active in the community and political arena. The lens that focuses on quality can help a union do all of these and more.

In many places, unions are struggling for their very life. American private sector unions have declined from representing almost 35 percent of the work force to about 12 percent in the private sector over a 40-year period. Instead of setting the standards in many industries, unions are trying the stem the tide of a downward spiral toward nonunion pay and conditions. They face massive economic change, legal barriers, and fierce employer resistance. Much discussion of union response has taken place concerning these fundamental external challenges. These are serious concerns that must be addressed. Without a credible counterbalance and independent voice in the workplace, the quality of employment is in danger of being dragged to the lowest common denominator rather than rising to an increased standard of living and working conditions, and subverting American quality possibilities along the way. For our purposes, however, simple survival doesn't guarantee high-quality unionism. Although a necessary condition, keeping their head above water is not enough to maximize labor's potential.

Unions effective in their own right can have a salutary effect on quality processes in a secondary way. Clarity of vision and goals allows the union to be clear about how it connects to quality processes and exercises leadership. Effective utilization of resources in the union frees up the energy, time, and funds required to effectively support joint processes at the local or corporate levels. In addition, the union that manages its own house in a high-quality way earns increased moral authority to challenge management to act on similar principles.

Our years of behind-the-scene involvement as consultants, teachers, and union staffers has utterly convinced us of the possibility of developing strong, effective, high-quality unions and simultaneously the highest-quality workplaces for union members. We by no means presume to think for international or local union decision makers. We do, however, lay out a general set of principles union leaders can use as they think through how to improve and reconfigure their union. Unions in many places have already taken this challenge seriously and have adopted practices that lead to high-quality unionism, several of which we will discuss later. When using this label of *quality unions*, we are describing the practice, not necessarily characterizing all other activities of the organization. Like any other organization, there are always areas for improvement and quality unions are no exception.

Each union must develop its own version of what it means to be a quality union. Indeed, the ability to generate local variations on the union theme is part of the strength of the labor movement. There is no single way that unions are organized or structured. There is no monolithic model of unionism. Each union must in its own way think through its options and adopt strategies that makes sense to it. Treading into this area can be risky. It is the internal democratic process that does and ought to make decisions on the internal operation of unions. This principle leads to their diversity in internal organization. The truism remains, however, that unions that challenge managements to live up to their principles and act in better ways must ask themselves the self-same questions—for even if those questions are at times uncomfortable, the answers truly are worth the effort.

Applying the language and perspective of quality is a valuable way to think about how unions might be managed and led. At the same time, one must be careful not to slip into corporatist views of unions. In one sense, union members are customers. They receive services and sometimes goods from their union, and hence need to be afforded the highest level of customer service. It is also true that many operations of a union mirror a business; there are accounting functions, membership records, communications departments, personnel managers, and so on. These functions also need to be conducted in a high-quality manner.

But union members are more than consumers of a commodity; they *are* the union, and hence take on a different character than mere customers. There is also a different nature to a union as an organization than one might find in companies or government agencies. This unique union character, this unique culture of a vital and energetic social movement, needs to be *accentuated* in a quality process, not ignored.

Since we assert that quality is *not* a concept solely in management's domain, it can be applied with integrity in thinking about the union as an organization. There is no Malcolm Baldrige Award for unions. Perhaps there should be a version that recognizes excellence in unions. Many of the categories used to judge the Baldrige Award winner also fit union situations, but there are others that don't seem to fit. Hence, quality unionism is a hybrid form of effective business organization *and* social movement.

From the successful experience of various unions, we have extracted a set of principles that could guide the application of quality to union operations. We outline some of these principles and a brief collection of practices below in a way that seeks to reflect the uniqueness of union organization.

## DEVELOP CLEAR, MOTIVATING, STRATEGIC VISION AND VALUES

Turn to the first page of most union constitutions and you find a stirring understanding of why unions exist. They articulate a broad vision of unionism. For example, the International Association of Machinist's constitution adopted in 1899 eloquently states:

> Believing that the right of those who toil to enjoy the full extent of the wealth created by their labor is a natural right . . . and recognizing the fact that those who toil should use their rights of citizenship intelligently, through organizations founded and acting along co-operative, economic and political lines, using the natural resources, means of production and distribution for the benefit of all the people, with the view of restoring the commonwealth to all those performing useful service to society. Now, therefore, we, the IAM, pledge ourselves to labor unitedly on behalf of the principles set forth.

The preamble to United Auto Workers constitution states:

> The precepts of democracy require that workers through their union participate meaningfully in making decisions affecting their welfare and that of the communities in which they live.
>
> Managerial decisions have far reaching impact upon the quality of life enjoyed by the workers, the family, the community. Management must recognize that it has basic responsibilities to advance the welfare of the workers and the whole society, and not alone to the stockholders.
>
> Essential to the UAW's purpose is to afford the opportunity for workers to master their work environment; to achieve not only improvements in their economic status but, of equal importance, to gain from their labors a greater measure of dignity, of self-fulfillment and selfworth.

The American Federation of State County and Municipal Employees declares in their constitution:

Workers organize labor unions primarily to secure better wages and better working conditions.

We hold that they also organize in order to participate in the decisions which affect them at work. One of the fundamental tenets of democratic government is the consent of the governed. Unions are an extension of that idea. . . . We are equally dedicated to exert ourselves, individually and collectively, to fulfill the promise of American life. Amidst unparalleled abundance, there should be no want. Surrounded by agricultural surpluses of all descriptions, there should be no hunger. With advanced science and medical research, sickness should not go untreated. A country that can shoot rockets to the moon can provide adequate education for all its children.

Powerful as the original mission statements of many unions were, they need to be revisited and updated often to adjust to current conditions. A review process that diplomatically asks what remains the same and what should be different is a powerful way to reaffirm core values and adjust to new times and new yearnings.

Many craft unions, which have seen craft skills and craft autonomy diminish, will find the quality movement provides an opportunity to reconnect to the pride of quality craftsmanship and the empowerment characteristic of craft workers. Industrial workers who have come to understand the importance of collective action can reinterpret the development of teamwork as an instrument of new solidarity and collective purpose. For service and government workers eager to provide public services of value, the quality movement provides a means for them and their unions to connect to public purposes and public missions that provide dignity and opportunity. Regardless of the industry, a quality union reconnects to the values and aspirations of its membership at a range of levels from the worksite to the public arena.

Yet in the life of a union, day-to-day struggles around the interpretation of particular contract clauses, coping with various crises, and confronting adverse economic conditions too often narrow the focus and crowd out a broad review of "why union?"

Today the need for clarity of vision for *why union?* is more pressing than ever before. When union membership and commitment passed from father to son or when working-class neighborhoods supported union values, a discussion of *why union?* was taken for granted. Today the world has changed: Sons and daughters often go into occupations that are not well organized. Workplaces are off the bus routes and long commutes dilute community. Media hostility to unions and a school system that poorly teaches labor's place in society means that understanding *why union?* can't be taken for granted.

Today's quality union has a vision that vividly connects to the needs of today's workers and articulates this vision clearly to its membership and the public. Members in a quality union may not be able to repeat verbatim the guiding principles in their union's constitution, but they should know it speaks to what is the heart of unionism and helps explain why they belong.

A vision of a quality labor movement has to be a broad and proud one. It has to include ways to provide community and support for union brothers and sisters in a world increasingly atomized. Part of the vision of the union movement is one where workers can find common ground and representation regardless of their diversity of backgrounds and particular concerns.

A quality union reaches such common ground in the daily life of workers in many specific ways. It affects what goes into the paycheck and the security and adequacy of benefits. It establishes additional services that help stretch those dollars. It finds ways to help those who are sick or down on their luck. It provides an avenue for justice and fair play on the job. It assures the highest standard of safety and health based on ergonomics and prevention. It reaches into workplaces to help assure the highest-quality products and the best quality of working life. In building trades and arts unions, it is the venue and advocate for jobs.

Our vision of a quality labor movement looks to long-term employment security at best and employability security at the very least. It is as concerned with the creation of wealth as it is with its distribution. It seeks a voice on the widest range of issues—including the strategic—and at the highest of levels—possibly up to the board of directors. This requires anticipation of the market and proactively challenging employers to keep up with the times. It requires developing skills training through either the employer or the union itself. The training should allow each member the ability to participate in the work force now and in the future. It challenges management to engage in the highest-quality production and/or service, both to preserve vitality in the market and as a source of pride for its membership. It recognizes that a quality union is adamantly for workers, not necessarily militantly antimanagement. It adopts cooperative strategies when they advance worker interests. In cases where the parties cooperate, the union adds value to the employer and the union sees a reciprocal return. It cooperates with management when it can but fights when it must.

In years past, for example, certain building trades locals gained a costly reputation for jurisdictional disputes, wildcat strikes, slowdowns, sickouts, and worksite arguments over the division of desirable tasks. Locals across the country eager to win back work from nonunion contractors have moved in recent years to change all such actions and their negative image.

Typical is a Philadelphia coalition of building trades locals, contractors, and construction users known as Built-Rite. It sponsors four task forces (productivity and cost-effectiveness, communications and training, safety and health and public policy, research and public information) that review all proposed work contracts and resolve problems before they materialize. They assess which (formerly rival) unions should do what job, discuss project budgets, clarify the quality of work that is expected, and review health and safety guidelines. They agree to a regular schedule of problem-solving meetings throughout the duration of the building project and exchange traditional defensiveness and posturing for the freest flow of communications ever known in the building industry. Above all, in project after project the parties are able to boast they finished ahead of schedule, below budget, without accidents, and without a single work stoppage . . . claims that help union builders beat out the nonunion competition for the next big job.

Our vision of a quality labor movement is not linked to one employer alone but to a broader notion of what is needed in society. Like any organization, it has validity when it has a clear sense of its core values. These values provide the compass for its concrete actions. Social unionism that seeks advancement for all workers, union members and nonunion members alike, is not only the right policy, but it is the smart policy. In countries such as Sweden and Australia which have broad social agendas for their labor movement, the percentage of the work force in unions is far higher than in the United States. In the United States, many unions have assumed that the larger the gap between union and nonunion workers, the greater the financial incentive for workers to organize. In fact, the large gap is the incentive that fuels intense employer resistance. Countries with a higher social floor that reduces the income gap between union and nonunion workers have higher levels of union affiliation. This doesn't imply that higher standards of living are not important for union members, but it does clearly demonstrate that social concern enhances the labor movement in very practical ways. It is a recognition that a rising tide lifts all boats.

A quality union learns new ways to spread a traditional union value of *solidarity*. It viscerally understands the strength of workers is enhanced when they stand together, not when they are broken apart by nationality, race, or creed. Yet solidarity must be more than a popular union song, and it must take on new meaning for a new generation.

Quality unions, for example, were among the first to recognize in the annual Workers Memorial Day observances, as initiated by the AFL-CIO in 1989, a rare and valuable opportunity to help "organize the unorganized" around health and safety. That is, long in advance of the day, progressive locals go out of their way to plan a stirring program, complete with the somber reading aloud of the names of men and women lost in the preceding year in unnecessary and preventable workplace accidents or workplace-based illnesses. In Philadelphia, to cite only one example, PHILAPOSH, a large coalition of area unions, rallies hundreds of members to walk behind a coffin preceded by a bagpiper, the entire spectacle making a strong prosafety (and prolabor) impression on everyone in and out of the parade. A major focus of union-backed pending OSHA reform efforts will establish joint labor-management health and safety committees in both union and nonunion workplaces to raise the level of protection for all workers, whether affiliated or not.

In many ways, the union of the future acts out the adage, think globally and act locally. In a global marketplace, unions have no choice but to engage in global unionism. Quality unions understand the way to protect jobs at home is to help create economic opportunity abroad by increasing buying power and diluting the draw of low-wage economies. They learn from successful strategies in various parts of the world and apply them in ways that make sense to their own membership and context. They seek new partnerships as part of a quality strategy. Max Ogden, a senior official on the Australian Council of Trade Unions (ACTU), demonstrates a way to conceptualize this strategic vision of the labor movement in Figure 1.[1]

Unions stirred by the rapidly increasing internationalization of business and the awesome loss of jobs to low-wage nations are starting to develop a new labor internationalism. Walter Reuther, the legendary UAW leader, conceived of global companywide unions in the 1950s and was among the first to call for global collective bargaining. That dream has proven quite ambitious and very difficult to achieve, but more and more unionists here and abroad agree the goal is sound.

---

[1]Max Ogden, *Towards Best Practice Unionism: The Future of Unions in Australia* (Leichhardt, NSW: Pluto Press Australia, Ltd, 1993), p. 10.

**FIGURE 1**
*Steps Toward a Global View for the Union Movement*

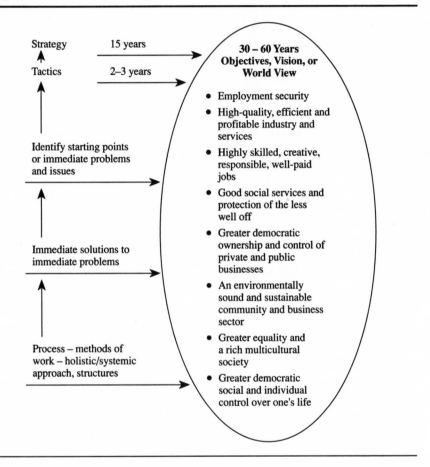

Accordingly, unions have long given critical support to democratic unions in Europe and more recently to the union-based Polish Solidarnocz. It is noteworthy that Nelson Mandella marched in a massive 1992 protest rally in South Africa wearing a cap from the United Auto Workers union—a tribute to the valuable ties forged by the UAW and other unions with anti-apartheid forces.

Quality unions are studying a new model for creating effective trans-frontier worker solidarity on economic and social issues. The model exists in Europe, where the unification of Europe has given way to increased

European Community-wide collective bargaining agreements. More and more European works councils have been set up to unite unions and workers from the same company but different nations under the leadership of the European Trade Union Council and the International Confederation of Free Trade Unions. Works councils for Digital, Ford, General Motors, Gillette, and Volkswagen are up and going. These may soon gain full legal recognition and protection throughout Europe. In America, there is increasing interest in works councils both for domestic reasons and to effectively step up to international challenges.

Global alliances provide an example of how quality unions can develop strategic partnerships and alliances. They can also ally with other American unions, community and nonprofit organizations, governmental bodies, and service vendors that will serve the broader interests of the union as an organization. These alliances can be found domestically as well with willing employers to help assure high-quality jobs. As a principle, no union can go it alone. It needs to develop appropriate partnerships with other organizations to achieve its objectives.

Typical here is what caring unions undertake in many charity drives sponsored annually by locals coast to coast. Major charities get a substantial boost from union-conducted golf tournaments, awards dinners, or plain old-fashioned coin-collection-box-shaking at area street corners. The work of the Letter Carriers Union for muscular dystrophy is an outstanding example of union involvement in these issues. Similarly, when a natural disaster strikes, such as a hurricane, tornado, or massive flood, the Red Cross looks to immediate aid from scores of trained volunteers from labor. Experienced unionists mobilized by labor community action programs show others the best way to do the most good in crisis situations or community involvement. Organized labor partners with reputable charities and relief organizations so that all in need, whether members or otherwise, can get such help.

But partnering can be in other, more tactical areas as well. In the battle over NAFTA, unions combined with environmental groups to raise issues that shaped the debate on trade and assured that labor and environmental concerns would be addressed. At Ravenswood Aluminum, where its workers were locked out in a bitter struggle, it was an alliance with local environmentalists who challenged the company's pollution practices that forced a settlement. Today, the community, management, and the union meet together to try to resolve environmental problems in their community. In Los Angeles, garment trades unions set up assistance programs for immigrants and illegal aliens who are being exploited by unscrupulous employers in sweatshops. Without asking for membership, unions have built alliances with churches and other community organizations to provide literacy, immigration, and legal assistance to the many who were disenfranchised and abused. In many of their countries of origin, unions too often held the keys to jobs through corruption. California AFL-CIO unionists worked with others in their community to show that unions can be honest and helpful.

In quality organizations, partnering goes beyond a joint communiqué or tossing issues over the transom. It means working together on solving common problems and building long-term relationships that add value past the immediate situation. Partnering is more than coalition building; it requires a greater overlap of interests and activity and a longer-term perspective than most traditional paper coalitions.

## SCAN THE ENVIRONMENT AND BE PROACTIVE ABOUT CHANGE

The world changes constantly and union members and union organizations are naturally affected by these changes. A quality union tries to stay ahead of the curve through active scanning of its industry and the world around it to identify what needs to be done ahead of time. It is anticipatory, helping to set the agenda for its membership and its counterpart employers.

Many have characterized unions as reactive institutions better able to tell management what it has done wrong than to advance an agenda of its own. Critics have long lambasted the labor movement as behind the times, stodgy, unresponsive, and out of date. Stung by the charge, quality unions have reacted constructively by pioneering in the use of long-range forecasts, scenario writing, and other powerful future-oriented tools.

Over the past decade a number of unions have set up blue-ribbon commissions on the future. Typical is the use made by the Communications Workers, Steelworkers, Teachers, Bakery Workers, Postal Workers, and other international unions of a committee established to put the thinking of leading futurists at the disposal of each union. The AFL-CIO established a high-level committee on the evolution of work. Many such committees, after a careful review of the literature and interviews with relevant forecasters such as Alvin Toffler, John Naisbitt, and others, draft alternative forecasts for the next 10–15 years, complete with the pros and cons of future-shaping policy options the union should consider as early as possible.

Known as *applied futuristics*, this approach drives a quality union to plan ahead, to make clear statements of priorities, to make difficult trade-off decisions after careful analysis, and to substantially improve its strategic information base. Neither an artificial exercise, nor a cover for rubber-stamping a set of predrawn conclusions, applied futuristics sets quality unions firmly on an empowering path the public and media associate only with cutting-edge business organizations. It enables the union to develop a profile of what a successful 21st-century union will look like, and allows it to identify the long-term goals, strategic options, and priorities it will need to come ever closer to that profile.

A quality union looks for new opportunities for its membership. Take, for example, the possibilities of new jobs in environmental industries. Some unions, such as the Laborers International Union of North America and the Operating Engineers, have begun to develop the training and capability to handle environmental cleanup safely and efficiently and to install and operate the new equipment that environmental action may require. When the Sheet Metal Workers developed a guarantee for solar panel installation, it was exercising positive leadership for its membership and for a society struggling with energy dependence. In coping with defense and aerospace conversion, the International Association of Machinists in California has looked to the development of high-speed rail lines and the technology it would require to provide jobs for skilled and willing workers who would otherwise be glumly out on the streets.

## BE PARTICIPATIVE, DEMOCRATIC, EMPOWERING

The union of the 1950s understandably mirrored the bureaucratic model of its times. The union of the next century will be based on the organizing model of unionism. Each and every part of the union will be geared towards mobilizing membership and helping the union grow. This implies broad and deep participation. In a manual on internal organizing, the AFL-CIO notes: "Many local union leaders are finding that using an 'organizing model'—involving the members in solutions—results in higher degree of organization and success." The manual went on to argue for an organizing model of unionism that involves and empowers "the membership in actions and decisions that affect them—whether bargaining for a contract, recruiting new members, settling a grievance, or lobbying on a bill in the legislature."[2]

An organizing model broadens the union's membership with greater involvement of women and minorities than ever before. Indeed, the fastest-growing segment of the labor movement comes from the ranks of women and minority workers. We see increasing leadership drawn from these communities at all levels. This diversity gives new strength and vitality to the labor movement. A quality union identifies ways to engage various constituencies as activists in the union. For example, many unions have established women's committees that are not the ladies' auxiliaries of the past, but provide skills and support to help union women advance in the union. Many attend Union Women's Summer Schools around the country or participate in Coalition of Labor Union Women (CLUW) chapter activities. They are expanding union concern for family issues and for equal opportunities at the workplace that shatter the glass ceiling and unglue the sticky floor that stop advancement opportunities.

Quality unions stand out in their concern for others, whether dues payers at the time or not. Typical is the effort made by the IAM CARES Program to pioneer innovative ways organized labor can bring disabled workers into the labor market and enable them to share in the rewards of economic independence as wage earners. The Machinists Union does such a fine job that it has received numerous federal grants and innumerable national and international honors. Two-thirds of the over 5,300 handicapped workers placed in jobs during the 1980s were not IAM members. This did not stop 20 IAM Lodges coast to coast from going all out to help disabled workers. Evaluation studies show that the retention rate of the workers helped by the union is higher than that of the labor force as a whole.

In a like manner, the Postal Workers Union set up a Hearing Impaired Task Force to look into the long-standing problems of the over 4,000 hearing-impaired workers in the postal service. At contract time, the union was successful in winning, for the first time, language requiring telephone devices for the deaf, open-captioned training films, certified interpreters as needed, and other overdue remedial aids.

Quality unions foster participation at every level and in new ways. At the worksite level, new methods are being employed to engage the mem-

---

[2]"An Organizing Model of Unionism," *Labor Research Review*, no. 17, Spring 1991, p. v11.

bership in the union—to move it beyond an insurance policy to a wellness program. Diverse members have many different ways of participating, through joint quality efforts, community service, union social functions, union benefit programs, volunteer organizer programs, employee assistance efforts, and a host of other possibilities. For example, *The Activist*, a regular newsletter published by the Letter Carriers Union, helps identify many ways to involve the membership and increase participation in the union.

In a quality union, a union meeting engages the membership in dialogue and problem solving on important issues. Union leadership uses a variety of techniques to involve the membership at such meetings and in other functions of the union. These include inviting guest speakers, use of labor arts, especially music, and small group discussions that focus on analyzing problems, not simply debating resolutions. At the Saturn plant, UAW leadership interviewed every member for 45 minutes on their concerns prior to contract negotiation as a way to involve everyone in the process.

At the national union level, participation is also increasing. The Oil Chemical and Atomic Workers, for example, developed a number of rank-and-file committees to examine ways to improve the union's operations and outreach to members including youth, women, and minorities. Still another major union, the Bricklayers, has regionalized and expanded participation on its executive council to give more voice to local leaders in the setting of national union policy.

Australian trade unionist Max Ogden terms the new union a *facilitative organization,* and says: "By facilitative is meant an organization whose focus is on developing the capacity of the members both as a collective and as individuals, to solve their own problems with as little need as possible to rely on the full time official. This strategy is not premised on the idea that the union plays a less significant role, but on the contrary, that the union becomes a much more powerful, living, robust organization at the enterprise level."[3] He goes on to say later, "The official is going to require extra knowledge and skills to act as a facilitator, be patient, understand and expect that mistakes will occur, but that these are important lessons, and that the shop stewards and members come out of such an experience with greater knowledge, competence and confidence."[4]

---

[3]Ogden, *Toward Best Practice*, p. 44.
[4]Ibid., p. 43.

Unions are democratic institutions. Members expect them to be. When there are lapses, members and the public are shocked and dismayed. Businesses are autocratic institutions. We expect them to act like bosses. When they act democratically, it is news. The particular forms of democratic participation vary from union to union. What needs to be central is the commitment to democratic participation. Unions open to debate, unions that encourage discussion and are open to diverse opinions are not undermined but strengthened. One of Edward Deming's most compelling principles is to drive out fear in the organization. A union is better off when it eliminates fear of expressing different ideas that aim for improvement of the union. Finding ways to express ideas fully and constructively is a major challenge for a quality union.

Healthy debate does not erode the solidarity of union activity. Nor does the recognition that elected leadership retains the right to speak for the union undermine democracy. In quality programs on the company side, top executives must exercise strong leadership and model the behaviors they expect of their subordinates. This difficult challenge is no less true for top leaders in labor unions. When they are clear and unequivocal in their support of a quality union and make every effort to conduct themselves in ways that reflect that quality commitment, it goes a long way towards creating the climate for quality change in the union organization as a whole.

Leadership means healthy doses of listening—but it also means being appropriately assertive. Ogden says: "It also means a leadership which does not take the easy road and simply agree with whatever the members are saying, but is prepared to take issue with them, argue and generate effective and competent debate. A most important role for the official is to constantly explain and keep the [local union] enterprise leaders abreast of the big picture, the strategic objectives. Otherwise we will fall into the trap of a narrow focus, even pitting enterprise against enterprise."[5]

## CREATE A LEARNING ORGANIZATION GROUNDED IN DIALOGUE, AWARENESS, AND DATA

The ability to do much of what we have discussed requires that the union become a learning organization. This means constantly learning organizationally, collectively, and individually about critical issues facing the

---

[5] Ibid., p. 44.

union. A quality union also seeks to empower and enable its union leadership and members with the skills necessary for effective participation. At the root of unionism is the moment when one worker talks to another worker and suggests that there can be a better way. They, in concert with their coworkers, eventually adopt this idea as one to be put forward. This learning from each other, debating what can be done, is the essence of a learning organization.

In Sweden, for example, the development of study circles have spread democratic learning methods that support democratic institutions. *Study circles* are small groups that meet with a facilitator to study together a common text around an issue for at least several sessions.[6] The labor movement is one of the prime institutions using study circles to build dialogue, involvement, and leadership. In fact, Swedish unions' largest expenditure is on education, with over 10 percent of members attending a union course or study circle each year. American unions spend far less on education. In the United States and Canada, the Bricklayers Union has used study circles extensively to build awareness and consensus including issues of the future of the industry, organizing, and ways to include women and minorities in the union. A study circle on health issues was developed and successfully used by the AFL-CIO Department of Professional Employees.

An extensive education effort is part of a high-quality union. It not only adds competence to the union, it provides a focus for increased union self-confidence. New membership orientation is the starting point. Initial contact with members should be an invitation to learn more about the union—not just about a payroll deduction. The building and construction trades, for example, sponsor extensive skills training activities through apprenticeship training. The union education side of apprenticeship needs to be beefed up. Apprentices are required to have 144 hours of related instruction, but little of it is related to the union and union-management relationship that afforded them this opportunity. A quality union in any industry will require participation in a session where the history, structure, benefits, and means to participate are discussed in an open and inviting way with new members.

Local and national leaders require additional competencies to be able to perform their tasks. The Bricklayers Union developed a competency-

---

[6]Leonard P. Oliver, *Study Circles: Coming Together for Personal Growth and Social Change* (Washington, DC: Seven Locks Press, 1987).

based model for local leadership that articulated 143 specific competencies needed by local business agents. This ranged from legal affairs, to how to run an office, to communications skills. It was generated with the active participation of business agents. They then sought a variety of means to improve their level of competency—such as finding a mentor, reading a book, listening to a tape, or taking a class. In any union, there are a set of competencies and skills that individuals need to master to be able to perform their roles better. A quality union not only touches the spirit and heart of unionism, but it also helps its leaders develop the specific skills needed to transfer intention into reality.

One of the emerging demands on and by unions at the end of this century has been the development of training and career development programs. Increasingly, it is the union which provides the member's avenue for career development, given the uncertainty of employment with any one employer. Lifelong learning supported by the union ranges from basic literacy, to career skills, to access to higher and adult education, to certication training. Australian unions are working with employers to develop flexible career ladders that lead to transferable skills which are linked to higher income and more capability. They are becoming the leading advocate for career development for workers.

For an American example, the Food and Beverage Workers Union Local 32 in Washington, D.C. very successfully developed a model program to help immigrant and other workers/members with low levels of literacy to learn new skills. This program has led to an increasing commitment of the local to further education. Contrary to the program proponents' initial thinking, those who leaped at the opportunity for education were high-seniority members finally able to pursue dreams of education. Literacy efforts run by unions increase union allegiance, help make better employees, and open up new windows on life to its membership.

There are also a number of extraordinary efforts to build career development paths. All of these are part of a strategy to develop high-skill, high-wage, high-quality, high-performance organizations. The Communications Workers of America, International Brotherhood of Electrical Workers, and AT&T have developed jointly administered programs such as the Alliance for Employee Growth and Development and Pathways to Learning which work with members/employees to open up new opportunities for learning from improved literacy to advanced degrees. Through counseling and placement programs, current and displaced workers are encouraged to develop themselves to improve their employment security, workplace performance, and personal development. In the auto industry, the United Auto Workers has negotiated the largest educational system in the United States with each of the Big Three domestic manufacturers. This system jointly provides an extensive array of educational benefits and options. Joint quality efforts are housed in the same organizations as these educational programs and are integrated with them. The Steelworkers Union has also recently begun such a massive effort with a multiemployer framework in the steel industry, the Institute for Career Development.[7]

Yet unions also have extensive programs on their own or in conjunction with universities. The Harvard Trade Union Program, created in 1942, annually brings together as many as 30 mid-career union officers and staff for an intensive 10-week session on the leadership response to the challenges for the future. Union-run campuses are found at the Steel worker's Linden Hall Center, the UAW's Black Lake facilities, and the Machinist's Education Center at Hollywood, Maryland. Perhaps the most unusual are the first-rate facilities run by the maritime unions. These facilities have the latest technological advances and the highest-quality training for the merchant marine. Computer-simulated decks train masters, mates, and pilots, while sea-bound classrooms introduce future seafarers.

Part of learning is generating data-based information that helps inform and guide the organization. Effective data can help decision makers make more informed judgments about the priorities and budgeting necessary to move forward. Generating data involves maintaining a research capability either in the union or through local universities that enables it to gather and analyze relevant information. It is also linked to information systems in the union, allowing it to measure and determine its progress against its goals.

A union has a clear-cut system of evaluation that lets it know whether it is meeting customer needs—an election. But better use between elections of evaluation data and budgetary information can also help in steering the union. Data in quality organizations is an overarching way to learn about what is being done and what can be improved. It also means moving to more data-based decision making and relying less on power or caucus politics at the local level. Some unions are using quality decision-

---

[7]Lewis Ferman, Michelle Hoyman, Joel Cutscher-Gershenfeld, and Ernest Savoie, et al., *Joint Training Program: A Union-Management Approach to Preparing Workers for the Future* (Ithaca, NY: ILR Press, 1991).

making tools, including root cause analysis, pareto diagrams, and other data collection and analysis tools used in quality processes. The use of such techniques can clarify options and open new opportunities to union decision makers.

No major corporation would engage in a significant competitive contest without having done thorough research on its competitor's strengths and weaknesses. Comprehensive campaigns, a research-intensive activity, continues to attract more and more support from quality unions that recognize in this new tool a powerful 21st-century response to the contemporary complexities of corporate life. Vulnerable characteristics of targeted companies are used as part of a strategy to win an organizing or contract campaign. Research uncovers an interlocking web of related interests propping up the targeted company. Pressure can be accurately and effectively placed on creditors, banks, stockholders, and others through informational picketing, leafleting, and other tools.

For example, when the United Steel Workers recently sought to force the Raytheon Company to reconsider its plant shutdowns, union strategists familiar with comprehensive campaigns were able to adroitly combine political pressure here and abroad and, with shareholder involvement, to expose mismanagement.

Best of all, comprehensive campaigns demonstrate to members that organized labor can unravel the most Byzantine relationships among parties of relevance to a campaign to win labor gains. Research has been shown to be an indispensable and potent ally in an age where information is increasingly coterminous with power.

## COMMUNICATE WITH ALL LEVELS
## FREQUENTLY AND CLEARLY

A quality union has an effective multidimensional communications system. First and foremost, a quality union listens and listens well to the voice of its membership. Unions have little value if they are not accurately reflecting the concerns of their membership—a corollary to the voice of the customer. Some unions have made extensive use of polling data and use focus groups and surveys to keep a pulse on membership concerns.

Internal communication within the union is configured for clear and rapid connections on fast-breaking issues. Democracy can spread when information is shared fully and in a timely manner—but effectiveness can also increase when communication is rapid and responsive. Sophisticated technology can help, but person-to-person union building through one-on-one programs can effectively gather and disseminate information.

Energetic public and legislative relations are also trademarks of a quality union. For some managers, emphasis on legislation and public relations may seem far afield from the day-to-day representation of membership. But the broader context of public opinion and legislative actions establishes the context for union action. On one level, what can be won at the bargaining table can be taken away in a legislature. But the legislative arena provides a venue to promote union goals and broader social issues key to coalition building. It is the court of public opinion that sets the tone for bargaining and organizing. Unions have always advocated for their membership in multiple arenas, and these are two critical venues for quality action. SEIU Local 790 in San Francisco, for example, reaches over a million northern California household members with a new magazine cable TV show, "Talking Union." The Chicago Committee for Labor Access has been airing a one-hour TV series, "Labor Beat," since 1986. The New York City American Federation of Teachers produces "Inside Your Schools," a half-hour magazine-style TV series that explores issues in public education. "Focus on Labor" is produced near Minneapolis by members of UAW Local 863 for viewing throughout the state. And in Nashville, trade unionists produce "Fraternally Yours," a creative television interview show focused on labor topics.

But quality unions are also concerned about the next generation of workers and have developed programs in the schools that lets students know what labor has accomplished and what its goals are. School-based programs—or innovative approaches such as the labor merit badge for the Boy Scouts—help young people learn more about what trade unionism is all about.

At the national level, a unifying theme of *Union YES!* has led to improved public perceptions of unions. The Labor Institute for Public Affairs, allied with the AFL-CIO, produces top-quality material to be used in union meetings and in public sessions. Some have aired on public television. This is coordinated out of the state-of-the-art studio on the first floor of the AFL-CIO headquarters in downtown Washington.

TV ads, videos, placards, buttons, and press releases done in a high-quality manner affect the current climate. Promotion of the union label and advertisements touting the quality of union workers and products are ways to communicate a proud union message on quality. All these methods—personal contact, newsletters, advertisements, video, and even on-line computers are all ways to communicate broadly and effectively.

## USE RESOURCES IN AN EFFECTIVE AND LEVERAGED MANNER

Union aggregate financial resources will always be less than the total financial resources of employers in an industry. That means the union must be particularly careful about using its hard-earned dues dollars wisely and leveraging them as much as possible. Sound administration that eliminates waste is a way to increase and leverage the resources available for the key activities of the union. Some unions have developed problem-solving groups, especially in administrative areas, to help in the more efficient and effective delivery of union services and functions. Better use of resources does not necessarily have to mean that union activities are shoddy or "on the cheap." High-quality presentation sends a symbolic message of high-quality unionism.

What the union is rich in is human resources. Encouraging the membership to participate in activities of the union is a way to magnify what can be done without adding very high costs. This means using staff in ways that leverage this human potential. Unions cannot have staffing levels that will completely eliminate grousing about "where is the union staff?" Staff cannot be in all places at all times, doing everything for the membership. Indeed, even if this would be physically or fiscally possible, this all-encompassing servicing model would be very disempowering of the membership.

Effective use of union staff means drawing on their commitment and experience in ways that use staff members to the fullest, while respecting their own quality of working life. The life of a union representative can be very stressful. Long hours, many nights away from home, and an unhealthy diet are too typical. These, when combined with other poor health habits, can lead to serious personal health problems that are also devastating for the staffer's home life and family. These also make it difficult to do an effective job for the membership. Relationships with union staff should model the best practices expected of employer counterparts.

Political control of the union must remain with elected officials, but these officials can empower and enable their staff to help get the union's work done effectively. This activity is not a political threat, but an opportunity to help political officers show their constituency how well they are addressing their concerns through effectively marshalling the union's resources.

There are specific ways that quality unions are looking to get more bang for their buck. Ford wouldn't pay its executives to buy General Motors cars, nor are unions willing to allow their investment dollars to be plowed into projects that undercut their competitive position. For example, the MFS Union Standard Trust Fund was launched in September 1993 to mark the first time that the AFL-CIO has ever advised a private asset management firm on an investment vehicle geared to unions and union members. It provides a vehicle to direct the over $350 billion pool of Taft-Hartley multi-employer pension funds. Although the AFL-CIO has stopped short of putting its formal seal of approval on the fund, MFS's close consultation with the federation is publicly acknowledged. Accordingly, MFS will invest in about 200 major national firms that meet such criteria as highly unionized, very cooperative with existing or organizing unions, exemplary labor-management relations, and support worker values in other vital ways—or at least, do not work against them.

Once a substantial number of union pension funds pool their assets in MFS, organized labor should have more influence when bringing issues to large corporations eager to have these pension funds. These investments are sound fiduciary decisions of their jointly trusteed boards that protect future pension checks and create better, more secure paychecks for American workers today through supporting the companies where union members work.

## COMMIT TO CONTINUOUS UNION IMPROVEMENT

The notion of continuous improvement is a central principle in quality improvement. Trade unionists since Samuel Gompers have understood continuous improvement, but instead called for "more." Even as a quality corporation consistently delivers high dividends and increasing stock value over the years, so too can a quality union be expected to improve the returns for its customers—the membership. This includes examining ways to improve overall compensation and benefits, quality of jobs, and health and safety. Improving compensation may not simply mean higher base wage rates, but also may include a variety of additional compensation strategies that create gainsharing and profit-sharing opportunities. The total package is also enhanced as benefits are improved, both in quantity and quality. When unions focus on retaining health care benefits through wellness approaches to cost containment, both coverage and health are enhanced.

There is nothing wrong with a quality union insisting that a quality workplace includes continuous financial growth for the member as well as the company. This is not necessarily at the expense of the employer, but can be in ways that help each succeed. Indeed, a quality union cannot win continuous financial growth for its members without helping to ensure continued growth in revenue or performance for the employer.

Quality unions appreciate how important it is to counter the popular misconception that all unions are after is more wages and benefits, a cruel misrepresentation of the response Samuel Gompers actually gave on August 23, 1893, when asked what labor seeks. Educational efforts in quality unions help new and old members alike grasp the full significance of Gompers' timeless insistence that organized labor "wants the earth and the fullness thereof. There is nothing too beautiful, too lofty, too ennobling unless it is within the scope and comprehension of labor's aspirations and wants. . . . We want . . . more of the opportunities to cultivate our better natures and make childhood more joyful, womanhood more beautiful and manhood more noble." *More* is not simply quantitative acquisition, but rather qualitative growth for the individual and society. *More* also includes greater dignity on the job and in the community as well as a greater sense of control over one's own destiny.

For a union, continuous improvement also means increasing membership. This is done through increased organizing efforts that seeks to bring higher standards of living for workers and a higher quality standard for the workplace to new companies and agencies. Organizing is broken into two categories: internal and external. A quality union never stops organizing the unorganized through membership drives and organizing the organized through membership involvement. But quality internal organizing is not simply a function of how spiffy the circular is, but of the connection to potential members that engages them in the union community.

External organizing is often a costly and frustrating affair that requires the boldest and most persistent efforts. The growth of volunteer organizers among dedicated members helps spread the union message more broadly. However, quality unions need to make hard choices about where to invest their limited resources in organizing campaigns. One method that has helped unions do this is extensive polling. Many unions, for example, rely on a professional telephone polling company linked to the United Food and Commercial Workers Union. Headed by a tough organizer and negotiator, Phil Comstock, Wilson Associates focuses on attitudes rather than opinions, on deep-reaching values rather than superficial responses to complex realities. It puts at the service of organized labor a data-based profile of nearly 500,000 completed telephone interviews with union and nonunion workers alike, a unique data bank of inestimable value to union researchers for organizing and for helping the union test possible initiatives.

Another area for continuous union improvement concerns how it appropriately services its membership. Over the past decade, labor has developed an impressive array of services that it provides to its membership as a way to increase the benefits of union affiliation. Typical of the advances here is the Union Privilege Benefit Program. Begun in 1986 and guided by ideas advanced by the AFL-CIO Committee on the Evolution of Work, the program offers valuable perks such as an inexpensive credit card, reduced rates on health and life insurance, an affordable auto club, and an eye care program. Over the years, the program has grown to include discount services for home mortgages and breaks for first-time home buyers. A travel club tries to feature union facilities. Also available to workers who cannot join unions because of the loss of an organizing drive or the shutdown of a workplace, benefits for "associate" members help the labor movement retain some useful connection with the millions who may someday help a quality union launch a fresh organizing or legislative effort.

Adding new services that add value to union members is one way to improve the union. But continuous union improvement looks to every aspect of member and local union support and asks how it can be done better and more efficiently. Answers have ranged from providing continuously upgraded computer services to local unions, to identifying new staff roles that can improve service to the membership, to new communications methods. An organizing model of unionism doesn't mean replacing high levels of service, but finding new and more effective ways to provide services of value to the membership.

Continuous union improvement is a never-ending struggle. At no point does a union reach a worker nirvana where there is no need to articulate the hopes for a better future for and with its members. There is an old labor song that says, "every generation has to win it again." This reminds us that continuous improvement means that each union must not take for granted what it has and rest on its laurels but must look for ways to build on its accomplishments in the future. In any organization—corporate, union, or other nonprofit—previous accomplishment does not guarantee future vitality.

## LOOK TO ADEQUACY OF SYSTEMIC RESPONSE

A quality approach is systemic. It looks to improving the whole system because it is systemic change that yields the best results. The hardest task for a quality union is to develop a comprehensive and effective plan that will really make a difference. All unions have at least several strategies running at the same time to address major problems.

An election-to-election set of strategies in unions is no more effective than dividend-to-dividend strategies in corporations. The sad fact is that all too often they are insufficient to the task they have been designed to address. In some cases, the time required to roll out a good program across a national jurisdiction is too long, and thus limited results are seen. In some cases, the resources available are insufficient and it winds up as watered-down soup. And frequently a lack of priorities, a limited range of responses, and a weak evaluation mechanism makes it feel like frantically plugging fingers in a dike. Sometimes because of the press of various issues, a union finds itself careening from one issue to another without ever truly resolving many.

Quality unions put in place long-term strategies that address the needs of the membership as whole people—workers, family members, and citizens. These strategies must have simultaneous short-term and long-term outcomes that are valued by the union's constituency, that are observable and often measurable. A quality union uses a variety of means of advocacy including political action, collective bargaining, industrial strategy, legal avenues, community partnering, self-help, and labor-management cooperative strategies. A sign of a union in trouble is one that is locked into only one strategy for advancing the interests of its members. A variety of strategies and tactics aligned to work together synergistically is best. This often requires cross-functional cooperation in the union and a rethinking and flattening of organizational structures to increase flexibility, response time, and efficacy. In some cases, this may require structural changes in how the union is organized. It may also mean seeking consolidations of unions through mergers to adjust to changing industry conditions and to provide certain economies of scale.

The other major barrier facing unions is their own version of what is called *cycle time* in quality management. Like many of their management counterparts, unions find frequently that they come up too short or too late to address the challenges that confront them. Often the time and energy it takes to get an issue resolved can allow the problems to grow or even to get ignored. The world is changing at such a rate that rapid response mechanisms from unions are needed in order to act in a timely and thorough fashion. Decisions need to be made, plans developed, implementation strategies deployed, and assessments of impact made in relatively short order. Unions can configure themselves to address this challenge or get tied up in frustrating knots. This need for response often feels in conflict with the demands of the democratic process and the need for building commitment and consensus. A solution is to spend the necessary time on developing agreement on principles and empowering those who need to implement policies with the authority and tools to get the job done.

## CAVEATS AND CONCLUSIONS

A union that wrestles with the principles we have outlined can be much better off. In many cases, they can engage as quality partners with employers in a common search for excellence. We hope that the ranks of these partnerships will expand and grow. But we are also painfully aware there will also be employers who choose to act unilaterally, engage in adversarial union avoidance or busting, or are just lousy managers oblivious to the possibilities of quality improvement. In all of these cases, a quality union can rise to the challenge.

Any quality organization goes beyond rhetoric and programmatic gimmicks to the hard work of doing the right things right, consistently. Likely, however, unions will mix inertia with reform, commingle yesteryear's mistakes with today's corrections. It will probably not be entirely of one piece, but will instead messily contain both regrettable and meritorious components. This not withstanding, a quality union is one that strives to be clear about its goals, strategies, tactics, and values. Drawing its strength from its members, it reflects its membership's needs. It develops strategies that address those needs. It continually assesses how well those needs are met and tracks the directions they can and do evolve. A quality union is recognized as such by its members and those in the community who see it as an instrument for the continuous advancement of the working people it represents, the places where they work, and the communities where they live.

# CASES OF JOINT QUALITY ACTION

## Chapter Five

# United Auto Workers and General Motors[1] Quality Network

## *General Motors Total Quality Management Process for Customer Satisfaction*

**Thomas L. Weekley**
*UAW-GM Quality Network*
*Assistant Director, General Motors Department*
*United Automobile, Aerospace and Agricultural Implement Workers of America, UAW*

**Jay C. Wilber**
*UAW-GM Quality Network*
*Executive Director, General Motors Corporation*

## A HISTORICAL LOOK AT THE UAW, GM, AND QUALITY

The importance of quality, particularly product quality, to business success and job security has been evident to the leadership of both General Motors (GM) and the United Automobile Workers' (UAW) union since

[1]We would like to acknowledge the contribution from Betsy Reid Creedon, consultant to the UAW-GM Quality Network. Her input and perspective provided the authors with important insight into the principles of total quality management and the necessity to focus on implementation and constancy of purpose.

87

their founding. Prior to the company's relationship with the United Automobile Workers, General Motors' leadership recognized that quality could only be achieved by all parties working together. In a 1934 letter to "All Employees in General Motors Factories," Alfred P. Sloan, Jr., then president of General Motors Corporation, wrote:

> Recently I sent you a pamphlet outlining the policies governing General Motors relations with factory employees. In that pamphlet it was said that the relationship between management and employees 'requires a harmonious working together to the end that the quality and cost of the product may be such that the business will prove continuously successful and will survive.' What this means is that we have got to make products which the public will buy, and we can do it only by all working together with that in mind. The buyers of our products are our real bosses. They are the ones who provide the money for the wages of every one of us. We must satisfy them or lose our jobs. . . . General Motors has been able to grow and provide more jobs only because we have had products of good quality at satisfactory prices. This has been possible because General Motors employees and management have worked together.[2]

Sloan finished his letter, "The spirit of fairness and cooperation in our relations with one another is necessary. It is only by real teamwork that we can maintain the quality of our products and satisfy the buyers upon whom all of us depend for our livelihood."[3]

When this letter was sent to all General Motors employees, independent unions were organizing workers in various auto plants. Teamwork, product quality, and satisfied customers, all characteristics of a total quality system, were not foremost in the minds of union organizers. They were concerned with the quality of the work procedures and practices, as well as the relationship between the worker and the company. At the time, the relationship between the unions and management was adversarial. In 1934, the American Federation of Labor (AF of L) agreed to hold the first national conference of the United Automobile Workers Federal Labor Unions. Two hundred delegates convened in Detroit, Michigan in August of 1935. The employees in General Motors factories had begun their fight for representation.

---

[2]Alfred P. Sloan, Jr., Letter to All Employees In General Motors Factories, October 15, 1934.

[3]Ibid.

The relationship between General Motors management and automotive workers in its plants began to formalize when, on February 11, 1937, the company agreed to negotiate with the union after a bitter 42-day sit-down strike at Fisher Body Plant No.1 in Flint, Michigan. A one-page agreement resulted, the first auto contract between the union and one of the Big Three, and the first of many joint documents between the UAW and General Motors.

In these early years, the union bargained for wage increases, a grievance procedure, and recognition of seniority in matters of layoff and recall. However, there was another issue that received attention. The earliest UAW-GM agreements specifically recognized and emphasized the importance of product quality to both parties. The 1940 UAW-GM national agreement, which had grown to 39 pages, stated in its introduction:

> The management of General Motors recognizes that it cannot get along without labor any more than labor can get along without the management. Both are in the same business and the success of that business is vital to all concerned. This requires that both management and the employees work together to the end that quality and cost of the product will prove increasingly attractive to the public so that the business will be continuously successful.

Thus, quality was viewed as a joint responsibility and remained so over the years. However, the primary focus of such quality efforts was not always the customer. As an example, a letter from George B. Morris, Jr., GM vice president, to Irving Bluestone, UAW vice president and director of the GM department, dated November 19, 1973, and included in the 1973 UAW-GM national agreement, reemphasized quality, focusing on the union and management working together to achieve it. It particularly emphasized improving the work environment for all employees, establishing an atmosphere "designed to improve the quality of work life, thereby advantaging the worker by making work a more satisfying experience, advantaging the Corporation by leading to a reduction in employe absenteeism and turnover, and advantaging the consumer through improvement in the quality of the products manufactured."

Here, social and physical environmental issues for hourly employees took precedence over stated productivity and product quality concerns. For the most part, such quality of work life (QWL) programs failed at General Motors because there were no structured mechanisms linking their efforts to plans for tangible productivity gains and quality improvements. However, where there were pockets of success, subsequent total quality efforts were facilitated. QWL was an important stepping stone for future joint quality efforts since it recognized people as important assets of General Motors. Over the years, various efforts addressed product quality; however, most efforts were management-driven, following traditional lines of thinking (e.g., additional inspection, post-production repair, and additional supervisory involvement).

The 1980s brought competitive pressures not faced in the past by domestic automobile manufacturers. Japanese automobiles, long regarded as cheap products of poor quality, seemed to suddenly appear as low-cost, high-quality alternatives to domestic vehicles. Domestic manufacturers continued to utilize antiquated, inefficient methods and systems that did not effectively integrate the needs and requirements of the people doing the work or respond adequately to customer requirements and demands. General Motors attempted to address this issue by installing high-tech, highly automated production systems to reduce labor costs. Japanese competitors, however, implemented lean manufacturing systems that better utilized people and technology to streamline and create efficient processes through small, incremental, continuous improvements. Additionally, the Japanese experienced major breakthrough improvements and innovations as a result of their continuous improvement efforts.

## EMPLOYEE INVOLVEMENT

QWL efforts had raised an awareness within General Motors management that company methods and systems must be modified to use the knowledge and talents of its most important resource, the men and women on the job. GM people, not just technology, were recognized as key to competitive advantage. People produce, apply, maintain, modify, and improve technology. In the late 1970s and early 1980s, the American automobile industry was comparable to foreign competition in automotive and production technology; where we were different was in how we managed people. The United Automobile Workers had encouraged worker participation in the decision-making process on the job for many years, through contract provisions establishing quality of work life programs, joint apprentice programs, joint health and safety programs, joint time-study methods, and other programs or methods. However, efforts were isolated and lacked a systems approach. They were often very narrowly focused. Lessons learned from one program did not migrate to others; organizational learning did not take place. As important as these early efforts were, neither party successfully bridged the gap between worker participation in the decision-making process and traditional management responsibilities and union rights. Negotiations subsequent to 1973 continued to address joint participation, searching for a balance between specific and joint responsibilities. This evolving dialogue increased understanding for both parties.

In the early 1980s, union leaders focused on the general need for worker participation in quality efforts in order to retain domestic jobs for American workers and to provide customers the best possible value. These issues were critical to the American automotive industry if the standard of living of the American worker was to be preserved. During the same period, some management officials began to recognize that an over-reliance on high-volume manufacturing resulted in inflexible processes. This inflexibility made it difficult for workers to respond quickly to the production changes necessary to meet customer quality requirements and ensure efficiency. At the same time, a recognition of people—the skills they possessed and the processes that allowed their input—became a greater focus of both parties. Within management, however, there was some confusion about the implications of worker participation. Some were concerned that such participation would open the door to higher levels of union involvement in the running of the business.

## ALIGNING QUALITY ACTIONS

Although traditional organizational structures and bureaucracy hindered radical change, efforts continued to better train workers and utilize their ideas in the manufacturing process. Distrust on the part of General Motors workers created political pressures within the UAW that hindered the union leaders' ability to fully participate in new processes. The overall lack of success of QWL had left workers skeptical that they could work with management. Such distrust was evidenced by the creation of new caucuses and special interest groups within the union structure.

In spite of this, both union and management leadership recognized they had to do something. Joint processes, mentioned above, had been written into a succession of national agreements. Management had sponsored several quality programs: Targets for Excellence, General Motors Quality Ethic, GM Mark of Excellence, and GM Quality Institute. GM employees, both hourly and salaried, had extensive exposure to quality-related subjects. All of these efforts were aimed at improving quality and thus satisfying customers. Unfortunately, due to the complexity, diversity, and size of General Motors, the results were often inconsistent and efforts were duplicated. The focus on customer satisfaction was not coordinated. All of the programs were aimed at the same target, but they did not line up. There was not a single, consistent approach that would result in a total impact greater than the sum of the individual efforts.

In July 1985, a joint committee comprised of international union and management representatives was formed to study the Philip Crosby quality process that was then prevalent within General Motors. A number of concerns from various locations had been raised regarding lack of jointness in this approach and limited union and worker involvement. The committee concluded that the Crosby process did not adequately recognize the need to involve the union structure in identifying appropriate members of a plant-level quality implementation team. Additionally, the workers' role in the quality improvement process was solely to identify problems; they were not involved in the resolution of problems. Further, there had been no attempt to communicate or explain the massive cultural and systemic changes that the Crosby process espoused.

Early in their examination, committee members determined that the study should be expanded beyond the Crosby quality process. They identified several quality programs that were being implemented throughout the corporation, many based on the work of W. Edwards Deming and Joseph Juran. All these efforts had begun before a joint agreement was reached on what was needed at GM to accomplish product and service quality improvement and job security. The committee's report, issued to Don Ephlin, UAW vice president and director of the GM department, and Alfred S. Warren, Jr., vice president of industrial relations for General Motors in March, 1986, recommended a national joint quality conference to determine who does what and why.

In February, 1987, continuing joint improvement efforts were brought into focus when General Motors and UAW leaders met in Toledo, Ohio, to discuss quality and the necessity of changing past practices and relationships. Each group/division in General Motors was invited to present

**FIGURE 1**
*The Toledo Accord*

---

The undersigned leadership of General Motors and the UAW is jointly committed to securing General Motors' position in the market and the job security of its employees in every phase of the corporation through an ongoing process of producing the highest quality customer valued products.

The parties agree that the production of world-class quality products is the key to our survival and jointly commit to pursue the implementation of the following jointly developed quality strategy:

- Ongoing UAW/GM top leadership commitment and involvement to a corporate quality stategy.
- Voice of the customer is understood and drives the whole process.
- Ongoing education and training to suppport the quality improvement process.
- Communication process to support the quality process.
- Create a plan and structure for a joint process for implementation.
- Total involvement for continuous improvement and elimination of waste.
- Reward system which supports the total quality process.

Signed by Robert Schultz, W. Blair Thompson, William Hoglund, Alfred Warren, John Debbink, Donald F. Ephlin, Donald Atwood, Charlie Best, Charles Katko, E. M. Mutchler, E. Czapor, Robert Stempel, L. C. Reuss, J. McDonald, and Robert Walker

---

its quality plan to the leadership. These presentations clarified the need for a single joint quality system for the corporation. This system would have to address each division's/group's needs, as well as those of the union. The resulting actions reflected more of a joint partnership, addressing each others' needs while working together on participative processes. This effort not only met the self-interests of both parties brought forcefully to the fore by economic pressures, but also demonstrated a maturing relationship between the parties. They recognized that their futures depended upon working together in areas previously recognized solely as management concerns or union concerns, with a strict line of demarcation between the two. The meeting resulted in what became known as the *Toledo Accord*, which envisioned a new partnership in addressing processes, engineering and manufacturing methods, and the working environment throughout General Motors. (See Figure 1.)

This broad understanding formed the foundation for a total quality management initiative named the *Quality Network*. This one process for managing General Motors was to be jointly developed by GM and UAW

**FIGURE 2**
*The Arrow Model of the Quality Network*

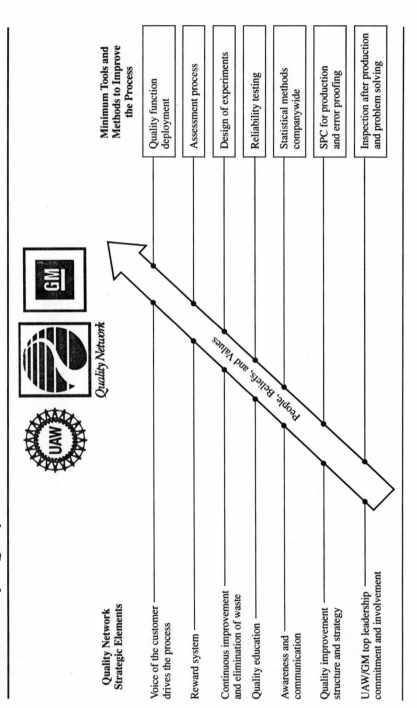

leadership, encompassing participative management at all levels of the corporation. At the Toledo meeting, an "arrow model" was created that depicted the early elements of the Quality Network. (See Figure 2.)

A joint task force was named to create an identity for this first-ever corporatewide joint quality effort. The resulting logo captures the ideas, philosophies and themes of the Quality Network. The UAW is represented by the circle and GM is illustrated by the outlaying square, each reflecting the shape of its respective logos. The circle and square design interrelationship along with the use of the UAW and GM logos represents the teamwork and cooperation pledged by the two parties. The UAW-GM Quality Network's journey to continuous improvement is depicted by the curving white line.

Previous efforts at participative management gave valuable insights into the obstacles that a total joint process might face. The architects of the Quality Network realized from the beginning that top leadership commitment across the board had to be in place. Quality and customer satisfaction provided a comfort zone for union and management to work together, a common goal that both parties did not have to fight about. Quality of work life (QWL) programs had allowed input from all parties but did not have the broad-based support and commitment to address critical processes throughout the corporation. Although successful in some areas of the corporation, QWL generally floundered without active and consistent commitment and support of both union and management leadership. Responsibility for implementation was at the discretion of individual locations. QWL lacked uniform plans and process; consequently, there was great variation in the results. This was a valuable lesson learned. Other joint programs, such as employee assistance, health and safety, and apprenticeship, showed that joint decisions can elicit a much broader base of support, creating an atmosphere of excitement and mutual commitment. These programs were national in scope and were recognized in the national agreement.

Union leaders were criticized by some for addressing issues that traditionally had been concerns of management; charges of "getting in bed with management" were not uncommon. Conversely, management officials were criticized for "selling out" to the union because of their efforts to invite the union to be full partners in the business. These reactions mirrored traditional viewpoints based on a history of union/management militancy and distrust. However, times and the marketplace had changed, and so had the way business was going to have to operate to survive. Change was inevitable, and both parties recognized the necessity to manage it and turn it into an opportunity for growth, prosperity, and security.

Top union officials, at their constitutional convention, received the support of delegates for joint programs. This support was based upon the compelling argument that early input into the decision-making process gave workers some say in their future and the future of the company.

Both union and management leaders made it clear to their constituents that neither party had sold out to the other, but that the decision to address mutual concerns jointly would benefit everyone involved.

At a Quality Network training workshop, Horst Schulze, chairman of the Ritz Carlton Hotel chain, gave an excellent example of why both parties must jointly address future issues. He began by saying that he did not understand why unions and companies could not work together. He likened the issue to two people sitting in a boat in the middle of the ocean with no chance of rescue. Suddenly, a leak develops in the boat. The management representative turns to the union representative and orders the individual to fix the leak. The union official responds by saying that management should fix the leak since he caused it. The management official then rationalizes that the problem was the union's fault because of faulty workmanship. The union official counters that if management would have authorized proper preventative maintenance and upkeep, the leak would never have happened. Charge is answered by countercharge until, ultimately, the boat sinks.

Obviously, the moral to the story is that management, workers, and their representatives are all in the same boat together. They can argue, as in the past, about cause and effect, and sink. Or they can work together, address mutual concerns, and save the ship.

## THE QUALITY NETWORK

The idea of a UAW-GM Quality Network clearly represented a departure from the antagonistic cycle Schulze talks about. It would provide an established process and environment for joint decision making and action. Following the *Toledo Accord*, top UAW and General Motors officials, led by Don Ephlin and Bob Stempel, were charged with creating a vision for the Quality Network and designing the framework for the process to be presented to their respective leadership. They did so, and the Quality Network was formally recognized in the 1987 national agreement:

"During the course of 1987 negotiations, General Motors and the International Union, UAW held extensive discussions about the subject of product quality. There was recognition on the part of both parties to the National Agreement that the cornerstone of job security for all General Motors employees is the production of highest quality, customer-valued products. This is reflected in the extensive efforts both parties have devoted to the subject of quality both on the national and local levels, exemplified by the formation of the UAW-GM Quality Network. . . ."

The 1990 UAW-GM national agreement further defined the role of the Quality Network. Document no. 119, *UAW-GM Memorandum of Commitment to Product Quality,* states: "General Motors process for total quality is the quality network—the one process for customer satisfaction. Although Management has the ultimate responsibility for the Quality Network, it is recognized that UAW leaders and members are valuable partners in the development of the process, the action strategies, and its implementation plans."

In a presentation titled "Theory of a System",[4] the authors gave an overview of the Quality Network and delineated its key elements. The Quality Network is defined as General Motors one total quality management process for the continuous improvement of the business system. The system in question, in a global perspective, is General Motors and its operational meaning draws heavily on the work of Dr. W. Edwards Deming. Deming defines a *system* as "an interconnected complex of functionally related components that work together to accomplish the aim of the system."[5] The North American Operations (NAO) is the primary profit center of the corporation and the primary component of the corporation. The vehicle, truck, component, and service groups are subsystems of NAO, with each in turn composed of platforms or divisions as their subsystems. Plants are the subsystems of the platforms or divisions. Finally, within any plant there are departments that are subsystems supporting plant operations. This entire system of nested subsystems (all business units and functions) is focused on optimizing NAO.

---

[4]"Theory of a System," presentation, August 1992; Accompanying booklet (QN #2051) published by Quality Network Publishing, 1992.

[5]Dr. W. Edwards Deming, *The New Economics for Industry, Education and Government,* seminar, July 14–17, 1992, module 3, "Introduction to a System," p. 46. Dr. Deming has since published a book by the same title drawn from a notebook used by Deming (Cambridge, MA: MIT Center for Advanced Engineering Study; 1993).

The Quality Network draws heavily from many recognized quality experts such as Joseph M. Juran, Philip B. Crosby, and in particular, W. Edwards Deming, whose methods have been tried and proven worldwide. Such experts agree that systems must be addressed *as a whole* to bring about long-term and lasting change. Short-term quick fixes cannot provide the lasting quality improvements necessary to compete in today's competitive world. The quick fix approach only results in "programs of the month" that do not encourage long-term employee commitment to change. Thus, the Quality Network encourages the establishment of standard processes and designs to ensure long-term change. More significantly, it emphasizes incremental improvements through employee suggestions rather than a search for the silver bullet to bring about system changes.

The Quality Network was premised upon union and management working together for mutual gain. For such a relationship to be feasible, both parties must be equally committed to the goal of creating a climate of mutual trust and respect. Creating such a climate was accomplished through a number of mechanisms. First, all communication concerning the Quality Network was jointly announced by the top leadership of both entities. The Quality Network was announced at the 7th Annual Quality Conference, broadcast throughout the corporation on January 13, 1988, and hosted by Don Ephlin and Bob Stempel. Although this was the seventh conference, it was the first joint quality conference and set the precedent for all subsequent quality forums.

Second, Quality Network awareness training was designed and delivered jointly. The Quality Network was rolled out to the corporation through a series of workshops delivered in the first quarter of 1989. Plant-level leaders from each corporate group (Truck & Bus, Chevrolet-Pontiac-GM Canada, Buick-Oldsmobile-Cadillac, Automotive Component Group, Power Products and Defense, Delco Electronics, Technical Staffs Group, Corporate Support Staffs, and Service Parts Operations) were led through two days of interactive team-building exercises as they learned about the Quality Network. Top UAW leaders and group executives presented the sessions together. Participants were seated at tables in groups of 10, including the "key four" from a plant—plant manager, chairperson of the bargaining committee, personnel director, and local union president—all seated together. In 10 sessions, over 4,000 union and management leaders attended the workshops together. Subsequent Quality Network materials, programs, workshops, and classes have all been jointly developed and implemented. A work environment education and training package has been designed for every location. Four strategies are presented for mutual consideration and understanding: support for the employee, top leadership commitment and involvement, communication, and cooperative union/management relations. These classes are designed to be jointly taught to groups with joint representation. Trust and respect cannot be mandated. However, much can be done in the design and execution of communication and education and training plans to help build these two critical factors.

## The Vision: Total Customer Satisfaction

General Motors' vision, as declared by the NAO Strategy Board, is total customer satisfaction leading to customer enthusiasm. The aim of the system is to establish an operational environment that provides for continuous quality improvement and results in total customer satisfaction. Every element of the organization is geared to satisfy the customer. *Satisfy* is defined as meeting and exceeding the needs, wants, and expectations of customers, resulting in repeat sales, owner loyalty, and new sales; using innovation and creativity to excite and delight. *Customer* is defined as all those affected by the system. General Motors has an obligation to its many customer groups to succeed: an obligation to its employees, shareholders, unions, suppliers, dealers, the communities in which it exists, the environment it affects, the industry to which it belongs, and the ultimate customers—the purchasers and users of General Motors products and services. Many customers belong to several of these customer groups. It is not uncommon for a purchaser of a new vehicle to be an employee, a union member, and a shareholder who lives in the community in which he or she is employed and is therefore affected by the environment surrounding the community. The system must:

- Provide a safe and healthful work place for its *employees*, where they have joy in their work, are confident in their job security, and are proud of the products and services they produce.
- Work in concert with its *unions* to support their efforts to ensure job security for their members.
- Ensure that its *shareholders* receive a fair return on their investments. It must be noted that many General Motors shareholders are pension plans of other large organizations.

- Develop long-lasting relationships with its *suppliers*, providing stability to their businesses and helping to improve the quality of their products.
- Produce exciting and highly valued products and services for its *dealers* to sell and to offer.
- Maintain a strong and healthy business which helps finance and sustain growth in a *community*.
- Improve products and processes that will contribute to the betterment of the *environment* for the good of all. This means that as the needs of all the various elements of the system are balanced out, the outcome must have a positive effect on the environment.
- Support and sustain a strong and healthy American automotive *industry*.
- Create and provide superior products and services for the *ultimate customer*, meeting and exceeding requirements and expectations while providing excitement and delight.

The Quality Network brings together all the components of this diverse, large and complex system for the purpose of attaining the vision of Total Customer Satisfaction. The Quality Network provides the four elements necessary to realize the vision: a value system, a structure, a process focus for analysis and understanding, and the tools and techniques for continuous quality improvement.

### *Quality Network Beliefs and Values*

Union and management leadership understood that a common set of beliefs and values was needed to define a basis for desired organizational behavior in any cooperative relationship. There had to be a shared value system for all. A group of General Motors top officials took on the task of articulating a value system for General Motors that would govern both the decision-making process and the treatment of people. A collaborative interview process obtained the views of union and management leadership. Input from all sources queried was startling and consistent. Most people wanted to be respected, trusted, and involved. Their responses reflected how people want to be treated in both their personal and professional lives and constituted a set of guidelines for successful relationships. In addition, respondents identified the customer as the final arbiter of products and services and affirmed that quality improvement is a never-ending journey.

The results were codified and became known as the *Quality Network Beliefs and Values*. They provide the cohesiveness necessary for a shared vision and have been adopted and championed by union and management alike. The *Beliefs and Values* of the Quality Network provide constancy of purpose.

**Customer satisfaction through people, teamwork, and continuous quality improvement.** The following are the *Beliefs and Values* of the Quality Network, fully endorsed by General Motors and the UAW:

*Customer satisfaction through people*

- Invite the people of GM to be full partners in the business.
- Recognize people as our greatest resource.
- Demonstrate our commitment to people.
- Treat people with respect.
- Never compromise our integrity.

*We believe that the people of GM and the UAW are General Motors greatest strength. Through their dedication and commitment to excellence, our people are the key to achieving our customer satisfaction goals.*

*Customer satisfaction through teamwork*

- Build through teamwork and joint action.
- Take responsibility for leadership.
- Make communications work.
- Trust one another.
- Demand consistency in the application of this value system.

*Joined as a team in a spirit of cooperation, union, management, hourly and salaried employees are working to achieve a common goal—customer satisfaction.*

*Customer satisfaction through continuous quality improvement*

- Make continuous improvement the goal of every individual.
- Put quality in everything we do.
- Eliminate every form of waste.
- Use technology as a tool.

- Accept change as an opportunity.
- Establish a learning environment at all levels.

*The people of General Motors are committed to the concept of continuous improvement in our treatment of people and in everything we do.*

The Quality Network is people, working together in the spirit of teamwork, continuously improving products, processes, services, and relationships. The *Beliefs and Values* serve as a creed for all GM employees, articulating how *all GM people* should behave as they work together to improve every aspect of the business. All decisions and actions are tested against them. This requirement allows the process to flourish and establishes what is OK-to-do in General Motors.


## THE STRUCTURE

A formal structure (see Figure 3), detailed in the 1987 national agreement, called for the creation of a corporate Quality Council (currently NAO UAW-GM Quality Council) consisting of the top GM operating officers and the top UAW administrative staff members. The president of General Motors and the UAW-GM department vice president cochair this council. The council meets three times per year, or more often if needed, to establish directives for joint action on quality issues.

The corporate Quality Council is an open forum where issues can be raised and discussed freely. An example of the impact discussions at these council meetings can have is evidenced in the 1993 national agreement. Between 1989 and 1992, GM North American Operations endured operating losses requiring elimination of waste, creation of more efficient processes, and development of a more focused approach to product quality. Efforts to address these concerns had resulted in the implementation of various quality improvement activities such as synchronous workshops, accelerated workshops (i.e., PICOS), lean manufacturing, and best practices. Implementation of these activities caused confusion in some locations as they appeared to rival Quality Network efforts. Although workplace improvements were realized in the areas of health and safety, ergonomics, and operations that affected the quality and cost of GM products and services, in many cases they caused certain jobs to be eliminated and some UAW-represented GM employees to be placed in a JOBS Bank (Job Opportunity Bank Security). From the 1993 national agreement:

**FIGURE 3**
*Original Quality Network Structure*

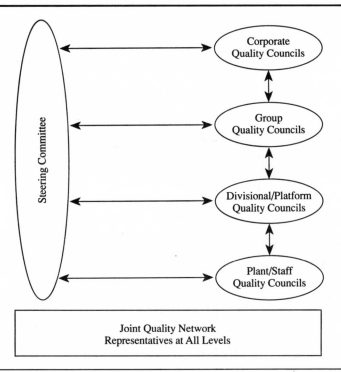

The Union leadership felt they could not be party to asking their members to assist in "working themselves out of a job" by supporting these efforts. In any joint effort, job security and "people issues" has to be considered so that people would be redeployed to meaningful work. The issue was discussed at the January 13, 1992 GM Quality Council meeting resulting in specific commitments to integrate synchronous efforts into the joint Quality Network Process and explore ways to employ people more effectively with meaningful work and help improve the business.

A joint steering committee handled the day-to-day implementation of Quality Council directives through interaction with various groups and divisions in General Motors. Each major group within General Motors (e.g., Truck and Bus, Chevrolet-Pontiac-Canada [C-P-C], Automotive Components Group [ACG], Buick-Oldsmobile-Cadillac [B-O-C], technical staffs, corporate support staffs) has established a jointly cochaired

**FIGURE 4**
*New NAO Quality Network Structure*

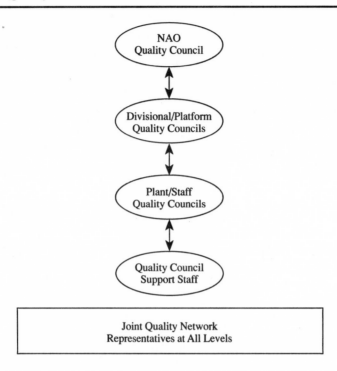

Quality Council to translate the corporate Quality Council and steering committee directives into action within their groups. The various divisions within each group also established Quality Councils to implement directives in their divisions (e.g., Lansing Automotive, Saginaw, and Delco Remy).

Finally, each plant has established a joint Quality Council to affect plant-level integration. These plant/staff Quality Councils are led by the "key four" leadership: plant manager, chairperson of the union shop committee, personnel director, and local union president. Quality Councils usually include members of the plant staff and other selected union leaders. In addition, a joint team of Quality Network representatives—one management person and one union person—is appointed at each plant to help carry out the plant-level objectives. These Quality Network representatives are the navigators, supporting their Quality Councils with implementation efforts. For example, they will be actively involved in seeing to it that their locations continue "to provide the necessary organizational support for employees to be trained and use Quality Network problem-solving techniques to improve product quality, reduce costs and become best-in-class in all products and services." In general, this interlocking structure of Quality Councils effectively communicates information across, as well as up and down, the corporate body.

From 1988 through October 1992, the Quality Network concentrated its work on the development of both the tools and techniques and the training and educational materials required to support them. The direction of the Quality Network was redirected in October 1992 at the first NAO UAW-GM Quality Council cochaired by Steve Yokich, vice president and director UAW General Motors Department, and Jack Smith, chief executive officer and president General Motors Corporation. The council acknowledged the development work of the previous years and then turned its efforts toward implementation.

In order to accelerate implementation efforts on the plant floor, in response to intensifying pressure for product quality improvement, a layer of the Quality Network structure and the steering committee were eliminated (see Figure 4). This restructuring better reflected changes within the General Motors corporate structure. The steering committee and group/staff level mirrored the group structure which was eliminated by the creation of the vehicle platform organization within NAO. Now, the divisional/platform Quality Councils would be a direct link between the NAO UAW-GM Quality Council and the plant/staff councils. Eliminating a layer of bureaucracy would speed up and simplify the communications process from top leadership to the plant floor. In addition, a full-time joint support staff would take over the duties of supporting the implementation process formerly held by the steering committee. Staff members would now interface directly with Quality Network representatives at all levels and work on specific assignments at the divisional, platform, and plant-floor level. For example, members of the support team who are experts in the new Quality Network suggestion plan are responsible for facilitating its implementation throughout the corporation. This fulfills a contractual obligation and one of the 1994 Quality Network objectives, "Each UAW-GM location to fully implement the Quality Network Suggestion Plan by May 1, 1994."

Also at this meeting, the leadership agreed that the primary focus for UAW-GM Quality Network efforts should be excellence in product quality. In a global effort, the Quality Network would continue to cultivate the larger scope of total quality management systems and philosophy. At NAO, the intensified focus on product quality improvement responded to a sense of market urgency, knowing that NAO was the prime profit center for the corporation. Cochairs Jack Smith and Steve Yokich announced the structural changes and the new product quality focus in a letter, dated November 5, 1992, to the leadership of both organizations. They concluded: "Our shared objectives are to satisfy our customers and competitively grow the business. We are committed to working in a spirit of cooperation consistent with the Quality Network *Beliefs and Values*." As codirectors of the Quality Network, the authors were empowered to take the responsibility to assist the organization in implementing the Quality Network process for immediate, specific focus on product quality improvements.

## THE PROCESS FLOW CHART

A system needs a plan. The third element of the Quality Network is a process focus. The Quality Network provides a road map for the corporation. (See Figure 5.) The GM product program management process (four-phase vehicle development process) depicts a uniform process for bringing GM products to market. The four-phase model lays out the structure and sequence to ensure that quality and conformance to the voice of the customer are defined and built into the products. The UAW was involved in the early stages of the four-phase action strategy development. Union and management key lead persons (KLPs) were assigned to chair the activity. Currently the strategy is being revised by a joint team. Members of the Quality Network support staff serve as consultants.

In essence, the four-phase model is a flow diagram of the production system. Each step in the process is clearly defined, and roles and responsibilities are described; work enters one stage, is changed in some way, and exits to the next step. Each step in the chain *has* a customer and *is* a customer. Various measurements and feedback mechanisms along the chain keep the process in check. By laying out the entire process, people see where they fit in the system and how their actions and work influence the whole. It provides a means to predict what will happen when any step in the process is changed.

**FIGURE 5**
*Product Program Management Process*

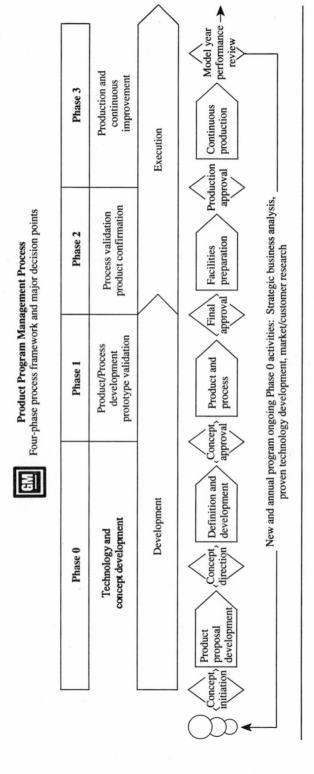

## THE QUALITY NETWORK PROCESS MODEL

The Quality Network process model (see Figure 6) is a standard way to analyze and understand a single stage in the four-phase Vehicle Development Process (VDP), as well as any other subprocesses. It defines the purpose of a particular stage and depicts the interaction of the various resources in that stage. If a work team should contemplate making an improvement in a process, use of the process model compels the team to examine all aspects of the process for full understanding of the effect of any change. All resources must be managed or blended to produce the correct output of the process. Additionally, the contemplated change can be tested against the production system process flow to predict its impact on the system as a whole. It is important to note that the heart of the process model is the *Beliefs and Values:* customer satisfaction through people, teamwork, and continuous quality improvement. Each process, no matter how small, engages people working together in the spirit of teamwork to continually improve their part of the whole.

If the process under study was to install a new material flow system, then customer requirements would have to include input from the operators involved as well as skilled trades, engineering, setup personnel, and others. Their requirements might include timeliness, correct parts, ergonomic considerations and accessibility. The people involved would include, in addition to those mention above, purchasing, health and safety representatives, material handlers, and others. Under methods and systems, implementation of a small lot strategy would be examined as well as workplace organization and visual controls. When considering materials, pull system and containerization strategies might be considered. The pull system would ensure that the correct material is replenished in the correct quantity in a timely fashion. Containerization would allow the optimum choice of packaging to work within the new material flow system. A planned maintenance process, an equipment strategy, will ensure the new system will operate at maximum uptime. The proper machine layout must be considered so that the new system will be synchronized with affected operations. Health and safety and ergonomic issues would be dealt with when studying the impact the new system will have on the work environment. They are integral to supporting the operator. As the new system is being designed, the voice of the customer will provide information

**FIGURE 6**
*Quality Network Process Model*

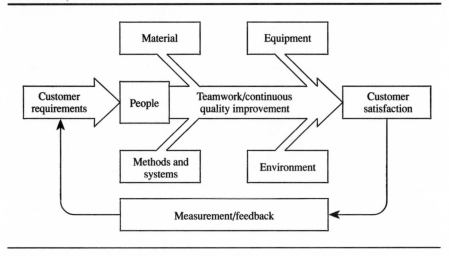

used to continuously update and refine the customer requirements. Without a measurement and feedback system in place, it would not be possible to know if customer requirements have been met. When all areas of a process are considered and balanced, customers should be satisfied.

## TOOLS AND TECHNIQUES

One of the first actions taken by the Quality Network was to establish standard methods and systems throughout General Motors. The strengths of the past had today become the weaknesses of General Motors. No longer could internal competition, division against division, be the driving force in improvement efforts. External competition had to be the focus of benchmarking and improvement efforts. Teamwork and cooperation had to replace internal competition. Best practices, whether from external *or internal* sources, had to be implemented. No longer could Chevrolet target Pontiac owners; both nameplates had to focus on their direct external competition. This was a major cultural change that has yet to be fully realized.

Initially, 36 basic strategies were identified as critical to ensure General Motors' competitiveness in the workplace: pull system, containerization, cooperative union/management relations, support for the employee, plant machine and office layout, and statistical methodologies, to name a few. Joint teams examined the best practices being used within the corporation, by the competition, and in other industries. These cross-functional "action strategy teams" represented all the stakeholders, union and management alike, affected by the strategy. The teams investigated, defined what is best for General Motors, and wrote guidelines for the strategies. These guidelines, 10-page process reference guides, were then developed to outline the basics of the strategies. They defined the strategy, its customers, its objectives, and implementation guidelines. Training materials, including videotapes, workshop guides, and training manuals, were then designed and produced by joint course development teams to supplement on-the-job training. The strategies were grouped under *initiatives*—actionable concepts that help focus their energies and illustrate the interdependency of the strategies.

- *Build a supportive environment.* Leaders and the organization focus on meeting the needs of our front-line people through demonstrated values, structures and systems, physical environment, rewards and measurements, job security, and leadership style.

- *Create an organizationwide customer focus.* Focus the organization on meeting and exceeding the needs of our internal and external customers—the people impacted by our processes, products, and services.

- *Synchronize the organization.* Utilize a systematic approach to identify and eliminate waste/non-value-added activities through continuous quality improvement of our products and services.

- *Detect, solve, and prevent product quality problems.* Encourage people to surface variation between the voice of the customer and the voice of the process (problems/opportunities), analyze and eliminate the root cause, and implement controls to prohibit recurrence. Constantly repeat this process as the catalyst for continuous quality improvement.[6]

---

[6]Quality Network Action Strategy Summary, (QN #1453: Quality Network Publishing) January, 1993, pp. 11, 23, 31, and 41.

These initiatives are closely interrelated. For example, it is extremely difficult to synchronize an organization without an open and honest workplace. Similarly, a workplace free from fear is achieved through building a supportive environment. Implementation of all four initiatives should be balanced to achieve the greatest benefit.

Training was presented to top leadership of both organizations through the Quality Council structure and cascaded to the plant floor level. This training was designed for leaders to present and support the strategies to their operating personnel at each level, all the way to the plant floor.

There has been much debate about this approach as it is very time-consuming. In the UAW-GM Quality Network, experience has shown that some leadership did not want to spend the time for full training in each strategy. The Quality Network responded by developing and providing to leadership overviews and awareness materials to introduce the training to their respective organizations as a means of showing support for the training content. In some cases, leadership deviated from the prescribed training design due to frustration with the amount of time it took to get results. Those who proceeded hastily have had to loop back, especially in the cases where environmental issues were not addressed from the beginning.

## DEFINING THE RELATIONSHIP

The Quality Network process identifies the union as a valuable partner and includes union involvement at all levels in almost every area of process management. The process does not envision a move to codetermination, although union concerns are considered in all aspects of decision making regarding Quality Council activities. The exercise of developing a current state chart (see Figure 7) drives understanding and defines a baseline of where the relationship between the union and management currently exists in the joint quality arena. Both parties agree to the need to work toward a defined future state.

The analysis of the current state builds on respect for each other's responsibilities and agreement to operate in an atmosphere of trust. Both parties recognize an obligation to perform as promised. This integrity ensures that trust given will be returned. Finally, open and honest communication becomes the basis for the relationship between the leaders of the Quality Network. Leadership agreed to discuss the previously undiscussable, to break down barriers that might make it impossible to work

**FIGURE 7**
*Current State Analysis*

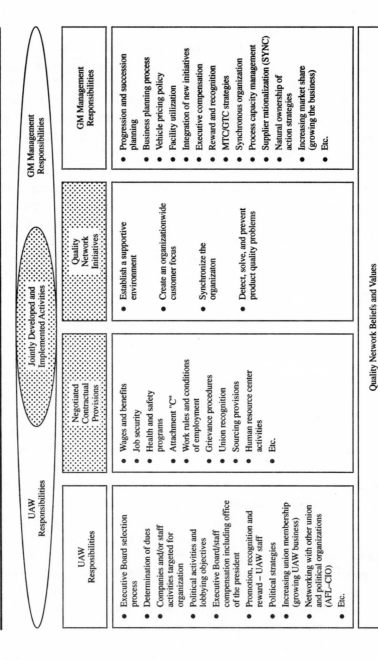

together. In the past, financial data was not shared to the extent it is today; the union learned of the financial state of the company through the annual report. However, in February 1993, GM President and CEO Jack Smith held a series of meetings with the top union leadership from unions across the country representing GM employees to discuss in great detail and frankness the financial state of the company.

The relationship between the union and the company is governed by many factors. Each organization has separate responsibilities, many required by law. For example, the National Labor Relations Act specifically defines management's responsibilities. These are restated in paragraph 8 of the UAW-GM national agreement: "The right to hire; promote; discharge or discipline for cause; and to maintain discipline and efficiency of employees, is the sole responsibility of the Corporation except that Union members shall not be discriminated against as such. In addition, the products to be manufactured, the location of the plants, the schedules of production, the methods, processes and means of manufacturing are solely and exclusively the responsibility of the Corporation." Unquestionably, it is management's job to run the business. However, empowering workers and encouraging their assistance and input into these decisions ensures a more successful organization. Today, represented employees participate in activities as far-reaching and nontraditional as marketing and supplier development.

The same provisions of the law define the union's roles and responsibilities, but do not require or encourage the union to consider problems the company may face. Clearly, self-preservation and common sense make such involvement necessary for a responsible organization concerned about its membership. There are many areas where interests overlap. These are depicted in the center of the chart in Figure 7. Specifically, they are the many common concerns found in national and local agreements, as well as the development and implementation of the Quality Network. These overlapping areas can be grown and shared. It is also incumbent on both parties to be mindful of the other parties' responsibilities. Decisions made by one part of a system cannot help but affect the total system. As each party's understanding of the other matures, decisions made by either side will reflect this knowledge.

In a recent nontraditional activity, the UAW, General Motors, Ford, and Chrysler worked together to demonstrate to members of the U.S. Congress the high quality of Big Three/UAW-produced vehicles. This event, Drive American Quality, highlighted joint program efforts that exist between the

UAW and the automobile companies. Further, it heightened awareness of component parts produced and the competitiveness of domestic manufactured vehicles and components. Sales, marketing, public relations, and increasing market share are clearly management responsibilities. But decisions made around these activities have a direct impact on the union and its membership.

## JOINT EDUCATION AND TRAINING

The education and training arena illustrates this point dramatically. Union and management facilitators deliver training at all levels, and encourage wide and enthusiastic participation. The national agreement provides for joint program representatives at each plant who are trained and certified in courses delivered at UAW-GM Human Resource Area Centers as well as the national center in Auburn Hills, Michigan. In addition, the Quality Network administers train-the-trainer (T3) classes in Quality Network action strategies in the plants. These representatives administer programs in the following functions: health and safety, joint activities, attendance, employee assistance program, human resource development, joint training, and Quality Network.

Through such activities, workers' talents and skills are recognized and used in a manner that, in the past, would not have happened. Hourly trainers and facilitators are extremely effective because of their plant-floor knowledge and experience. Success on the plant floor is tangible. It can be measured in reduced cycle time, reduced motion, less scrap, more ergonomically designed jobs, safer jobs, and high first-time quality rate, all of which affect the bottom line and solicit the support of leadership.

Everyone wants success and a way to achieve it. Success stories, hoarded as secret strategies in the past, are now openly and enthusiastically shared. At the GM Knowledge Center in Warren, Michigan, a joint task force from the Quality Network has developed a living display highlighting implementation successes from across the corporation. The Fort Wayne truck and bus plant, winner of the 1993 J.D. Power Silver Award, duplicated its display highlighting its successful product quality improvement activities back in its home location to share with all employees.

The excitement of success is infectious. Several annual joint conferences and workshops are held to allow representatives from across the corporation to share information and build understanding: health and safety conference, leadership conference, Quality Network representatives' workshop, key four conference, and joint training representatives, to name a few. A knowledge transfer network and database is currently under development, spearheaded by UAW and salaried communication resource people of the Quality Network. The purpose is to exchange lessons learned and to attempt to prevent the reinvent-the-wheel scenario.

The learning process is ongoing. Based on new ideas and benchmark studies, action strategies applied for continuous improvement are used to evaluate current training and education efforts and ask the tough questions necessary to drive change. This renewal process keeps training materials and methods and systems at the cutting edge of the industry's latest developments and monitors other industries for applicable concepts and ideas.

## THE PEOPLE COMPONENT

The overall success of the process depends on a constant awareness of people issues that must be considered in every decision. This basic concern for people must permeate every aspect of the labor-management relationship. When capital expenditures are contemplated, health and safety questions are the first issues addressed. If processes are to be changed or new processes implemented, the first consideration is the effect these changes will have on the workers. Market fluctuations affecting volume have a direct impact on workers; therefore, there must be a long-term commitment to job security that can withstand the swings in the market. Employee involvement at every level of the decision-making process has become commonplace. Access to top management is widespread; changes such as common cafeterias and parking lots and casual dress have erased much of the class structure differences between salaried and hourly workers. A components plant in Flint, Michigan made a ceremony out of taking down the wall between management's private dining room and the workers' cafeteria. It symbolized the changes that had occurred. Such changes affect most labor relations issues, which were traditionally resolved through the grievance procedure or left to fester due to the lack of an adequate process for employee input.

Both sides have found it desirable to discuss issues "before the concrete is poured" and financial constraints prohibit meaningful change. For example, traditionally when installing a new production operation, the engineer provided blueprints and the line was installed as shown on the prints. Skilled tradespersons modified the line to get it to operate and then production operators were worked into the line. Problems with ventilation, platform height, mechanical adjustments, and the like, were so costly and/or time prohibitive that changes at this stage were, at best, compromises that were less than satisfactory. Through the proper use of Quality Network action strategies such as people-focused practices, workplace organization, plant, machine and office layout, people who will eventually install and run the line are consulted first, before any plans are finalized. In many instances, mockups are made to test ideas and plan job assignments. The entire operation is then planned to fit the line to the needs of people rather than the other way around. This eliminates many disputes over health and safety, environment, skilled trades, and other issues that, in the past, have caused problems for everyone. Addressing people issues and getting advance input realizes tremendous benefits toward the aim of total customer satisfaction; reduction of waste leads to lower costs, higher quality, and faster model changeover. This simple, common-sense approach creates opportunity for both management and labor to win and engender teamwork.

Another paradigm concerning reconstruction and improvement has been redefined. Like the example of the installation of a new production operation, the redesign and reconstruction of existing production operations were often stuck in interminable planning stages. Some improvement ideas were informally touted, but never accomplished. People on the plant floor were frustrated; they knew how to make their processes better, more efficient, more capable, but they were not often part of the redesign team. Today there are quality and productivity improvement teams that are comprised of experts in all facets of the production operation, specifically including job setters and operators. Quality Network action strategies are their tools for effective change. An area is analyzed for improvement opportunities and the team agrees on the changes to be made. When necessary, bulldozers that have been literally waiting in the aisles move in and the changes are made then and there. If modifications or refinements to the changes are deemed necessary, they are made with as much dispatch. This activity could not happen without the cooperation of union and management leadership in the plant. A commitment to a redeployment plan for affected workers is a fundamental. In fact, cooperation and understanding is critical on the part of all affected functional groups: operators, job setters, the skilled trades, engineers, financial planners, schedulers, material handlers, health and safety representatives, and so on. In addition, production workers both upstream and downstream of the affected area must be informed and considered. The result of these efforts have been gratifying. Workers like it because they are being listened to and their workplace is being improved; ergonomic and safety considerations are always a factor in the changes made. Non-value-added wait time is minimized. Quick, if not immediate, response is gratifying to those involved and boosts morale. Better processes support the operators and lead to better products and better bottom lines.

## QUALITY NETWORK AND LABOR RELATIONS

The evolution of the Quality Network process has affected all areas of labor relations. Advance discussion, total information sharing, and mutual concern for problems have improved the worker-management relationship. The relationship between union and management has changed. Trust is being built. Today there exists a joint action process, epitomized in the design of the Quality Network, in which both parties resolve to solve mutual and common problems in a co-equal environment. Document 40 of the national agreement is an operational example of this belief. It spells out a process for "employees to raise product quality concerns in the course of carrying out their required work assignments." What is significant about this provision is that it specifies that this process is outside the grievance procedure. A concern may be settled immediately on the plant floor, or it could go as far as the NAO UAW-GM Quality Council should the resolution require resources or policy changes that go beyond plant or divisional jurisdiction. Recently an operator in an Arlington, Texas car assembly plant raised a concern about the fabric fit on the bucket seats he was installing. He personally experimented by sewing an extra piece of material to the area that had been pulling out further up the assembly line. Using the Document 40 process, he notified his supervisor and together they brought the problem, and in this case the solution, forward. Ultimately the supplier, a GM component plant, changed the specifications and eliminated a quality problem. Document 40 manifests this new philosophy of joint action in a co-equal environment. It also helps solve problems, engenders trust, improves quality, and positively impacts the bottom line. Both parties are demonstrating a tangible and visible commitment to this change.

This change in approach to labor relations has affected unions and workers directly and has strengthened the union's ability to effectively represent employees. Although this interactive approach requires a change in traditional union roles and functions, union officials are able to influence decisions that affect their membership much earlier in the process, with greater success. This increased involvement requires additional time and resources. Administrative functions within the union have increased, requiring additional resources and advanced training. Overall, joint involvement in the decision-making process has secured the union's position as an effective instrument for worker advancement and has changed the union's role from adversary to partner in areas that benefit workers.

Contract negotiations can be based on an attitude of mutual concern and address issues of competitiveness and quality as joint initiatives to the benefit of all parties involved. There are still basic philosophical differences that can only be resolved through collective bargaining efforts. Time spent on bargaining grievances can be better spent jointly resolving the issues that cause the grievances in the first place. It is more important to spend less time on disputes and more time on understanding people issues. For instance, determining ways to work together to improve the ergonomics of a work site results, in the long run, on less absenteeism, less injury, and less stress. When employees do not have to strain to do their jobs, when they are not fighting the system, quality improves. Counterbalanced tools, platforms of an appropriate height, and stock delivery at a constant level have helped reduce back injuries.

In General Motors, collective bargaining proposals and resolutions have created a better working environment, one in which workers have input into their own destiny. The Quality Network provides a foundation for the cultural transformation of the organization to a total quality system. Figure 8 depicts some of the characteristics of our culture as they have been in the past and as the Quality Network would like them to be. It is process focused, surfacing differences and addressing issues in a way in which they can be handled. The Quality Network helps create a better climate for labor relations, a climate in which other contract provisions that support employee involvement—such as outsourcing, subcontracting, job security, health and safety—may be dealt with. Viewing other contractual provisions on the basis of the *Beliefs and Values* helps promote a win-win attitude and changes the bargaining environment.

These changes are widely supported by the UAW membership, tempered by a natural reluctance to change. Previous experience with quality of work life (QWL) activities caused caution and, in some locations, distrust. Dissenting sentiments warned of the dangers of cooperating with management. They saw joint activities as a serious threat to union solidarity.

The Quality Network attempts to balance the WIIFM (what's in it for me?) consideration among the stakeholders:

- Management—improved quality and productivity.
- Employees—improved work site ergonomics, health and safety, and job security.
- Union—improved response and concern from management regarding historical areas of difficult negotiations such as employee workplace issues and training.

The evolution of traditional union roles had been a hotly debated issue throughout the UAW. An active debate ensued at the Collective Bargaining Convention in Kansas City, Missouri, in preparation for 1990 negotiations. Union leadership understood that a significant change in emphasis of the union's role was necessary to protect workers. The UAW felt it could no longer allow companies to make decisions prior to UAW involvement and that workers' equity should be considered *up front*, along with the interests of stockholders and others. Delegates to the convention overwhelmingly accepted the premise that the union must be proactive in seeking further input into areas previously left up to managers in order to successfully represent workers in the future. The 1990 and 1993 collective bargaining proposals reflect this new attitude and collective bargaining will continue to do so in the future. Contract ratification in 1990 was very high, and support for the notion that job security was provided in exchange for working with the company on improved quality and productivity has remained high through the life of the agreement as shown by internal and external surveys.

General Motors has also changed in its view of labor relations, recognizing the need for open information sharing and joint processes in every aspect of the business. This has required an extensive change in labor relations practices; the same changes faced within the union confronted the General Motors Corporation. More resources had to be redeployed into joint problem-solving and decision-making processes. This required a change in the working environment at every level of the corporation and remains an ongoing challenge today. People skills are now important considerations in promotions; rewarding people for different skills than those required in the past.

Trust can only be developed in an atmosphere of totally honest and open communication requiring sharing of previously confidential materials.

**FIGURE 8**
*Comparative Approaches*

| Characteristics | Traditional Union Point Of View | Traditional Management Point Of View | Quality Network Point Of View |
|---|---|---|---|
| Problem treatment | Management's problem | Crisis | Prevent problems |
| View of customers | Only management can influence | Sell | Satisfy and delight |
| View of workers | Responsibility (health, safety, ergonomics) | Burden | Assets, greatest resource |
| Shop floor | Part of the business they can influence | Source of problems | Continuing source of improvements |
| Shop floor methods | Tedious and boring | Static and routine, minimum of skills | Meaningful and continuously improving |
| Measures of success | Doing what you are told | Only in the end result | Improvement trends in product, process, service, and relationships |
| Focus on solutions | Management's responsibility | People, someone to blame | Improve the system |
| Treatment of information | "I'd like to know why. Why won't someone tell me?" | Confidential, restricted access | Open, honest, and shared |
| Focus of appraisal | Focus on weaknesses | Focus on weaknesses | Focus on strengths |
| Training | Part of the job | Necessary evil | Ongoing, positive contribution |
| Supervisors | Policemen | Inspectors | Coaches, team members |
| The way we view each other | Adversaries | Adversaries | Partners |
| Vehicle design | Not involved. "Why didn't you ask?" | Fix it later | Design in quality |

Source: This chart is adapted by the authors from a chart used by Dr. Jim Kowalick in association with the California Technical University.

During the 1993 national negotiation, the company openly disclosed financial data and future product plans. Plant operations considered for closing as well as those requiring new tooling and modernization were also discussed. Only a few short years ago, this would have been unheard of; information of this nature would not have been shared until the very last moments before implementation of the decision. The management of an organization cannot expect the leadership of the union to support decisions that affect the people they represent unless information is forthcoming.

The attitude concerning communication in general has changed. Employees have become used to seeing joint teleconferences and receiving jointly published letters. The Quality Network leadership hosts "Representative Conversations," a video program that addresses topics of the day. A recent session in January 1994 explained all the new contract provisions affecting the Quality Network. These programs are typically taped before a live audience with a spontaneous and often lively question and answer period. Copies of these programs are distributed to all Quality Councils via their Quality Network representatives with facilitation hints to promote discussion at Quality Council meetings.

## THE QUALITY NETWORK AND THE MALCOLM BALDRIGE AWARD

On August 20, 1987, Congress established the Malcolm Baldrige National Quality Award to recognize "U.S. companies that excel in quality management and quality achievement."[7] The *1992 Award Criteria* state that "the award promotes:

- Awareness of quality as an increasingly important element in competitiveness,
- Understanding of the requirements for quality excellence, and
- Sharing of information on successful quality strategies and the benefits derived from implementation of these strategies."[8]

The criteria list 10 core values and concepts that are embodied in seven examination categories. The values listed are customer-driven quality,

---

[7]*1992 Award Criteria, Malcolm Baldrige National Quality Award,* United States Department of Commerce, Technology Administration, National Institute of Standards and Technology, Gaithersburg, MD, p. 1.

[8]Ibid.

leadership, continuous improvement, full participation, fast response, design quality and prevention, long-range outlook, management by fact, partnership development, and public responsibility. Candidates for the award are judged in the following categories: leadership, information and analysis, strategic quality planning, human resource development and management, management of process quality, quality and operational results, and customer focus and satisfaction.

In 1990, the Cadillac Motor Car Company became the first automobile company to earn the prestigious Malcolm Baldrige National Quality Award in the manufacturing category. In a publication written to capture Cadillac's quality journey culminating with the Baldrige Award titled *Cadillac: The Quality Story*, the company revealed that the early 1980s brought the first real challenge to Cadillac's quality leadership since its founding in 1902. Response to this challenge did not "completely meet customer expectations. By the mid-1980s, Cadillac's prestigious image was in jeopardy."[9] It was Cadillac's answer to this challenge and the company's ultimate transformation that garnered the Baldrige Award. Three strategies were behind this transformation: a cultural change, a constant customer focus, and a disciplined approach to planning. The Quality Network played a major role in the execution of these strategies and is particularly credited for its effects on teamwork and employee involvement, the heart of Cadillac's cultural change.

Cadillac Quality Councils oversee quality improvement activities and are involved in the business plan implementation. The *Beliefs and Values* focus the entire organization on the customer. Cadillac's business plan is its quality plan, directed toward continuous improvement of products, processes, and services. The four-phase process is the disciplined road map Cadillac followed to execute each product program. The implementation of the Quality Network principle strongly supported Cadillac in meeting the Baldrige criteria. Figure 9 is illustrative of the relationships of some of the Quality Network action strategies with the Baldrige examination categories. The Quality Network is characterized by a participative management style, customer focus, and continuous quality improvement.

---

[9]*Cadillac, the Quality Story*, (Detroit, MI: Cadillac Motor Car Division), p. 1.

**FIGURE 9**
*Quality Network Linkage with the Malcolm Baldrige National Quality Award
(Summary Correlation of Malcolm Baldrige Examination Criteria to Quality
Network)*

| Baldrige Examination Category | Quality Network Primary Correlation |
|---|---|
| Leadership | Environment action strategies: top leadership commitment and involvement, support for the employee, cooperative union/management relations, communication |
| Information analysis | Technique strategies that provide data systems: design of experiments, statistical methodology, machine/process capability, validation, reduction of variation. |
| Quality planning | Technique strategies that provide customer requirements and planning skills: quality function deployment (QFD), voice of the customer (VOC). |
| Human resource utilization | People action strategies: people recognition, suggestion plan, employee excellence development. |
| Quality assurance of products and services | Technique strategies that provide the how-to tools to assist our people in assuring quality: workplace organization and visual controls, quality verification, pull system, lead time reduction, error proofing. |
| Quality results | The results from implementing technique strategies (measurement and feedback) |
| Customer satisfaction | Customer satisfaction action strategies: voice of the customer, quality function deployment, four phase. |

Application of the Quality Network philosophy and principles was the success at fulfilling the Baldrige criteria was the result of a total quality process that was Quality Network principle-driven. Upon winning the Malcolm Baldrige National Quality Award, the cochairs of the Cadillac Quality Council, Bill Capshaw, UAW international representative, and John Grettenberger, vice president, General Motors Corporation and general manager, Cadillac Motor Car Division, issued a joint statement:

> The Malcolm Baldrige National Quality Award process has helped us to review, as a company, our total quality system. What we learned has been invaluable—giving us the assurance that we have the right processes in place and strengthening our commitment to stay the course. . . . Winning the Baldrige Award is a great thrill for Cadillac, the United Auto Workers, our partners

in General Motors, our dealers nationwide, and our suppliers. . . . But we know that the Baldrige Award is just a stepping stone on our path of continuous improvement.[10]

## THE QUALITY JOURNEY

Dr. Deming speaks of the "quality journey" which is ongoing and continual. Both the International union, UAW, and the corporation, General Motors, have been on this journey since their respective inceptions. The first joint relationship between General Motors and the UAW began in 1937 with the first labor agreement between the two organizations. Both parties brought quality to the table. Today, the UAW-GM Quality Network is recognized as the process for product quality that has resulted from the progression of the quality journey and the maturation of the relationship between the union and management.

President Franklin D. Roosevelt foreshadowed this cooperative spirit in an address following the creation of the Automobile Labor Board organized to support the implementation of obligations decreed by the National Industrial Recovery Act. He is quoted in the General Motors 26th annual report in 1934:

> I would like you to know that in the settlement just reached in the automobile industry we have charted a new course in social engineering in the United States. It is my hope that out of this will come a new realization of the opportunities of capital and labor not only to compose their differences at the conference table and to recognize their respective rights and responsibilities but also to establish a foundation on which they can cooperate in bettering the human relationships involved in any large industrial enterprise.[11]

Almost 50 years later, on January 15, 1993, in a teleconference broadcast from the General Motors Building in Detroit, Michigan, Steve Yokich and Jack Smith candidly discussed their mutual concern for product quality and their relationship based on working together for the common good of both the union and the corporation. The theme of the teleconference

---

[10]Ibid., p. 8.

[11]*Twenty-sixth Annual Report of General Motors Corporation,* year ended December 31, 1934, as prepared for presentation to stockholders at the Annual Meeting to be held in Wilmington, Delaware, Tuesday, April 30, 1935, p. 11.

was "Quality, Our Futures Depend On It." The audience was every Quality Council in the corporation; a total of 528 locations viewed the broadcast.

Jack Smith was asked about the importance of trust and the role of the *Beliefs and Values* in the decision-making process. "If we don't build mutual trust for one another, we won't be successful. And we've had a history that hasn't been great. And yet, we know today that if we don't work together, we're not going to have the quality we need for a really satisfied customer. So, we're all in it together and when we're in it together, we can win."

Steve Yokich continued, "And I'd like to add to that because we just had a national UAW-GM council meeting, and . . . I said, we're all faced with our sins of the past—a large corporation that used to make decisions and . . . just announce them, and then argue about what we're going to do. . . . And we were a large union doing the same thing. "Well, let them make their decision and we'll just take them on." In today's world, it's a different world. A union that can't change in a fast-changing society will not survive. . . . I've seen a change in attitude; we are in this together. I think it's important that people understand that."

The teleconference presented product quality information heretofore kept guarded and limited to a small group of top management leaders. GM workers were used to using quality data retrieved on the job and therefore very job specific. The teleconference presented the quality picture in the macro sense, looking at the whole system and sharing competitive data. Audience feedback was immediate and positive, indicating a strong interest in knowing and understanding corporate product quality data and its relevance to an individual and his or her job. Audience reaction was consistent with employee surveys, confirming that there is a strong desire on the part of the work force to be the best at quality. Later in the telecast Yokich went on to state, "Quality is everybody's business—every individual that works for this corporation, UAW or non-UAW, it's still their business."

Jack Smith followed, "It's a total team effort. I certainly echo what Steve is saying. Clearly, the focus has to be on the best in class as our vision. . . . The GM Mark of Excellence should be the symbol of quality on a world basis. . . . We're going to push very hard to be best in class in everything we do. Then, we have a catalyst for change and with that catalyst everyone is going to win. The company is going to win, and everybody on the team is going to win."

It is clear that the jointly developed Quality Network has changed the relationship between General Motors Corporation and the UAW and permits and encourages joint decision making without forfeiting responsibilities required of each organization. The success of General Motors and the future of workers represented by the United Auto Workers Union depend upon a mutual concern for each other's welfare and interests. Mutual respect and trust must be the foundation for the success of each organization. The destiny of both organizations is inextricably linked and depends on the success of each. Neither can make decisions detrimental to the other without hurting its own organization. Joint decision making does not compromise either organization's effectiveness, but is a way of looking after each other's interests while assuring one's own success.

## THE RIGHT QUESTIONS

The evolving relationship between the UAW and General Motors in the quality arena over the past seven years has generated several questions that remain as valid today as they were in 1987. The answers to these questions have a life of their own. They are not constant, not defined in stone. Many forces, internal and external, controllable and uncontrollable, knowable and unknown, impact their composition. What can be constant are the principles, methods, and systems used to pursue their answers.

Every organization needs to ask itself several key questions, including the following:

**Who is our customer? Are we satisfying our customer's requirements? How do we know?**   This is the heart of why an organization is in business. The voice of the customer tells us how we are doing and helps us predict what we will have to do in the future. There are many voices of many customers and it is crucial that they are all recognized and understood.

**What's in it for me? (WIIFM)**   All stakeholders must understand how they fit into the total plan and how they will benefit from its success.

**What's going to happen to me?**   Job security for all workers, represented and unrepresented, is a key issue. As Dr. Deming points out, *secure* means without fear. Bargaining issues must be kept separate from quality management issues with the exception of the bridging issue of job security. Plans must be developed that provide redeployment of people to meaningful work. If downsizing of an organization is necessary, then it should be accomplished to the extent possible through the principle of attrition.

### What are the key success factors in a quality system?

- Management and union leadership support: constant, consistent, visible, and sustained.
- All stakeholders involved from the inception. Like the design of the production operation described earlier, all affected functions should be represented.
- Operationally defined leadership involvement that will endure changes in leaders, on both sides. For example, since 1987 General Motors has had three new presidents and two new chairpersons. The UAW has had one new vice president and four new administrative assistants.
- A shared value system that is fundamental and profound with enduring impact that can withstand outside forces.

**How can there be a win-win situation?**   Balance and harmony must exist, and they are based on trust and respect. Turf battles can no longer be tolerated. *Balance* means:

- A systems approach that balances considerations for people and teamwork, business needs, and technological innovation.
- A process that is generic enough to be accepted as a common process, yet flexible enough to allow for local cultural and systemic differences.
- An understanding and respect for each party's responsibilities and obligations, with the agreement to work together on commonalities.

**How is this different from all the other programs of the month?**   The answer to this question must be lived. This is not a program. This is the ongoing transformation of a business system with its partners, customer driven and continuously improved.

For the UAW and General Motors, the Quality Network *Beliefs and Values* capture it all: customer satisfaction through people, teamwork, and continuous quality improvement. General Motors and the UAW know that they must work together to secure their futures by satisfying all their customers. Corporate and union leadership have agreed that the way to satisfy their customers is through joint involvement and action focusing on quality improvements and innovation.

## Chapter Six

# Total Quality at Corning
### The Role of the American Flint Glass Workers Union

**Larry Bankowski**
President
American Flint Glass Workers Union

**Hank Jonas**
Organizational Consultant
Corning, Inc.

**Mario Scarselletta**
Cornell University
Ph.D. Candidate

*The quality process at Corning really began when the Union got intimately involved. . . .*

Gary Emmick, *Vice President of Employee Relations,*
*Corning, Incorporated*

## CORNING AND THE "FLINTS": EARLY HISTORY

The roots of the total quality approach at Corning, Incorporated, can be traced to the small handshops of the emerging glass industry during the 1850s. Skilled glassworkers from New York, New England, and across the Ohio Valley developed an artisan's image of quality in those early products—signal lenses for railroad lanterns, pharmaceutical glass, and blanks for Thomas Edison's new incandescent lamps—which consisted of sight, shape, and feel. In many ways this close identification of workers with their products formed the foundation for an appreciation of quality that would blossom over 100 years later with the introduction of total quality at Corning.

In the newly emerging glass industry, wages for skilled glassblowers were based strictly on the number of good pieces produced following rigid inspection at the end of the tempering lehr or oven. If glass quality was "seedy" or bad, workers could be sent home with only a partial day's pay.

The 19th century glassworkers benefited from the 1878 formation of the American Flint Glass Workers Union (AFGWU) in Pittsburgh. In December 1886, when the American Federation of Labor (AFL) was formed in Columbus, Ohio, the "Flints" were among its founding affiliates. Like all AFL unions in those early days, the Flints were comprised exclusively of skilled glassworkers. With the passage of the Wagner Act in 1935 and the national drive spearheaded by John L. Lewis and the CIO, the AFGWU organized the semiskilled and unskilled workers in most of the country's glass plants.

The Flints, (or "Traveling Flints," as they came to be known for their willingness to move from state to state in search of year-round work), pushed hard for fair wages and decent working conditions in the hot, sweaty handshops and factories that were springing up across the northeastern United States and moving westward as cheaper sources of coal and natural gas were discovered. Among those early companies was the Corning Glass Works, originally founded in 1868 by Amory Houghton as the Brooklyn Glass Company.

The AFGWU also battled the tough, adversarial climate that was typically displayed towards fledgling unions by the early barons of industry. In many ways, the Corning Glass Works of the late 1800s was no different in its stance towards unionization than other glass companies. The company resisted early companywide organizing attempts that had been successful in Pennsylvania, Ohio, and Indiana, and by 1891 remained the largest unorganized glass maker in America.

Under pressure from its own members to organize the Glass Works, the Flints gained a foothold among a few glassblowers engaged in blowing bulbs for Thomas Edison's newly invented incandescent lamps. When some workers were dismissed, a strike ensued and they were forced to find employment elsewhere, some as far away as Ohio. Unfortunately, while those workers were returning home to Corning by train, their coach cars were struck by a freight train and 18 young men lost their lives in the massive fire.

---

**A Demonstration of Concern**

In July of 1993 Local Union 1000, representing all production and maintenance employees in the Corning area, celebrated its 50th anniversary with
a picnic attended by more than 400 employees, including family members.
Jamie Houghton chose the occasion to make his first public appearance
since suffering a serious accident several months earlier. Jamie's presence
on crutches to express his appreciation to the men and women from the factory floor for their contribution to the success of the Partnership program
demonstrated to those present his interest and concern for their welfare.

---

To honor their labor brothers, the Flints held their 1892 convention in
Corning and erected a huge memorial at the mens' common grave site at
St. Mary's cemetery. That monument still stands today, and each
Memorial Day and Labor Day the AFGWU decorates the site with flow-
ers. According to George Parker, national president from 1961 until his
retirement in 1989:

> It was a paternalistic company back then and still is, having great concern for
> both the welfare of its employees and the community. The early Houghtons
> were not exploiters of labor but there is little doubt they hated unions. I've
> always wondered whether that tragic train wreck and that monument to the
> young men who died may not have had an effect on later generations of
> Houghtons that rose to positions of leadership in the company. I know that if
> I were a young Houghton and viewed that touching memorial I would have
> said to myself, "I believe my grandfather may have been wrong."

In fact, founder Amory Houghton was different than his fellow industry executives in several important ways. First, he signaled his commitment to the community of Corning, New York by taking up residence in
the town whose name he borrowed for his company, a tradition that has
continued uninterrupted by the Houghton family to this day. Second, he
established a philanthropic tradition of help to the community that later
generations also continued, most notably following the 1972 flood that
devastated the small town and might have wiped it out altogether were it
not for the steadfast assistance of the Glass Works. Last but not least, he
demonstrated a concern for workers and their families—a positive form of

paternalism—that again was communicated consistently to later generations of family, as well as nonfamily, leaders of the company.

A story is told of young Amo Houghton, Amory's great-great-grandson and now a U.S. congressman, welcoming national union officials to the dedication of some new office buildings in 1955. Houghton asked one of the older officials if he would like a cold drink. The official accepted and fully expected Houghton, then a senior executive in the company, to ask an aide to fetch the drink. Instead, Houghton himself sprinted nearly 100 yards across the field to order and deliver the drink himself. These characteristics helped convince later generations of union leaders, naturally skeptical of top management, that Corning's leadership possessed a fundamental respect for trade unionists and their work.

## BACKGROUND ON LABOR RELATIONS

Before the Flints officially organized Corning, other unions were vying to organize Corning's glassworkers. For its part, the company had established a labor council to handle worker issues, no doubt as a means of avoiding unionization. At the time, the AFL and the CIO had split over the issue of whether to include unskilled industrial workers. In 1943, the Flints won the right to organize the Glass Works and at the same time agreed to the company's request to consolidate all production and maintenance workers into one local union, versus the multiple unions for various job classifications that were in vogue in most AFGWU plants at the time. Thus, for the balance of the modern era leading up to the advent of the total quality effort, and with the exception of a few of its branch locations, Corning and the Flints enjoyed an exclusive labor-management relationship.

According to George Parker, Corning also selected men to advise the process of labor relations who brought a variety of professional backgrounds, plus a consistent sensitivity to the needs of the individual while attending to their responsibilities as spokesmen for the company's interests. Attorneys like Nick Unkovic balanced his advice to the company with a sensitivity to unions and rank-and-file workers. Industrial relations leaders like Dick Marks, Bill Bradshaw, and Dave Miller quickly grasped the subtleties of their positions—the tough-minded give-and-take of negotiations—while also mirroring the Houghton family's respect for, and acknowledgment of, their counterparts in the union leadership.

For example, it was not unusual for Amo Houghton to invite union officials to his home, or for his younger brother Jamie to be a frequent speaker at union functions. In turn, the industrial relations managers endeavored to consistently practice the company's informal motto at the time: "Be firm, be fair, be friendly." So while there were many disagreements over substantive issues, a respect began to grow between the leaderships of Corning and the Flints as to the proper way to conduct business.

## INITIATION OF TOTAL QUALITY AT CORNING GLASS

In the 1950s and 1960s, both Corning and the Flints experienced considerable prosperity. Union membership climbed within Corning's plants while its products, in particular dishware products such as Corelle™ that are so well-known to consumers, were selling so well that plants could not produce enough. In a sense, both the company and the union enjoyed perhaps their last period of relative stability and quiescence.

The 1970s brought a wake-up call. During that period and on into the 1980s, Corning closed or sold 35 of its manufacturing facilities, while from 1980 to 1988 the Flints lost 35 percent of their membership. Overseas competition and greater attention to quality by the Japanese combined to seriously threaten Corning's businesses. A sense of urgency began to be felt by leadership from both sides, and the respect that had been carefully built during the preceding decades was put to the test.

A good example was the television business. Corning had invented the TV picture tube in the 1950s and at one time had five plants producing tubes to satisfy America's apparently insatiable appetite for television. By the early 1970s the company was fighting to survive in a business increasingly dominated by the Japanese. In response, then Chairman Amo Houghton and President Parker created a joint committee comprised of television executives and union leaders to lobby Congress for action on behalf of American color television manufacturers. Such efforts laid a foundation for later cooperation in the total quality arena.

In 1983, Jamie Houghton became chief executive officer at Corning and challenged the Glass Works to adopt total quality principles. Prior to becoming CEO, Jamie had served as the company's chief strategic officer, responsible for understanding many of the challenges to Corning's traditional manufacturing businesses, such as those coming from Japan.

Houghton had concluded that the company's businesses were too vulnerable to cyclical fluctuations and that diversification was critical. He also decided that excellence in business practices, and manufacturing processes in particular, was the key to Corning's future success. No longer could the company rely on its technological innovations and patents; it would have to compete in manufacturing.

Houghton's early commitment to his vision was impressive. All 28,000 Corning employees went through initial quality training, which consisted of learning basic quality principles, practicing methods for treating everyone as customers, and understanding their requirements. Quality managers were designated in every business in the company. Executives and managers made frequent trips to Japan to study Japanese manufacturing methods. Regular reviews and checkpoints were instituted, not only corporatewide but in each plant facility, to assess progress.

The initial quality approach was based on four principles:

- Meeting customer requirements.
- Delivering error-free work.
- Managing by prevention.
- Measuring by the cost of quality.

Of these, the most appealing and immediately understandable to the average worker was the importance of error-free work. It resonated with the workers' close identification with their products that was the legacy of their fellow glassblowers 100 years earlier. As managers began to discuss the importance of quality in the plants, workers were sensitized to the amount of scrap and rework that had previously been tolerated as business as usual. They were also confronted with a contradiction: producing and shipping a quality product was the espoused goal; yet, decisions to ship inferior products were routinely made. Quite naturally, workers began to raise questions about the company's commitment to real quality. Richard Aiken, former president of Local 1000 and now national representative, recalls:

> Sometimes, we'd build a product and feel like it wasn't good, and just watch it be packed. We'd have orders on Monday and it wasn't good so it went into the cullet hopper [scrap]. By Thursday the customer was yelling so loudly that even though we hadn't fixed the problem, hadn't even identified what was causing it to be wrong, we'd just begin packing the ware because it had to go. So we knew that the quality of what we were building and shipping wasn't what it should have been. We knew it should be better.

## THE UNION'S ROLE IN THE EARLY STAGES

In the years leading up to and just following Chairman Houghton's challenge to the company, the role of the Flints was more passive, at least on the surface. Rank-and-file union members participated in early corrective action teams and quality circles, while national union leaders attended the initial quality training sessions and even visited Japan with Corning managers to learn about the motivations behind the Japanese workers' widespread passion for quality methods. Behind the scenes, however, national union officers were quite active, arguing for meaningful incentives and financial rewards for individual involvement in the quality efforts, monitoring middle management commitment to the process, and benchmarking other union organizations such as the UAW for suggestions on direction and approach. George Parker gives an example of lobbying for rewards:

> In our meetings I was quite frank about it. I said I know your top executives get money, stock options, bonuses. You don't give them jackets. But that's what makes the wheels turn around, that's what people work for—earnings and a better life. Somewhere along the way you're going to have to turn this thing around where the workers get some of that green stuff.

In 1986, three years after the inception of the total quality effort, Corning and the Flints entered into their triennial labor negotiations. The leadership of Local 1000, the largest Corning local, decided to put a stake in the ground. There was a growing feeling that while progress had been made generally within the businesses, the vision of total quality was still elusive in many of the manufacturing locations. Discussions of the quality program dominated the negotiations, and continued in the weeks and months following their conclusion.

Responding to these concerns, Dave Miller, director of labor relations, suggested to Chairman Jamie Houghton and Corporate Quality Director David Luther that they meet with the local leadership of the Flints. The officers, led by Local 1000 President Richard Aiken, were respectful but blunt: quality was not as pervasive in the plants as the corporate leadership believed, poor quality ware was still being shipped, and many worker ideas for improved quality were not being implemented.

Houghton and Luther were disappointed but they also got the message. Things began to happen quickly. Miller, Luther, and Aiken were joined by the Flints' Assistant Secretary Larry Bankowski for a series of visits to each plant—quality progress reviews—where barriers to quality were scrupulously inventoried and discussed with plant management and workers at all levels. At the conclusion of each quality review, the visitors left a list of action steps to be implemented by local plant steering committees, consisting of management and union representatives, to be followed up at regular intervals.

Stories began to roll in that dramatized the shifting perspectives. In one of the larger plants, a batch of glassware had been produced that was found to be slightly off-color by a team of workers. Middle management was ready to pick up the phone to see if the customer would accept product that was slightly off specifications—an acceptable practice then and occasionally even today—when the plant manager gave orders to drain the tank of molten glass in order to correct the problem, an expensive proposition that cost the plant thousands of dollars in gross margin. The message soon went out, not only inside but outside the company as well: Corning was serious about quality.

## PARTNERSHIP AND EMPLOYEE INVOLVEMENT

*The essence of quality is partnership.*
Jamie Houghton

By 1987, Corning and the Flints were ready to take the next step on their quality journey. Competitive pressures continued to affect Corning's businesses. While clear progress had been made, the competition had discovered quality as well. The logical extension of greater worker involvement in how quality was achieved meant further experimentation into the conditions of work itself.

An opportunity presented itself with the reopening of a closed Corning facility in Blacksburg, Virginia. At this juncture, visionary leadership came from Norm Garrity, who headed the business group, Dick Marks, head of human resources, and Dave Miller, head of industrial relations. These men had studied some of the best American examples of what were known at the time as high-performance work organizations. Yet, the phrase *high-performance* felt too impersonal and jargony. "Why don't you just say, *partnership*?" suggested George Parker.

Larry Bankowski would soon succeed Parker as president of the Flints, and together with Garrity, Marks, and others they would rewrite the book on how to design a factory. At Blacksburg, jobs were defined broadly, supervisory levels reduced, rewards and incentives redesigned, intensive training programs instituted, and teams of "operations associates" given major responsibility for managing the work. Bankowski remembers:

> Blacksburg was the first very sharp break with traditional labor contracts that we experienced in our union. We tried new things with seniority rights, job descriptions, and other things. It was a risky thing to do for any labor leader. But we worked it out jointly. It was a sharp departure over what we had fought for and struck for over the years, but at the same time it was an improved, enlightened look at what was going on in America and what we had to do to change. And certainly the Blacksburg results have been good for the company, the union, and the members.

The Blacksburg results, although consistent with similar experiments in other companies, were astonishing. Learning curves to achieve profitability were cut dramatically, initial quality levels eclipsed those of older, more established plants, and worker morale and commitment was so positive it literally could not be measured using the company's conventional methods. Today, associates conduct regular tours of the factory for visitors from across the country, knowledgeably answering questions about the entire plant's operations.

The Blacksburg experience, coupled with several examples of redesigning more traditional plants in the Corning, New York area, led company and union leaders to draft a bold visionary statement entitled, "A Partnership in the Workplace"—known today as the *gray book*—outlining the principles of work force partnership. In fact, many of the statements were written by union members themselves. The following excerpt gives a flavor of that document:

> Corning Glass Works and the American Flint Glass Workers Union recognize that now is the time to take yet another step in improving union-management cooperation in a very tangible way. While endorsing the continuation of our traditional collective bargaining relationship, the Company and the Union also join together in support of greater employee involvement in the identification and solution of product and process quality problems and in improving the quality of work life and job security of the work force.
>
> Jointly we recognize that our objectives cannot be reached unless a true partnership exists. In fostering this process trust, communication and respect for the dignity of the individual are absolutely essential. Just as the Union is concerned with the competitive problems of the Company, the Company is

---

### Essential Values for Partnership

* Recognition of the rights of workers to participate in decisions that affect their working lives.
* Acknowledgment of the worth of all individuals and their right to be treated with dignity and respect.
* Recognition that workers are a valuable resource, in mind as well as body and that such resources should be preserved.
* An atmosphere within the plants of trust and openness in a work environment free of arbitrary and authoritarian attitudes.
* Encouragement for individual creativity and participation to maximize the human potential.
* Provision of avenues for individual growth and development within the workplace and the Company.

Source: "A Partnership in the Workplace," Corning Incorporated and the American Flint Glass Workers Union.

---

equally concerned regarding the job security of the work force, in a safe and fulfilling work environment.

For the Flints, *quality* initially referred to the products produced, but now extended much further to encompass the type of organization that is created when people value one another, utilize all their capacities, and cooperate to achieve a higher purpose. The evidence that quality exists in peoples' day-to-day behavior is when they—managers as well as workers—regularly go beyond what is required in their contributions, and seek opportunities to surprise and delight their customers by offering superior products and services.

*Partnership* is about creating the ideal work environment that will allow everyone to fully participate in helping to satisfy their customers— internal, external, or both. If these two definitions sound similar, it's because for the Flints they are synonymous. The gray book represented a vision of how, through partnership, workers could successfully implement quality principles. Yet, achieving the vision required no less than a cultural revolution within the company. Up until this time, union and management together had proven that such a revolution was possible through bold experiments like Blacksburg. As impressive as these were, however, they were still isolated examples.

What was needed was a more far-reaching revolution that would affect the entire corporation, much the same way as Chairman Houghton's initial quality challenge had altered the day-to-day practices of much of the salaried work force. The Flints and the company faced the daunting challenge of capturing the commitment of over 28,000 workers. Clearly, further inspiration was required.

## ACCELERATING QUALITY THROUGH PARTNERSHIP

After the success of Blacksburg, all eyes turned to the remaining Corning plants, nearly 30 in all, that had been established in earlier times and under far different assumptions about quality and employee involvement. Could these plants, using existing workers and equipment, achieve the same spectacular gains as a start-up facility? Experts and consultants, as well as examples from other companies, gave little cause for optimism.

Meanwhile, competitive pressures continued to dominate the thinking of both Corning and union leaderships. The good news was that top leaders from both sides understood and recognized those pressures; they had the information; they had been educated; they knew what had to be done. Usually, such critical information was only reluctantly shared with union leaders. But the Flint leaders had been to Japan, had maintained close ties with their colleagues in the auto and steel unions, and by the beginning of the 1990s had recognized the implications of sagging memberships that had decimated union strength. In the plants, education had been delivered by corporate staff professionals on the basic ingredients of working in teams, the changing roles of supervisors, and the new personal risk taking that would be required.

The bad news was that not all of the rank and file could see what Corning's top managers saw, or feel what the Flint leadership felt. In the end, both groups knew it made little difference to give workers a greater say over the conditions of their workplace—"reshuffling the deck chairs on the Titanic," as one worker put it—if they couldn't see *outside* their workplace by experiencing the anxieties of their customers, understanding at a gut level the same trend information that management leaders took for granted, and essentially "stepping out of the box." Achieving true quality under those conditions was unlikely. To have any hope in the so-called retrofit plants, the process needed a shot in the arm.

In late 1990, following a few smaller-scale experiments where large groups were given a concentrated dose of business information, Corning business leaders and top Flint officials invited all the plant Partnership Steering Committees—union-management committees charged with implementing quality through partnership in their locations—to a four-day meeting in Corning, New York. Keynote speakers included Larry Bankowski and Jamie Houghton. Titled, "Global Competition: Winning through Partnership," the conference allowed the local committees to hear first-hand from the real customers of their products, share best practices as well as problems experienced in the plants, ask questions of company and union leaders in interactive sessions, hear other examples of worker involvement in other companies, and most importantly, contribute to building a vision for work force partnership that would sustain and direct them back in their own facilities.

Five strategic goals were presented for fully achieving partnership in all of Corning's factories. These were:

- *Information.* Employees will be provided with all the information needed to understand their businesses.
- *Training.* Employees will be the best trained, most flexible, productive, and secure in their areas of employment.
- *Empowerment.* Employees will be empowered to make operational decisions across a broad range of tasks.
- *Redesign.* Each unit will develop and implement a plan to redesign their operations.
- *Rewards.* All employees will participate and share in the success and financial prosperity of the business.

The momentum from this event has carried well into the present. The process of partnership has been more fully documented. Quality of work life issues began to be addressed. Grievances began to be processed and disposed of at lower levels. Union officials running in support of quality and partnership were elected or reelected. Perhaps most important for the union as a whole was that the membership decline that was such a conspicuous feature of the 1980s has been reversed. Since the advent of the

---

### The Turning Point

Richard Aiken, former president of Local 1000, is often asked when he became convinced that a different approach was needed in union-management relationships at Corning:

> We would go into negotiations and we'd always have quite a bunch of grievances we'd have to deal with. The company would win theirs, and I'd win mine. I used to win quite a few, and I'd feel pretty good about it, but I realized that really, I wasn't winning at all. After a while, I began to come out of those negotiations feeling I hadn't accomplished a damn thing. We were winning grievances, but nothing was changing! We weren't dealing with the really big problems. That's when I started telling people, "We've got to do this differently, or it's not going to work."

---

Flints' commitment to total quality and partnership, their membership in Corning plants has increased in the last several years.

Specific attention has been given to fully implementing the five strategic goals outlined above. In terms of information, many plants conducted similar global competition events for their own work force, a commitment that in many cases involved suspending operations for a day or more so workers could see and hear first-hand the same things their steering committees had heard.

In terms of training and empowerment, many facilities have implemented cross-training programs, job combinations, pay-for-skill approaches, and self-directed work teams. The redesign goal is perhaps the most ambitious, involving chartering design teams that meticulously examine plant layout, workflow processes, customer and supplier relationships, and in many cases investment in new equipment.

Finally, in the area of rewards, for the last several years Corning and the Flints have jointly pioneered GoalSharing™, a unique form of gainsharing that involves setting, and continuously improving, targets covering not only traditional manufacturing measures, but also quality and customer satisfaction objectives. Goals are set in such a way as to acknowledge the competitive realities in each location. For example, plants in breakeven, or even money-losing, businesses can earn Goal Sharing financial bonuses as long as they beat their manufacturing efficiency or quality goals. An example of the effectiveness of Goal Sharing was demonstrated by the Blacksburg plant, which for the last two years has exceeded the corporate bonus paid to salaried workers.

## CURRENT STRUCTURE OF QUALITY AT CORNING

Tim Tuttle, national union representative and former President of Corning's Local 1000, sums up the current state of quality in Corning Incorporated today:

> Quality has grown from just a program—guiding principles, etc.— to really focusing on the individual through the partnership process, which had to happen to make the quality program work. The quality program itself didn't start until people began to be listened to by the people that were really the policy makers. And when that happened, that's when we started to see improvements in product quality, productivity gains in the factories, and the quality of work life improve.

The structure of the quality effort at Corning today is definitely in transition. Ten years after Jamie Houghton's original championing, leadership for quality is being diffused throughout Corning's many decentralized business groups, to the smallest work teams and individuals, not just centralized at the top. The success of the company's optical fiber business, a Baldrige finalist in 1989, has helped to institutionalize periodic quality assessments using the Baldrige and ISO frameworks. In keeping with the partnership focus on sharing business information, quality objectives—or *key results indicators*—are communicated at all levels and responsibility is shared for their accomplishment. Benchmarking, both internal and external, is encouraged as a regular practice.

The union's role has been to drive quality through partnership. President Bankowski has been influential in *policy setting* at the national level, providing advice based on the Corning model to other companies in the glass industry as well as in other industries, meeting regularly with current U.S. government officials on trade policy and job retraining, and spearheading efforts to organize a benchmarking process between unions to share policies and practices.

At the local level, of course, the Flints have the greatest impact on the direction of Corning's quality process. The Corporate Quality Council, responsible for overall direction of the process, currently has two members from Local 1000. By agreement, each Partnership Steering Committee consists of elected union officials working side by side with plant management and other rank and file members as needed. The Steering Committee sets the broad policy guidelines for the partnership process, monitors quality results, selects and gives direction to redesign teams, and often establishes GoalSharing targets.

In the area of *training,* the steering committees are also active by pushing for the establishment of job certification approaches and sponsoring specialized training programs, such as statistical process control techniques, to help facilitate partnership objectives. Recently, a task force consisting of Local 1000 officers helped to create training modules that plants could use to sensitize workers to gender and ethnic differences so that the benefits of partnership extend to everyone, regardless of sex or color.

In terms of *measurement and evaluation,* partnership progress reviews are regularly conducted in each plant, involving national and local union officers, division business executives, industrial relations representatives, and the local steering committee members. Modeled after the original quality progress reviews, the visiting delegation talks widely with plant employees about progress and barriers to the partnership process, then formulates its recommendations for the local steering committee. Corporate officers also regularly review plant partnership progress.

Several plants have trained union members to act as *facilitators* of work teams, steering committees, and redesign teams. Supervisory assistants, a bargaining unit position, are often responsible for team leadership functions that previously were handled by first-line supervisors. At the corporate level, one of the Local 1000 officers has worked full time as a member of a corporate staff group responsible for consulting with plants on their partnership implementation.

*Benchmarking presentations* are conducted jointly by Local 1000 officers and company staff managers. "Partnership days" are scheduled quarterly to handle the large volume of requests from companies eager to learn about Corning's partnership process. In addition to the national benchmarking efforts between major unions currently being organized by President Bankowski, there are joint visits to other companies. For example, a group of national and local AFGWU officers, Corning managers, and staff professionals recently visited the Saturn plant in Spring Hill, Tennessee.

Finally, *process improvement and work redesign* could encompass its own chapter. As mentioned earlier, plant steering committees regularly charter design and redesign teams to help develop plans that will improve efficiency, productivity, and quality of work life. Some plants historically have taken an approach of continuous improvement, and have used traditional quality tools such as statistical process control and root-cause analysis to correct process problems.

## APPLYING TOTAL QUALITY TO THE AFGWU ORGANIZATION

In the recently concluded negotiations between Corning and the Flints, a new spirit was evident. The struggle and the learning on both sides of the union-management table that has accompanied the quality journey permeated each group's approach to the negotiations. Joint issue teams worked on special issues such as retiree insurance prior to the beginning of the formal negotiations. Union representatives gave frequent debriefings with rank and file members so that there were no surprises. Both sides joined together to present a united perspective to the news media. Recalls Larry Bankowski:

> There are times in our negotiations when I swell with pride when I hear our union fellows get up there and talk about increasing productivity at one of our plants by 180 percent. Twenty years ago if a union fellow said that they'd run him out of town. But we're all striving for that end now, and it shows in our negotiations.

In the end, as measured by the quality principle of error-free work, the negotiations were a great success. The evidence was the final contract vote, one of the highest favorable results in history. With results like these, it's hard to imagine how to improve the process.

Yet, in the spirit of continuous improvement, the Flints have taken a hard look at the process of negotiations. Richard Aiken gives a perspective:

> People organized because they needed a voice in wages, working conditions, and all those things that unions deal with. I don't think we should ignore those traditional things, but I think we have to focus less on them and more on the things that we didn't see as our problems before, and that's to help make

Corning a more productive work environment. We can't go to negotiations and ignore that anymore.

Aiken foresees the day when the union and the company will prepare for negotiations together, rather than separately. And Tim Tuttle imagines a time when national union officers will be subject matter experts in particular fields, such as education and training, or employee involvement. These responsibilities may eventually replace more traditional roles, such as inside/outside guard, that were needed in a different era.

## SUMMARY

The story of the American Flint Glass Workers' contribution to total quality at Corning Incorporated has highlighted some important streams of activity that have produced successful outcomes and benefited both sides. First, there was the traditional artisan's focus on quality products that helped workers feel receptive to later formal programs. Second, there was the positive concern for both their employees and the community by the Houghton family, which created a background of trust and further receptivity to Jamie's quality challenge. Third, there was the historical relationship between the union and the company, a bitter struggle at first but one that eventually produced mutual respect. Fourth, there was the leadership of key individuals both in management and the union. Last but not least was the urgent economic environment, which legitimized the personal risk taking required to make quality and partnership a reality at Corning. Without any of these ingredients, the outcomes of these essential programs very well might have been different.

Yet, as the current proverb states, change is the only constant. And despite the obvious successes achieved by Corning Incorporated and the Flints, there can be no slacking off in the pursuit towards total quality. Both sides have learned tough lessons which combine, on a daily basis, to influence the level of progress—positively and negatively—of living quality through partnership. In the spirit of continuous improvement, we would summarize these lessons as follows:

- *Awareness is the "booby prize."* Using large-scale interactive sessions to help workers understand the business environment and contribute to shaping a vision for the future are important first steps. But unless these efforts are linked to a meaningful plan to make major changes in the way work gets done, including process improvement that eliminates non-value-added tasks and promotes genuine worker empowerment, much energy and momentum is lost.

- *Training is often the first casualty.* More and more evidence points to a link between customer satisfaction and employee satisfaction. Satisfied employees are those who have the knowledge and ability to meet changing customer demands, Yet, training budgets are often sacrificed to meet short-term objectives, and training, when it is offered, does not draw on the full range of learning technology now available. True commitment to quality must value training, as well as education.

- *Self-direction can be premature.* In today's rush towards self-directed teams, care must be given to support tentative steps towards independent functioning. In many cases, this means maintaining a strong supervisory presence and gradually introducing team responsibilities, rather than eliminating supervisors to achieve short-term cost savings and leaving the teams to fend for themselves. Union stewards can play a positive role in this transition.

- *Leadership at all levels is critical.* Middle managers and local union officials must be given the flexibility from short-term financial demands to implement the culture change required for long-term performance.

- *Courage is the bottom line.* The above lessons must be dealt with and dealt with head-on. Once resolved, they will reoccur in a different form. A true revolution in the workplace involves courage, expressed by many people from the ranks of management and the union, every day. But in the end, that's what makes work interesting and worth the effort.

## Chapter Seven

# Building the Future through Quality Unions in the Telecommunications Industry
## Communications Workers of America and U S WEST

**Kevin Boyle**
Internal Consultant
Communications Workers of America

**Sue Pisha**
Vice President, District 7
Communications Workers of America

In 1977, the Communications Workers of America organized a nationwide Job Pressures Day. Workers in the telecommunications industry drew attention to the increasing stress and job pressures in their work environment. This was, in part, the union's response to the increasing difficulty we experienced when sitting down with management within the guidelines of the traditional labor contract to deal with issues of stress due to work pressure, technology change, and constant management observation.

Consider for example, the work life of a typical telephone operator. Supervisors of operators had been trained to employ the principles of Frederick Winslow Taylor. Supervisors designed the work standards and made sure that they were adhered to through direct, close, and constant observation. This was facilitated through a computerized electronic monitoring system enabling management to evaluate individual operators at 15-second intervals. In addition to continuous monitoring, operators were subjected to incredibly condescending work rules. Examples of such rules included raising your hand or turning on a light in order to be released to go to the bathroom. The resulting stress was intense and very unhealthy. While some managers understood the dehumanizing impact of these types of practices, the union was not able to make great inroads to solve these problems at either the local or international level.

As new technology became more common in the workplace, new sources of stress emerged among workers. The union found itself trying to find common themes in this stress in order to identify common causes. With very little knowledge about new technology—the science of ergonomics was in its embryonic stage as it related to the computerized workplace—it was virtually impossible to prove the workplace as a cause. Yet we were talking with members who once were enthusiastic about their work, but now lacked motivation; workers who had no energy and often found themselves physically ill. They were suffering from stiff necks, tingling hands, colitis, chest pains, blurry eyes, and headaches. But these symptoms were situational and it seemed some individuals were more susceptible than others. As local union officers, we were becoming more and more frustrated because we were sure continuous management observation and technological change were part of the problem, but did not have the knowledge or the contractual mechanisms to address these issues.

The Communications Workers of America (CWA) has always been aware of the critical position that technology plays for its membership and the industry. In fact, CWA is a product of modern technology. The birth of the telephone and modern telecommunications gave birth to a union of telecommunications workers. CWA has never been opposed to technological advancements, but the increasingly rapid pace of change has given rise to new issues. What was needed was a rethinking about how these issues were going to be dealt with in the future. In 1979, the CWA convened a conference on technological change. The goals of the conference were threefold: first, to gather together the tremendous amounts of information available from local officers who were becoming increasingly concerned with the health of union members; second, to develop a proactive and creative response to technological advances, rather than one which was reactive and defensive; and third, to be sure that any process for dealing with technological change incorporated the basic principles of democratic participation.

The scenarios which emerged from the conference on technological change called for a CWA that was more flexible and responsive to the members, the industry, and communities at large. We would become a union informed well in advance of any proposed changes, and involved in negotiating methods of implementation to minimize negative impacts on the membership. CWA's role would not be to resist change, but to anticipate change and ensure that it would benefit its membership. The conference recognized that there was going to be greater competition and a need for more organizing in the industry. Collective bargaining would look toward greater protection of workers against dehumanizing procedures, better employment security, and labor and management cooperation in future projects. As we look back from today, the outcomes of the conference on technological change were prophetic in nature. They became the basis for the union's bargaining proposal on quality of work life to AT&T in 1980.

## QUALITY OF WORK LIFE

In an effort to find new ways to deal with emerging issues and to remedy the ills of the existing workplace, CWA, under the leadership of President Glenn Watts and Executive Vice President John Carroll, hammered out an agreement with AT&T to embark on new ways of working that directly involve workers and the union in decisions previously viewed as management's sole prerogative. The quality of work life (QWL) effort, as defined by the CWA/AT&T national committee, is a process in which the union, management, and workers jointly participate in decisions on the job that affect their working life. What QWL is and what it is not was also spelled out in the agreement. Frank Mailloux, area director for CWA in the Pacific Northwest, designed the union's role in QWL to include the values and goals of CWA. This would mean that everyone would be more involved in the goals of the business and the union, giving each member a say in the improvement of the whole working environment.

The ink had barely dried on this breakthrough agreement when, in February of 1981, Pacific Northwest Bell, one of the AT&T operating companies serving Washington, Oregon, and Western Idaho, announced consolidation of some of their marketing, sales, and service offices. This reorganization affected over 150 members of the local in Western Oregon. The official announcement of this closure was given to us less than 24 hours before notice was to be given to the people impacted. Many of the service representatives impacted by this closure were women who were either single heads of household or supporting spouses attending Oregon State University. There were no comparable employment opportunities in the community for these people, and if there had been there was no time to prepare the members or the community for this change. The result of this closure was disastrous to the workers and their families, as well as the local itself. Over half of our local union was destroyed in less than a year.

As local union officers and representatives, we began to contemplate the QWL language in the recently negotiated contract as it applied to these situations.

The agreement outlined principles which dealt with:

- *Employees participating in decisions on the job.* The employees impacted by the office consolidations did not participate in any of these decisions, and if they had, they certainly wouldn't have treated themselves this way.

- *Employing people in a profitable business.* There is certainly a debate about which of these principles carries the greatest priority, but from our perspective at this point, employing people was at the top. Our knowledge of these workers led us to believe that if they had had some say about their employment future, the corporation would be *more* profitable.

- *Creating work conditions which are fulfilling.* The knowledge level of the workers we represented was increasing continuously. They had proven that given the opportunity and support, they could create work processes that are more productive, provide better quality service, and are safer and healthier than the current situation.

- *Maintaining the integrity of the bargaining process.* If continuous technological change and its resultant impact on the work environment were defined as falling under management's prerogative, some of us were not convinced that the results of collective bargaining had any integrity or value at all.

As a local union president, it was virtually impossible to do anything but react in very angry and militant ways. There were no processes available to support the dignity and development of people in furthering their work career. QWL had not modified the union's role at all in addressing the detrimental effects of change on the membership.

To deal with this situation we had two alternatives. On the one hand, we could fight the corporation at every turn—in the community, through the legislature, at the grievance table, and in the workplace. On the other hand, we could support the members concerned for their future because of these changes; negotiate whatever deals we could with the corporation and the community; and begin exploring ways to democratize change processes in the future.

We did both. The hurt and anger was so deep and it had hit with such surprise that we came out swinging. As we carried on our battle, impacted members would call to ask what their alternatives were and to find out what they were entitled to in terms of severance pay or transfer rights. At times, they would just cry. It soon became evident that we did not have the energy to both fight and be supportive. Our main concern had to be the membership, but we also committed ourselves to the ideal that people would never be treated as an afterthought to change again. CWA had negotiated excellent contract language to help facilitate the changes caused by technological change and economic downturn. Downsizing was resulting in fewer opportunities for people to work in communities of their choice. Human dignity and development are the values of the trade union movement and only through the union's involvement and understanding of the human side of work will the social needs and participation of workers truly become principles of workplace change.

## ESTABLISHING LABOR-MANAGEMENT CHANGE OBJECTIVES

The fundamental changes in technology, markets, and world trade predicted in 1979 at the conference on technological change, had by 1982 altered CWA's assumed role in dealing with the changing workplace. Marvin Weisbord, a well-known organizational change specialist, has suggested that the surge of change in the work world is different from anything that has happened before.[1] He uses futurist Alvin Toffler's term the *third wave* to differentiate this change from the agricultural and industrial revolutions of bygone eras. As a union, we can no longer sit back and ser-

---

[1]Marvin Weisbord, *Productive Workplaces: Organizing and Managing for Dignity, Meaning and Community* (San Francisco: Jossey-Bass Publishers, 1988).

vice members' grievances on a daily basis and not involve ourselves in the larger global issues. CWA found it necessary to assess where their energy and resources were to be expended if the union was to grow and prosper in the future.

The union had identified a number of solid reasons for management to welcome them into joint worker participation processes. Previously, management had attempted a number of participation processes, many fashioned after the early forms of participation attempted in nonunion organizations. The suggestion box and climate survey gave a limited voice to workers on the shop floor, but only included employee views on how to improve productivity and workplace policies. The development and implementation of these ideas were done solely from a management perspective. So in many if not most cases, the intended improvements were never realized.

Morton Bahr, international president of the CWA, says, "I'm convinced, after years of negotiating with management at the bargaining table, that remarkable creativity often results from struggle and conflict over opposing ideas. The constructive conflict which exists at the table can, and often has resulted in tremendous progress for both organizations and for the workers associated with them." In the June 1987 issue of *The Quality Circles Journal,* President Bahr went on to say, "In order to meet the needs of the membership in this changing workplace relationship, there are specific advantages to involving the union in worker participation."[2]

- Workers feel safer when the union is part of the transition from a conventional organizational design to one which brings them into the decision-making process. With the presence of the union, workers are more likely to support and accept the joint worker participation process.
- With union involvement, a formal structure exists to resolve the difficulties that will arise anytime change is implemented. The union's involvement assures participants that the whole system of the workplace will be incorporated in the change process. The whole system is not formalized in nonunion settings—just the immediate work environment.

---

[2]"CWA's Approach: Participative Decision Making," Morton Bahr, *The Quality Circles Journal* 10 (June 2, 1987), pp. 20–21.

- The union is a valuable advocate for the change process. Workers recognize that their union will represent their views and ensure that the worker participation process will meet their needs and any benefits will be distributed equitably.
- The union is the central point of contact for management in designing, implementing, and evaluating worker participation processes. Taken as a whole, the union structure is certainly more effective than in cases where management attempts to negotiate with each individual employee or work site.
- The union is the focal point for communication. The increased amount of information usually accompanying these processes is more effectively transmitted through both union and management structures. This ensures that all people throughout both organizations from the shop floor to the higher levels of each organization will receive the information they need.
- A union can provide extraordinarily valuable people resources recognized by the work force as legitimate. For example, within CWA today, besides the front line knowledge of the work force, there is a very large network of highly trained facilitators, internal consultants, researchers, trainers, and other resources that gives expert support to these processes.

By being proactive in identifying the advantages of union involvement, CWA has accelerated the change process within some companies. These advantages provided a foundation for CWA's joint activities with U S West Communications. The union's presence can enhance and foster understanding and acceptance of a new participatory culture by managers trained in a traditional, more authoritarian management style. The union balances the process; without the union, management is more likely to view worker participative processes as a means to get what they wanted beforehand. The union can emphasize that workers can think, be creative, and meaningfully participate in the decision-making process. Once this is realized, a wealth of creativity can be released within the organization. Finally, the collective bargaining process has two distinct advantages; it formalizes the system so everyone understands it, and it offers opportunities for additional progress. The bargaining relationship also offers the opportunity for grappling with interim changes in the organization and its systems of governance by providing a forum for strategic decisions to be made while maintaining the checks and balances of the relationship.

## INTERNAL RESOURCES FOR CHANGE

In 1984, there was enormous and permanent change in the telecommunications industry caused by AT&T's divestiture of its operating companies.
Pacific Northwest Bell began to prepare for an increasing level of competitive pressure in the marketplace. In order to adapt and survive in the
continually changing environment, the company intensified its exploration of new methods and technology to maintain its ability to provide
high-quality service to its customers along with a satisfying workplace for
its employees. While these new approaches enhanced the ability to compete, they had a history of reducing the work force. Thus, Pacific
Northwest Bell, the Communications Workers of America, and the Order
of Repeatermen and Toll Test Boardmen Local 1011—the International
Brotherhood of Electrical Workers (IBEW) began a revolutionary partnership.

In the previous bargaining cycle, the unions and Pacific Northwest Bell
negotiated a Common Interest Forum providing the top union and company leaders with a formal mechanism for discussing issues of mutual
concern. This was an opportunity to open strategic discussions between
labor and management, but did not provide the necessary resources to
jointly manage strategic changes.

While the contractual processes provided forums for strategic discussions and shop-floor problem solving, these processes were inadequately
tied together. As a result, many of the local issues were still being
addressed in an adversarial way by both management and the unions.
Time was being spent by all parties attempting to resolve issues of organizational or technological change through the grievance procedure.

Both the union and company became aware of the effect that strategic
and operations plans could have on people in the workplace when those
people did not participate in the design of the change efforts. On many
occasions, the implementation of these plans had a negative effect on
working conditions and consequently on the success of the plans. Labor-
management conflict usually arose as a result of such situations.

Because of the limitations identified by existing agreements, Pacific
Northwest Bell, the CWA, and IBEW agreed to jointly explore expanded
approaches to organizational change. In order to do this, all three organizations agreed to form and support internal organizational consultants to
manage joint change efforts. These consultants would serve both the com-

pany and union leadership as well as local management and union representatives throughout the region.

The leadership of this effort—Marvin Glass (PNB-Network), Sue
Pisha (CWA), and Russ Cook (IBEW)—agreed to four principal goals
that would guide the consultants' change activity:

1. To foster joint ventures at the working levels of all three
   organizations.
2. To jointly explore ways to utilize the creativity, knowledge,
   experience, and innovativeness of management and unionized
   employees in enhancing the corporation's competitive position,
   while increasing employment security and employment
   opportunity.
3. To provide a forum for company leaders and union officers to
   establish a closer working relationship.
4. To demonstrate the mutual benefit of a joint approach in the
   development of strategic and operations plans.

As a result of these goals and the work of the joint consultants, the Federal
Mediation and Conciliation Services awarded the organizations a grant of
$50,000 to support increased activity in jointly managing organization
change. The consultants developed skills and expertise among union and
management participants in organizational effectiveness and conflict
management. By becoming familiar with these skills, local union and
management representatives began to engage in workplace change activities that were jointly planned and implemented. Many of the technology
and process changes that were once imposed by management were now
being designed and implemented jointly. However, this comprehensive
approach to organizational development and technological change raised
a whole new set of issues.

The organizational interdependence between labor and management
became very obvious. Unions had spent the last 20 years reacting to management change and now were faced with having to clarify labor's agenda
in order to respond to the flurry of new activity in the employer. At the
same time, workers were being faced with technological change that was
both decreasing traditional work and demanding new skills.

An early example of how these issues were dealt with concerns the
marketing of technicians' skills and the billing of nonregulated work. The
joint consultants pulled together a cross section of workers and managers

to identify new ways to increase revenue and job security. A joint committee developed a process for technicians to charge for nonregulated
equipment installation and wiring. In the past, the company saw very little revenue generated by technicians for labor hours spent, so it had
stopped marketing the technician's services. The technicians knew this
could be profitable work if they were given the opportunity to learn and
clarify billing procedures. The committee agreed to measure the revenues
generated by time and material billing, so that these revenues could be
weighed against labor costs in layoff decisions.

Two days of training were delivered to 400 installation and maintenance technicians. The instructors were all bargaining unit members. The
results of the training were phenomenal. In January 1985, before the training, technicians had billed $589 for their nonregulated work. In April,
after half of the workers had completed the training, the technicians billed
$21,000. By February of 1986, billing for customized work had reached
$180,000. Total revenues for 1985 and the first two months of 1986 were
about $1.4 million, or nearly twice the joint committee's projection of
$831,000. In addition to achieving the company's goal of enhancing revenues, the joint committee's efforts have led to increased job security for
installation and maintenance technicians. Demand for their services has
grown with increased bidding and more technicians have been added, providing CWA members in other jobs the opportunities for promotion into
this work. In 1992, one crew of technicians in Seattle, Washington generated over $200,000 in new revenue. This is an example of what is possible when labor and management identify their objectives and work to
accomplish each other's needs.

## UNION DEVELOPS A STRATEGY

The massive changes brought on by divestiture put every aspect of work
into question: structures, skills, and even ideas about work itself. These
dynamic changes in technology caused a monumental gap between new
job demands and workers' skills. It began to be evident to local and international union leadership that simply reacting to the changes in the workplace and community was not going to be enough. The CWA locals were
going to have to develop a long-term strategy that would meet the needs
of the membership.

During this time, U S WEST consolidated its three former operating
companies—Northwestern Bell, Mountain Bell, and Pacific Northwest

Bell—into a new corporation called U S WEST Communications. This company would now provide telecommunications to the largest single geographic area in the United States, with arguably the most potential for growth, of any American telecommunications company. U S WEST Communications and the unions knew that unless they worked to develop human capital, the drive to improve technology and productivity would flounder on a shortage of competent workers.

CWA knew that the structures and roles of the past were not going to serve a strong labor movement in the future. The introduction of new technology often destroyed old jobs. On the other hand, such new technology, together with entry into new markets, created new job opportunities. While new work might be available, it was often consolidated in other cities, requiring workers to uproot their families and move. Thus, new technology impacted not only individual members, but also whole communities. These issues would require the union to set new strategies and be proactive in implementing them.

During bargaining in 1989 and 1992, CWA looked to broaden recognition and jurisdiction of work within U S WEST, so jobs would not be created outside the reach of the current membership. CWA saw the need to ensure that existing members be prepared for the new jobs to be created in the coming years. There were three forces combining to produce the changes that CWA was going to have to deal with in the changing economy. First, technology was upgrading the skills required to do most of the emerging jobs. The new workplaces would require people with high reading and math capabilities. There are not enough people entering the work force with these skills and most projections did not indicate this trend would change. People already working would need massive retraining to keep pace with changing job requirements.

Second, job growth would be fast in the high-skill occupations, such as telecommunications and electronics. This kind of work would require knowledge and quality assurance capabilities that were not necessary 20 years ago.

Finally, the way work was now being organized would require a completely new set of skills. As U S WEST Communications transformed its bureaucracy, CWA members would have the *technical* skills necessary to totally rebuild the information industry, but neither management nor workers had the skills to manage such a tremendous organizational transformation. Both workers and management would have to go through intensive training in group dynamics, problem solving, and continuous systemic improvement in order for increases in productivity and true employment security to be realized.

Based on this joint look into the future, CWA and U S WEST negotiated two very comprehensive initiatives to deal with their future strategic challenges. The first was a training/retraining program known as Pathways to the Future. Pathways is a jointly developed and managed nonprofit education and training corporation. Pathways allows union members, at company expense and on the member's time, to attend classes to further develop their careers, or in the event that existing jobs were displaced, to train for new work either inside or outside the organization.

The second initiative was a negotiated agreement focused on quality customer service. Both the company and the union contractually committed themselves to improving the quality of customer service through employee involvement and process improvement. To improve the systems and processes to the extent necessary to exceed marketplace expectations, the union and the company agreed on an increased need for internal consulting resources to facilitate change. An additional 40 labor-management change agents were trained to design and facilitate this massive change effort. Using a systemic approach to workplace change and education, the union and the corporation hoped to realize a trained, productive, and secure work force. CWA had developed a system with real input into the design and implementation of new technology, innovative work design, and development of training and retraining curriculum, as well as an opportunity for growth in membership. The customer would see the result as improved quality of service and increased innovation of new products in the marketplace.

Early in the process, CWA established basic objectives for the union and integrated these objectives in any relationship the union had with companies, legislatures, and communities. These objectives included:

- Give top priority to quality products.
- Organize workers for the purpose of collective bargaining.
- Improve working conditions in respect to wages, hours, and conditions of employment.
- Propose new approaches to greater job security and a genuine workers' voice in workplace decision making.
- Reform America's labor laws to allow workers to freely exercise their desire for democratic participation.

- Respond to change in pragmatic and creative ways to deal with the problems of today and tomorrow's workplace and society as a whole.
- Improve the conditions of life for all in our democratic society through political and legislative action.
- Involve the union in the design of new technology to enhance worker control of the job and to liberate workers from tedious and dangerous workplaces.
- Develop health and safety standards through collective bargaining dealing with issues of job stress, ergonomics, chemical hazards, VDTs, and noise control.

As the locals began to work toward these objectives, they became aware that the skills and structures within the locals themselves were geared to a reactive, adversarial approach. Their future would require that these objectives be proactively integrated into the union's major strategies of organizing, community/political action, and member representation.

## A QUALITY WORKPLACE DEPENDS ON A QUALITY UNION

Local union representatives were being bombarded with requests from management to appoint union members to joint committees to discuss and design changes to the existing workplace. Initially this was seen as progress—management was finally coming to the union prior to making decisions. But as it turned out, the existing steward structure was already overworked, and they saw the role and skills expected in working jointly with management as in opposition to their work as union representatives. They had developed their goals and skills to counterbalance management and could not envision themselves supporting a common strategy.

The most common responses to these requests by management were either to not participate at all and grieve whatever change was not consistent with their interpretation of the contract, or appoint a worker representative who was supportive of the union to sit in these meetings with management as a "watchdog." The watchdog's role was to communicate to the union any changes or issues that it may need to be aware of.

This caused great debate and controversy within the union. First, local leadership often found themselves reacting to changes in the workplace that their own members had helped to design. In change efforts that the union had decided not to formally participate in, union members were devising strategies that in some cases were in direct opposition to the labor agreement ratified by the whole membership. But when the strategies were questioned by the union representatives, management would respond by pointing out that it was their own membership who had devised these strategies. Local leaders then began to react by calling for the discontinuation of all joint programs because they were pitting some members against their own union. This same controversy was being experienced by other unions in different industries across the country. Indeed, Mike Parker in his book *Inside the Circle* had suggested that this was precisely the danger of worker participation; it would undermine union power.

The second controversy involved situations where stewards or worker representatives sat in on joint committees. These union representatives saw opportunities to greatly affect potentially detrimental change actions prior to their implementation. The role of watch dog had expanded to one of full partner in some cases. These representatives recognized the benefit of having the worker's voice heard during the design of workplace changes while at the same time maintaining the integrity of the labor agreement. In some cases, the union's values were actually influencing the behavior of managers in U S WEST. Managers were calling local union representatives for their input and participation prior to any change strategy being devised. Also there was a willingness to debate value-based issues on both sides and not declare a winner or a loser, so everyone would gain respect and understanding of the others' reality and concerns.

An early example of this occurred during a meeting of labor and management representatives discussing and designing a process to deal with the employment and training impacts of new digital technology to be installed throughout the company. The labor and management representatives were selected to represent different geographical areas, and therefore had to travel to different cities for their meetings. Both labor and management representatives often used Alaska Airlines when traveling to these meetings. During this time, the machinists and flight attendants of Alaska Airlines went out on strike. For obvious reasons, the unionists on the committee chose not to use Alaska Airlines and made alternative flight arrangements for the next joint meeting. When the union representatives arrived at the meeting, the managers were waiting, some very impatiently, for the meeting to begin. The unionists, on the other hand, felt betrayed by management crossing a picket line and then sitting in a room expecting to work cooperatively with them.

Some very heated and emotional discussion ensued, with a clear understanding by most in the room of the values that the unionists felt had been denied. A manager spoke up and said, "I understand your values, but I appreciate the great service I receive on this airline. They serve champagne, and to change flights would cost my department $25 and that's a value to me." The following day, Ray Gonzalez, a strong trade unionist and the executive vice president of the local union, brought the manager a bottle of the finest champagne and the difference of her rebooked flight. He said, "I respect your values, can you respect mine?" This one act probably changed the whole complexion of this committee's work. They went on to develop excellent worker retraining, career counseling, and new work opportunities.

This success, however only served to intensify the debate within the union about the value of sanctioning and participating in these activities. Both sides of this debate were correct. The union had experienced some disastrous failures as well as some revolutionary breakthroughs. One of the greatest successes of this committee's work was the development of new work for union members impacted by the installation of new digital central offices. U S WEST Communications had traditionally contracted this installation to the vendor that manufactured the equipment. This committee studied the project, called Operation Avalanche, and proposed a savings of over $50 million by using U S WEST technicians to install, test, and maintain the new digital equipment. This project turned a potential downsizing into new work for highly trained technicians; it has since become a line of business for U S WEST Communications and created work for union members. This was a win for both the union and U S WEST.

On the other hand, there were other initiatives that were not as successful. U S WEST Communications had determined that it was going to consolidate the customer service and technical monitoring centers throughout the 14-state region. After the decision had been made to consolidate, the union was asked to participate in developing the consolidation plan. Regional representatives were appointed by CWA and IBEW to work with management to develop an overall consolidation plan. Then on a state-by-state basis, joint implementation teams were appointed by management and the unions to work through the local issues of this massive change. This was not an ideal joint initiative because the union and its representatives were not involved in the initial decision, but the leadership felt that union involvement might be able to temper the negative impact on the union membership and bring the human element to the forefront of the discussions. It was very difficult working through the issues, but with the help of joint consultants in each state, a workable consolidation of the customer service and technical centers was proposed. Just prior to implementation of the center study plan, U S WEST changed strategies and embarked on a reengineering initiative which did not include union involvement. The joint plans were scrapped.

The union saw reengineering as today's corporate buzzword for continuing to streamline and downsize the work force. The union felt that without their involvement the technical systems would be improved and workers would be manipulated from one city to another like pawns. This caused great controversy and questioning of the commitment management had to this joint relationship. The leadership of CWA was in debate over whether there was any reason to trust the relationship with U S WEST. On the other side of the debate were examples of skills upgrading and work-saving initiatives that had been breakthroughs. There was no leader who could deny that both were true, nor could one person point to any one thing that seemed to equate a success or failure. This debate was tearing the leadership of CWA District 7 apart.

The internal union consultants had been involved as facilitators in most of the successes and failures. They were already discussing some of the common criteria for both, but for the most part were not allowed into the internal union debate because they were seen as company resources even though they had been appointed by union leadership.

There were three fundamental areas that the CWA consultants identified as opportunities for the union to use participation by the membership as a tool for union building. The areas of opportunity were: establishing a strong union presence; establishing and maintaining necessary communication links; and developing and stating union expectations and goals.

They outlined these areas in a workbook for union representatives. The book was entitled, *Joint Labor/Management Process: A Workbook for Union Representatives*.[3] The workbook was designed to respond to some

---

[3] Jagoda Perich-Anderson, Leah Be, Kevin Boyle, Dennis Hutchinson, and Kevin Wilson, *The Joint Labor/Management Process: A Workbook for Union Representatives* (CWA, 1988).

of the questions being raised internally in CWA. The workbook provided information and interactive exercises for union representatives to work through prior to meeting with management in any joint activity.

The workbook helped local representatives identify the ways the union could strengthen their representation of the membership, educate a broader base of the work force about the benefits of unionism, and be proactive in dealing with workplace issues that have not traditionally been addressed. The workbook also helped local union representatives communicate to members and "not-yet-signed members" about the union's role in improvements, positive changes, and successful problem resolutions. Joint labor-management initiatives where union representatives were clear about their roles and their objectives led the membership to see the union in a more positive light. Union members were gaining skills to participate as union advocates in work redesign. These skills also strengthened their ability to more proactively exercise control in other areas of their work and personal lives. This introduced a whole new set of issues for the CWA locals. In many cases, the locals were not structured to include diversity and greater membership participation. Indeed, some noninvolved members were even running political campaigns for local offices. Some local officers found this increased participation in the union unnerving and were convinced that this joint labor-management stuff must end. Others, however, seized the opportunity to assess the needs of the local membership and restructured their locals to meet the long-term objectives of the union and its members.

Even today, despite great turmoil and the eventual downsizing of the traditional telecommunications work force within U S WEST, the locals which have best integrated the skills and knowledge of improving the workplace and building the union are attracting new members. Some of this increase comes from having a clear picture of union needs in the changing workplace, as well as from taking proactive action in expressing those needs.

Another outcome of this work is the connection of the local's purpose and structures to the needs of the larger community. For example, CWA Local 7704 of Salt Lake City had traditionally supported a limited number of community causes or activities. According to Local President Randy Warner, "These were the community activities we had always supported. No one asked any questions." But when this local did a needs assessment of their membership, they found that their members were less interested in what the union had traditionally supported although they were very involved in other community activities. The assumption had been that if the members weren't active in the locals' community service activities, then they must be complacent about their community. In fact the exact opposite was true. This local is now reaching out to support the activities that are of interest to its members.

As local unions become better at building quality unions using the tools of organizational development and total quality, they will become more proactive and proficient at building quality workplaces and quality communities. And this will result in world-class products and services with a union label.

## REDESIGN OF HIGH-TECH /SERVICE WORK

During the 1989 negotiations, CWA and U S WEST Communications attempted to use an interest-based bargaining process. These negotiations were affected by a number of major influences, both internal and external to the two organizations. U S WEST was under increasing competitive pressure in its carrier and local network markets. This also caused some concern to CWA, as most of these competitors were nonunion and were constricting the union's ability to bargain. Technological change within the industry was increasing unabated. This was raising serious concerns in the union about whether the company would invest in new technology or the development of new skills for union workers. Trade-offs between technology and skills were definitely a point of contention throughout this bargaining session. And finally, if these issues were not complex enough, these negotiations would combine three major operating companies' contracts into one agreement.

During negotiations, CWA raised the issue of U S WEST management assigning computer software production and ongoing software processing outside the bargaining unit. This work was being assigned to management-grade computer specialists. This high-tech software work did not fit the traditional functionalized jurisdiction of other bargaining unit work, because the same physical technology was used for the design and implementation of these software program applications, (i.e., payroll accounting, sales and service billing, and capital expenditure) as was used in the running and ongoing maintenance of each application. The company and the union were both faced with bargaining issues that did not fit into the traditional distinction between *managing* work and *doing* work.

The complexity of this task was increased by the fact that each of the three former U S WEST subsidiaries defined and compensated this work differently. The workers who raised the issue were computer specialists in the former Mountain States Telephone Co. that had been paid at the highest wage band in the agreement. The former Northwestern Bell Telephone Co. had split the work into two lesser-paid titles—a clerical title and a systems administrator title—while the higher-skilled software development and program implementation was left to management. In the third company, Pacific Northwest Bell, all of the work was done by management. The bargaining committees had agreed at the bargaining table to divide the work into two categories—one the computer specialist paid at the top wage scale and a management position. With many issues left to work through, they agreed to name a joint committee to define and delineate this work.

Both sides had moved from their initial bargaining positions. Management had agreed that they would work with the union to add approximately 250 people to the top wage scale in the bargaining unit, provide all of the training necessary to help them be successful and engage in a work-design effort to implement this new relationship. The union had moved on their position of wanting to include all of the software work within the unit, including software development, programming, implementation, and maintenance. The bargaining teams delineated the work as *preproduction,* done by management, and *production,* done by union members. It was up to the joint team to define those terms and then design the work accordingly. The group of managers and unionists appointed by the bargaining agents used labor-management consulting assistance and a sociotechnical approach to redesign the work. They also defined some of the organizational changes necessary for the new design to be successful.

Though many may believe *sociotechnical work redesign* is another buzzword or new program, it is actually an approach to improving work that encompasses both the social and technical aspects of the whole system. This was one of the earliest attempts of labor and management in a high-tech service industry to redesign work in a way which would not only delineate work between management and the bargaining unit, but would also recognize that this work would be continuously changing due to technological advancement and customer expectations.

As this team began to map the technology and organizational systems in the existing workplace, it became evident very early that they were going to have to work from a different set of assumptions than had been used in delineating work in the past. Work was going to be changing so fast and so frequently that in order to create a long-term and meaningful job, most of the specific references to the "how to" of today's job were going to have to be deleted. Thus, the first agreement between labor and management was an acknowledgment that the constituencies of both sides were going to have a difficult time accepting a job description free of vendor and tool-specific references. Most job descriptions described the value of the work in specific areas and the use of limited tools. The new work had to be designed in such a way that it would survive technological changes and would remain long term and meaningful.

The new work design had to allow workers the ability to work and interface with software users, organizational clients, and any computer support groups within the system. The design team agreed to an end-to-end work process that allowed workers to analyze, troubleshoot and resolve problems in any of the five areas of software batch production. In the past, each of these tasks had been handled by a separate functional group under the direction of a functional manager. Such functionalization often caused the ball to be dropped for the customer in handoffs between functions. Additionally, changes in technology tended to negatively impact one of these functions, creating a possibility of bargaining unit job loss. The new work design called for skills to be developed in all of the work processes. To facilitate the skill development in this entire work process, the work design team developed a self-assessment tool that could be used by workers to determine their own skill level and training needs. The team then created what was known as a *training pipeline*. A computer specialist would enter the pipeline at what ever level she/he chose and would begin a training track from there. The name *pipeline* came from the recognition that once inside the development track, there would always be something new to learn, given the dynamic nature of the work. Such learning would thus be career-long.

This self-assessment tool and training pipeline marked a couple of firsts for the union. First, there was a joint recognition of the need for continuous learning throughout a work career. And individuals would finally have some say about their own training needs without being held accountable to some subjective management approval. Joint work teams would schedule release for training based on training availability, work load, and seniority.

The pipeline was also unique as it identified social skills necessary to perform this high-tech work. These skills included interpersonal communications skills such as conflict management, the giving and receiving of feedback, and negotiating tools. These were core curriculum training classes that everyone was expected to have. The core curriculum also included training on the labor contract and self-management techniques. Since some of these workplaces were unionized for the first time, the development and understanding of the union and its workplace role were imperative in managing ongoing change in a unionized environment.

As a first attempt in redesigning work using a joint labor-management process, this team met all of the requirements set forth by the bargaining process. They were able to delineate management and bargaining unit work processes in the world of software preproduction (design) and production (ongoing processing activities). They also developed a process that focused on creating meaningful and challenging work, designed to survive technological change. While this approach developed a process for continuous learning throughout the union and the corporation, it did not create a nirvana of participation. The sociotechnical approach used to design computer specialist work certainly looked at that work from a whole-system perspective internal to Information Technology Services. But it did not address the linkages between Information Technology Services and other departments, nor the systems and cultures of those departments.

The greatest learning for the union was that while participation in workplace design can meet the goals of membership development and education, it is only through organizational redesign, using a whole-system approach, that true partnership, learning, and continuous improvement for both organizations can be attained. Whole-system approaches recognize the union and the company as independent as well as interdependent systems. As the union becomes involved in work redesign, the critical questions of how the enterprise and union are organized and governed must be dealt with. Otherwise, the pressure to return to the old system is too much to overcome. There were many lessons learned during this process, but both the union and management knew that unless they could balance their interdependence with their independence and be open to each other's needs during the change, the long-term success would be in question.

## REDESIGN OF KNOWLEDGE WORK

In 1990, the high stress of customer-contact sales and service workers and the increased work volumes and market pressures on U S WEST Communications began to converge. At the annual CWA marketing conference held in Denver, sales and service workers from across the country gathered to discuss the sales pressure, the monitoring of workers, and other job stress issues. The traditional response to such stress had been to mobilize pressure against the different companies to bring attention to the sweatshop-like conditions in the business offices. During the planning of this activity at the conference there was some discussion about the technical expertise necessary to do this work and the inequities which existed between the technical work force and those in the sales and service job titles. Based on what we had learned in the Information Technology Services job design, there was enough information available to indicate that the way jobs had been compensated and designed in the past were sexist and may not be relevant to work in the telecommunications service industry today. While this provided some very interesting conversation at the conference, the energy was focused on developing workplace job action to get the union's point across to management.

As the union continued to hammer home its concern about stress in the workplace, U S WEST Communications hired a new vice president for its home and personal services (HPS) division. It was in the home and personal services division that the worst conditions were identified by the workers and the union representatives. Jane Evans was hired to turn around the division. Very soon after taking her post, she expressed a desire to work with the union. She joined the Employee Involvement Quality Council (EIQC), a joint union-management board that oversees all employee involvement activities in HPS. At Ms. Evans' first meeting with the EIQC, the local unions from across the 14-state region sent her a bouquet of black balloons and asked her to change the sweatshop conditions in the residential and collections marketing centers. Her response, a surprise to many, was to ask the local officers on the EIQC to join her in changing the organization. Based on the union's experience of workplace redesign, this looked like an opportunity to help redesign an entire organization.

The local officers were initially hesitant to agree to this offer since they had great concern about the future of the members' jobs and wages. This was a real fear, since U S WEST had forced through arbitration the split of the former service representative job into sales and collections job titles, with collections being paid less. After meeting with the union bargaining agents to discuss this opportunity, the local presidents created an ad hoc committee to develop objectives and guidelines for this partnership based on the list of objectives the union created earlier to integrate the union's agenda in all activities. These objectives and guidelines were taken back to the locals for their review and ratification. The local presidents believed this was necessary in order to gain rank-and-file support for developing major changes in HPS.

The overwhelming union opinion was that these objectives would not be agreed to by Evans and HPS, but to their surprise she agreed to every demand. According to Carla Floyd, a union president in Portland, Oregon, "We believed that by demanding the union's agenda we would not have to worry about participating beyond our comfort level. Now we were being held accountable for our agenda."[4] The agenda included an agreement on the critical issue of employment security. Evans believed that she could reduce costs and increase revenue by redesigning the organization. The union officers believed that they could improve the unhealthy working conditions, develop new skills for the membership, and organize new members by meeting the needs of the work force. They also believed that there was a greater opportunity for success, as the union had set its agenda for change up front, and there was an opportunity to change the entire organization, not just one job title.

The EIQC identified management and union cochairs to lead this redesign process and then hired a union and management internal consulting team to develop the redesign process. It took a team of union representatives and managers from the work units almost 18 months to work through a sociotechnical redesign of the HPS organization.

The design team researched the technical and social systems of all of the customer contact positions. At the outset there were three functionalized job titles—customer service representatives, credit consultants, and telemarketing sales representatives. The design team assessed the technical tools and the social environment, including the relationships workers have with customers and secondary relationships in support of the customer. The team mapped each one of these processes individually in order to identify variances which prevented quality customer service. There were over 100 of these work flow maps for the team to research and as, expected, the complexities were immense. Only about 30 of these work processes directly impacted the customer.

---

[4]Carla Floyd is the local president from Local 7901-Portland, Oregon. Comments are from an interview the authors conducted with union representatives on the HPS/CWA EIQC.

It was during this research process that the team began to identify how technical software or new systems designed and implemented by engineers outside the workplace impacted the social system within the workplace. If the technical solution did not fit the need of the service representatives, they would develop their own way to work around it to resolve their issues. The workers were very creative in developing the "work around" and would often ignore the technical solution altogether because it did not support the end result of quality customer service. The design team found through their technical analysis that in addition to hard technology such as computer systems, tools, and procedures, a large amount of technology existed in the minds of the worker. It was at this point that the idea of continuous improvement took on an entirely new perspective for the team.

Many of the models used to redesign work had been developed in manufacturing or production organizations that would take system knowledge and develop physical technology or tools to meet the needs of the production process or the worker. So a traditional technical system would be looked at from a work flow perspective—in a linear fashion. The steps of a linear work process are visible and easily identified. The initial approach to the HPS work was to use this linear model. It worked fine in identifying technology and the different systems that the service representatives and credit consultants needed to access to meet the customer request. But there was something missing as the design team attempted to identify the technical variances in their existing work design. They were not able to identify the sequential order of how and when technology would be used to service the customer. In fact, the technical systems were really only an information storage process usually accessed after the work process was well underway. The credit consultant-service representative jobs are mostly knowledge-based and the work process is nonlinear. Many steps may occur simultaneously and unpredictably. Variances then are controlled by the base of knowledge a worker possesses. This knowledge includes what the workers personally know about the products they sell, who their market base consists of, and in many cases, who the customer is.

Some customers will attempt to buy telephone service numerous times after being denied previously. The denial is usually a result of past due bills, poor credit ratings, or fraud. Workers would draw on past scenarios, knowledge of their customers, and their intuition about the situation to determine the next step. Most of this work would be done prior to accessing any physical tool or technology.

Throughout the customer contact, service representatives-credit consultants are fact finding, relating to the customer, solving problems, and making decisions based on a myriad of information. The knowledge technology consisted of listening skills, instinct, intuition, understanding, empathy, and self-control. Using this knowledge technology, the workers would translate what the customer says to what the customer means, and what the computer says to what the customer will understand. They will use recall from previous experiences and consider new data to solve problems and make recommendations. Each decision to meet the customer's needs would be customized to the individual customer.

This is where the traditional approach to technical system analysis proved inadequate. As consultants to this process, we found ourselves confused about where to go next. Our frustration was feeling the need to assess the nonlinear knowledge of 5,000 workers and managers in order to be truly able to assess the technical system within the organization. This was made especially complex when dealing with the merging of three former operating companies. Each had their own technologies, work processes, and management systems. Even though we now had a common labor contract, the three still had separate sets of informal rules and cultures.

Once we realized that we were dealing with a knowledge-based, nonlinear work model shoved into a linear, compliance-driven, computer-based mold, we had to define a new model for design. We found few resources that talked about a nonlinear model. William Pasmore, Larry Hirschorn, and Cal Pava had explored nonlinear work design. But even after researching these resources, most of what was learned still left us with the unique issue of redesigning work for a large organization spread over 14 western states that had very diverse ways of doing work from one office to the next. Each area also had a very diverse collection of customers based on culture and geography.

The design team felt under the gun at this point because the EIQC were expecting a product soon and the team felt it had hit a roadblock. Bargaining had begun and the rank-and-file were expecting some sort of increased compensation based on what had been communicated to them. The bargaining teams had expressed an interest in getting input from this team on how to structure skill-based pay. But the design team was confronted with the realization that everything they had assumed about work in HPS was still a question mark at this point. The design team, the EIQC, and the joint consulting team were feeling a great amount of pressure to develop a product. It felt like we were at the ground floor after six months of learning and research.

As consultants, we decided we would break the team into their three former company and union structures and have each team walk through each work process as it was designed. We asked them to insert the nonlinear knowledge needed to complete the task of giving customers high-quality service. There was a great amount of resistance to doing this because from their point of view they were only reworking what they had already done. As consultants, we acknowledged this, but felt it was necessary for the knowledge base to be documented so we could identify the entire system along with the different variances. This zapped the energy out of the team and as consultants we weren't even sure at this point if a whole-system redesign of work could be done in a high-tech, unionized, service organization. But we struggled through the mapping, adding the nonlinear fact-finding, relating to the customer, problem-solving and decision-making processes to each step. It was at this point that, almost simultaneously, everyone's jaw dropped on the table. The steps identified as nonlinear in each work process were identical throughout the three former companies. They were identical regardless of which technology was used, or work process methods, or management structure, or former labor contract. (See Figure 1.)

There was a common base of knowledge technology which had developed throughout the 14 states based on customer needs. It was amazing to the team that this had not been documented or shared between any office or persons until now. It was at this moment that the team as a design organization increased and improved their own capacity to learn. The resources they had read up to now were transformed into working technology.

This was a breakthrough, not only in understanding the context for the work design, but also for the creativity of the work design process. Up to this point, the consultants had served as process knowledge experts and resources for educating the design team on sociotechnical and whole-system change. But it became very clear that from now on the consultants would only serve as process facilitators because the knowledge needed to complete this task now existed within the design team. The model in Figure 2 represents the core of the new work design in HPS. The workers in this new workplace would be known as *service consultants* because this new work would include knowledge of all functions necessary to provide-high-quality telecommunications service to the customer.

**FIGURE 1**
*Design Process*

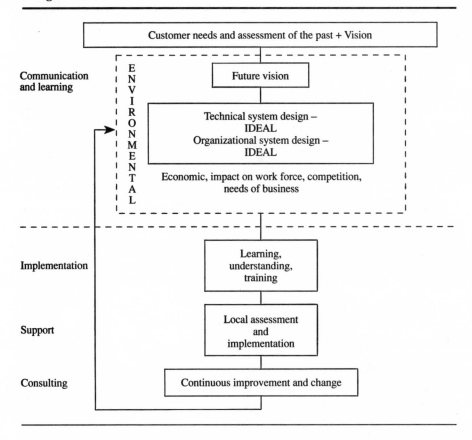

In order for this work to be seamless to the customer, it was evident that each service consultant was going to inherit the customer's needs and actually become the customer to other departments. The nonlinear work process then begins all over again. Prior to his death, Cal Pava identified this process as *deliberation* and recognized it as a very important technical process. Deliberations may be formal meetings or informal discussions which shape the ways knowledge is applied to organizational tasks. Upon understanding this, the work design team knew that the organizational systems within HPS as well as the organizational systems internal to CWA were going to need to

**FIGURE 2**
*Nonlinear Technical System*

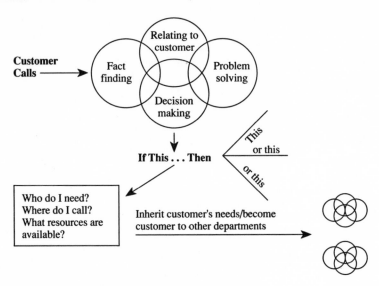

Source: Model designed by CWA/HPS job design team, May 1992.

change. The work system that was being designed was not consistent with the control and compliance governance of the past.

Throughout the design process, the team used a whole-system model based on the organizational universe model created by John Jones.[5] In working in joint labor-management environments, we had identified this interdependence of the union's reaction to independent action by a company and vice versa. Kevin Boyle built a mobile (Figure 3) that physically demonstrated that each organization had its independent systems which governed the organization and the importance of balance between them. Using Jones' work, the systems were identified as decision making, accountability, reporting relationships, rewards, norms, and communication patterns. Jones also states that besides the formal and accepted system there is also an informal and sometimes more powerful system which develops in organizations over time. The model developed for this process

[5]John E. Jones, "The Organizational Universe," in *1981 Annual Handbook for Group Facilitators* (San Diego, CA: University Associates Publishers, 1981), pp. 155–64.

**FIGURE 3**
*Whole Systems Change Model*

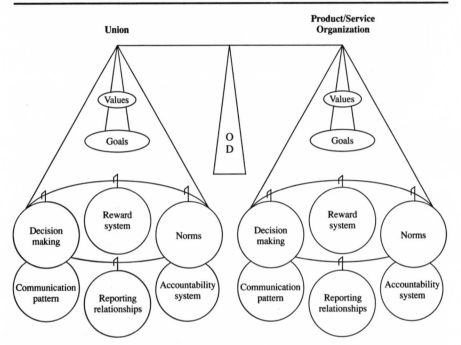

Source: Based on a model designed by Kevin Boyle and Associates, 1990, in conjunction with the Joint Organizational Development Task Force of representatives from Communications Workers of America, International Brotherhood of Electrical Workers, and U S WEST.

suggests that the informal systems in the union will act and react to the formal systems within a company in order to hold them in balance. The same holds true for the informal systems in a company reacting to hold the formal systems of the union in balance. In designing change in this work system, it was important that the design team had a whole-system understanding of the impact their design would have on the existing systems in each organization.

The work design team knew that they were not going to be able to develop and implement an incremental problem-solving process in each location. There were two reasons for this. The first was that none of them felt they would live long enough. Secondly, they were conceptualizing a total transformation of the way customers would be served, and the technical and social systems in place today were not adequate to accomplish this task. The unionists on the team were also thinking through the issues of how the union would bargain and represent members in a knowledge-based, nonlinear workplace. So instead of designing a model for contingency planning, the design team completed their analysis of the technical and social systems and assessed the needs of the customers and the workers in these offices.

The design team would travel to different cities during the design phase. Depending on what information was needed, they would develop their research and gather data in the local offices they visited. This allowed the design team to use real-time data from people doing the work and insured that the needs of the actual workers who would be responsible for the change would be included in the work redesign. This action research also allowed the design team to communicate with their constituency about their progress. On a monthly basis, Ms. Evans would hold a Home and Personal Services "sharing rally" that kept managers and local union representatives up to date on process improvements within the division. Unfortunately, there was no way to truly communicate the complexities or magnitude of the team's task.

Based on what they had learned, the team developed a future vision of the workplace in the year 2000. The team attempted to design the ideal organizational systems that would support this new workplace and then integrated continual reassessment of the environment. The environmental reassessment would involve continually examining economic forces, impacts on the work force, competition, and the needs of an ever-changing business. Labor and management leadership would be expected to assess the external environment and deliberate with the internal work force, who would then change the organization based on the need. This kind of workplace would consist of teams learning and communicating throughout the company, the community, and the union. It would also assume that continuous learning would insure continuous improvement. This process will continually cycle back to assessing and redesigning the ideal systems. The design team used a visioning process to determine that these ideal structures, shown in Figure 4, would facilitate the implementation of their future workplace.

Often technical systems are given the highest priority and the structures are left to informal development, which results in continuation of the status quo. Besides envisioning the ideal organization(s), the design team

**FIGURE 4**
*Ideal Systems Identification*

### Systems Changes within the Union

**Reporting Relationships**

- Members will begin to organize themselves and others into workplace coalitions.
- A broader participation and understanding of workplace, social, and economic issues.
- A higher expectation of local leadership skills.
- A demand for structural changes and closer relationships between local unions.

**Rewards**

- Recognize the diversity of members and compensation.
- Go beyond the wage bargaining model of unionism.

**Communications Patterns**

- A well-defined steward and resource network in the workplace and community.
- Share openly information from the shop floor to the union hall.
- An open and focused network between locals.
- Locals share information beyond their jurisdiction.

**Accountability**

- Leaders are expected to have more market and technical knowledge.
- Local leadership is expected to be a source of information and support for the members' individual and collective goals.
- Develop a broader view of what labor and unionism is.
- Be a source of learning and training in the local and the community.
- Collective bargaining addresses community as well as workplace issues.

**Decision Making**

- Democratization will move toward the workplace.
- Members will demand and share more information across local and functional boundaries.

**Norms**

- Members will drive change and begin to provide direction for the union.
- Risk-taking for change versus political risk.

### Systems Changes within the Company

**Reporting Relationships**

- Directly responsible to customer, team, and self.
- Union and company leaders coordinate networking with other work units.
- Leaders provide support, feedback, and mentoring.
- Environment has no visible boundaries.

**Rewards**

- Fair and equitable and supports high skills.
- Focuses on customer while offering personal growth, diversity of work, and promotes team.

**Communications Patterns**

- Timely communication with real time data.
- Open, honest, and shared dialogue across all levels.
- Supports work unit's other departments in benefiting customer and front-line employee.

**Accountability**

- Customer focused.
- Balanced by commitment to self and team.
- As team, set goals and objectives, problem solve, and plan for future.
- Understand entire business and competition in order to anticipate customer needs.
- Foundation is training and education.

**Decision Making**

- Front-line employee makes customer-based decisions.
- Information and resources shared for risk-free decisions.
- Interaction with other work units to make strategic customer decisions.

**Norms**

- Employees encourage change, welcome challenges, and focus on vision.
- Willing to take risks with no fear of reprisal.

recognized that learning, understanding, and training was going to be needed at the local level. Local implementation of this vision could differ depending on the type of technology, level of employee involvement, labor-management relationship, and management reporting relationship. The team developed a local assessment to be undertaken in each location to provide local management and union representatives with quantitative information about the existing relationships and organizational systems.[6] This information is to be used as a base of knowledge to help local implementation of the new work design, as shown in Figure 5.

A prototype center of this design is being developed in Phoenix, Arizona. The center is known as the Center for Customer Service. This prototype is combining the work design vision with a test of new technology to be used in U S WEST Communications. The learning from this prototype will be used in implementing these centers throughout the 14-state region. During a recent visit to CWA Local 7019 in Phoenix, we sat in on a TQM process improvement class being held for stewards and members from the prototype. On the easel under *Expectations* it read, "To be at least as knowledgeable as management in process improvement." Through this whole work design process, the union has increased its level of knowledge and is working to provide this information through union-designed and presented training classes.

The work design effort had been knocked off track for a period of time due to U S WEST's announcement of downsizing and consolidation of work. The local union officers on the EIQC were concerned about how their work in HPS would be viewed, based on the corporate announcements. The work design team encouraged the union officers to stay on the council and focus on the vision. The work design team members knew there would be roadblocks, but are convinced that it is the correct way to go in order to create healthy, unionized, productive workplaces. They also know that increased improvement in nonlinear, knowledge-based systems will create more opportunity over time, not less. This situation has raised new questions for CWA about its changing role in helping to develop these opportunities for members in the future.

---

[6]Local Assessment Tool developed by Winnie Nelson and Joyce Trimble. Unpublished paper. *Transforming Whole Systems: Tools for Organization Redesign* by Winnie Nelson 1993. (Phoenix: A2, U S WEST, 1993).

**FIGURE 5**
*HPS Job Design Future Vision*

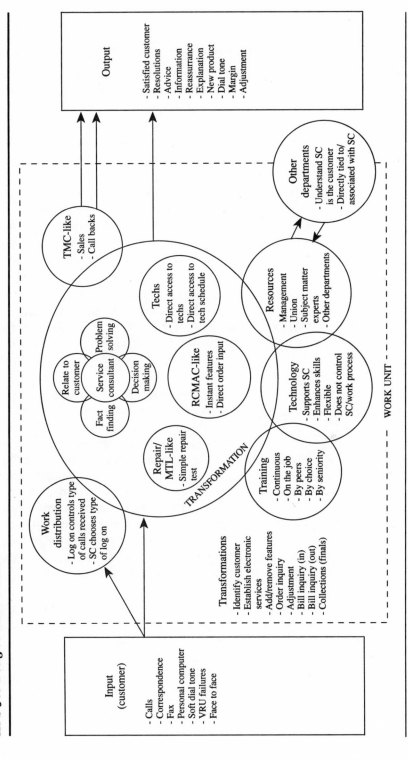

Key lessons from this joint work design are as follows:

- *Establish a clear union agenda prior to starting such an endeavor.* The issues are very complex and at times overwhelming, but clearly stated objectives can help keep union representatives focused.

- *Conduct training for union participants in total quality process tools, sociotechnical and whole-system change philosophy.* This will help participants integrate *their* learning—rather than the consultants— into the organizational systems.

- *Do not try to simplify the design process.* Whole systems composed of the union and the company are complex and contain many checks and balances that impact complex change efforts. Attempts to circumvent the realities of either one of these organizations will result in a failure to implement true process improvement.

- *Continually teach organizational leaders what you have learned in this redesign process as it becomes known to you.* Through the 6 to 24 months that a team may work on a redesign, the way team members see the organizations is much different than the way the leadership may see it. If this is not done, we have found that the changes recommended may not make any sense, or may be viewed as too drastic to implement.

- *Most important, communicate, communicate, communicate.* It may be difficult to communicate on an ongoing basis, but it will be more difficult to gain support if the people impacted have no idea why change is being recommended. In this redesign, the team communicated and researched with managers and workers in the workplace, did a couple of videos to be sent to every work location, reported out monthly at the sharing rallies, sent their meeting minutes to both organizations, and were in continuous verbal communication with the leadership of both organizations. It still wasn't enough for the organizations to understand the magnitude and complexities of the change in enough detail to make it happen without reverting back to old organizational structures and processes.

- *Commit to change for the long haul.* Continually remind people that it can only be done by them and it is going to take lots of time, commitment, and personal energy.

## BUILDING THE FUTURE UNION

Today, the labor movement and CWA specifically are at a crossroads. The question is whether the objectives, structures, and approaches that have raised the standard of living for working people in this country for the past century are still appropriate today. There is no doubt about the mission of labor and the values that have driven changes to our economy and society as a whole. The mission has been to create democratic structures for participation both in the workplace and the community. The debate is whether the structures of participation in the union from the past truly create democratic forms of participation for the future. The changes in communities, economies, technologies, and demographics of the work force have raised serious questions about whether labor itself is ready for the next century.

Through the successes and failures of CWA's participation with U S WEST Communications and AT&T, we have built a base of knowledge and competency around managing change both in the workplace and in the union hall. We believe this increased knowledge can be used in creating a stronger union. There is no doubt that the technology and changing regulatory environment impacting telecommunications in the United States and Canada is going to turn everything we know about the industry on its head. We believe it is going to be necessary for us to mobilize everything we have learned in the past 10 years about managing change with employers and integrate it into a move to recreate CWA. Once we can clearly express the ideals and vision of CWA from the leadership, it is going to be important to share this message with the membership to engender their participation in insuring equality and democracy in building our future.

Sue Pisha talked about her vision for leadership in addressing the leadership of District 7:

> I began this process when I campaigned for vice president of CWA District 7. District 7 included a huge geographic territory, including 15 western states and 4 provinces of western Canada. It was virtually impossible in this campaign to meet every member or leader for that matter. In early 1989, I assembled elected leaders, union staff representatives, secondary and informal local leaders, and union-trained consultants to help us envision the future of CWA District 7 and then fashion a campaign around this vision. We were told a number of times that an election could not be won on an ideal vision for the future, but must be run on concrete objectives for the present. I felt this

approach assumed the membership to be out of touch with the realities of today. I believed that the members of CWA are more in touch with the future than any group of workers anywhere and I was counting on the rank-and-file becoming engaged in this election. It was the correct assumption, and the election was a success.

The key to this victory was an approach that looked to the future and engaged the membership in deciding the role CWA would play in the future. Expectations had been heightened and it was going to be important to work to continue this participation. Corporations had worked to engage employees in participating in the workplace, and in many cases we had helped and encouraged that participation. But it was time that we began to balance this participation between labor and capital and engage the thoughts, beliefs, and creativity of the members for the purpose of a stronger, flourishing Communications Workers. And more importantly, it was time to mobilize the increased expectations of working people throughout all communities in the United States and Canada.

As a movement, it was important to look into the next century and develop a vision that would impact workers and their employers in ways that remain consistent with the core values of a progressive, proactive, and militant union. This was a vision that sees beyond the boundaries of our contracts, union halls, communities, and nations. It is a vision that truly gives meaning to the words, "An injury to one is an injury to all."

In May 1993 in St. Paul, Minnesota, 300 leaders and rank-and-file members throughout District 7 assembled to begin the process of building the future. The planning process was inclusive of the entire district. The intent was to develop common strategies regardless of the industry or bargaining unit. There is a strong recognition that technologies, economies, markets, and labor forces are becoming increasingly similar regardless of the industry. So the intent was to involve a more diverse group than is normally included, take a much broader view of the issues facing the membership, and most importantly, do it together.

Vice president Pisha opened the planning conference by saying, "The staff, local leaders, and members each have pieces of a very complex puzzle known as the future of our union. As we begin to plan, we need a shared view of what is going on in the world, our hopes for the future, what is going well for us, what is not, and agree on what we want to do about it. The starting place is not getting to know each other better, but getting to know the wider world and then identifying the union's relationship to it."

The objective of the planning conference, entitled "Building the Future," was to create a *democratic strategy design*—a design that assumed participation by locals prior to arriving at the conference and intended for follow-up after the conference. Prior to coming to the conference, surveys were sent to every local to be distributed among leaders and rank-and-file members to be completed and sent back to the district office. Union-trained consultants analyzed and assessed the raw data into a report that outlined the major themes and strategies. There were four major themes that emerged from the surveys: economics, technology, community diversity, and learning. Within these themes, there were four to six strategic objectives which emerged (e.g., bargaining, employment security, organizing, educating members about diversity, and visibility within the community), supported by action ideas. These strategies and objectives sparked debate and helped formulate overall strategies for the union during the conference.

The conference was an open design that allowed each participant to decide which of the major themes and strategic objectives they were interested in developing. Trained union facilitators and union staff helped to lead and facilitate each planning session. In each planning session, participants identified their dissatisfaction with the way things are right now, then developed a positive vision of what they wanted it to be in the year 2000 and determined the first steps towards recognizing their vision.

The energy level of the participants was high and very focused on the proactive work that could be done to build the union. As participants listened to the readouts from each group, there was a real feeling of what the future could be. At the end of the day, a motion was made on the floor of the conference to set aside two full days to continue this process at the expense of the locals. This was unprecedented.

In order to insure continuity with the international CWA, the delegates used the preamble of the CWA constitution as the basic values on which to build the preferred future of the district. At the end of the follow-up session in Las Vegas, the delegates had developed and agreed upon a statement of preferred future, strategic directions, and action items that individuals, locals, and the district could implement.

The preferred future and strategies set the focus for a proactive movement, mobilized to meet the needs of working people in the future. The preferred future for CWA District 7 is:

CWA is at the leading edge for worker rights in the Information Age. In the future we are one movement; rank-and-file, elected and appointed leadership, and inclusive of the unorganized. Our Union expands communications, services and benefits to members through bargaining, which is a continuous process driven by individual and organizational needs. The Union is recognized as a positive force in the global community protecting the human and civil rights of all people.

We practice diversity in attitude, action, involvement and commitments to our communities. CWA's educational, communication focus, both within our Union and our community, extends Union values. Continuous learning is embraced by members and employers. We are actively involved in creating and maintaining a peaceful, pollution free world. We continue to create the future we envision, prefer, and deserve. We have a society in which everyone has equitable working and social benefits standards guaranteed by legislative action and the right to improve those standards through unionization. All workers have guaranteed work at a job they enjoy in their community of choice. And all people are treated with dignity and respect.[7]

Following the development of this statement the planning groups completed and agreed to strategies and specific action items and time lines. The locals and staff representatives are meeting in area meetings to further develop action and time lines to integrate the strategies of community, diversity and participation; economics and bargaining; education and learning; and organizing and mobilization into all union activities. The union consultants who participated in the analysis, design, and facilitation of the future-planning conferences have each identified staff representatives and locals within geographic areas to help continue this process. This planning for the future is a continuous process that can be used for developing strategies around any issues that may impact members of CWA.

The skills which developed in the areas of organization development and continuous improvement since first embarking on quality of work life in 1980 have proved to be an advantage to the local union officers and rank-and-file membership in CWA District 7. When these skills are used to the benefit of the union, they become the basis for a proactive, community-focused, and continuously learning rank-and-file necessary for the labor movement to reemerge as a leading organization for progressive social change.

---

[7] CWA Distict 7 Union Statement, adopted July 24, 1993.

## CONCLUSION

CWA's involvement with U S WEST Communications, Inc. and AT&T in quality of work life, employee involvement, quality, and other processes, has raised many concerns in the labor movement about whether there is anything to be gained by cooperating with management. What our decade of involvement suggests is that the focus and the objective is not labor-management cooperation. The union must commit to develop an agenda for the future. At times, the means to accomplish this agenda may be labor and management cooperating to meet their respective agendas. At times, the agenda may be in common, such as developing high-skilled employees, creating new work and revenue opportunities, and producing quality products and services. At other times, the agendas of labor and management may be different. Then it is also possible for labor and management to support each other in achieving those separate agendas as long as everyone is clear and open about expressing their needs and objectives, and as long as those objectives do not harm the other party.

The union can use these processes to empower the rank-and-file membership to develop healthy and interesting work, which in turn will create employment opportunities and profitable organizations. Joint processes with a clear union agenda can balance the power of capital and labor on the shop floor as well as at the bargaining table. Labor-management programs certainly offer new challenges to unions and their locals, especially given the rapid change in technology and markets that we will continue to experience in the coming years. They also offer great opportunities to use the skills to revitalize the union as an organization for positive, progressive change, not only in the workplace, but in society as a whole.

For true success to be realized for workers and their unions, it is important to redefine the core values as CWA District 7 has done in "Building the Future." The basic assumptions that have guided the union and its structures have changed. The Communications Workers of America has looked to the participation and quality movement in the workplace as an opportunity to increase participation and quality within the union, as well as to increase the viability of our member's employers. The challenges that face CWA and other unions will not be eliminated because of involvement in these processes alone, even if progress can be made. Since the goal of involvement is success in accomplishing each organization's respective agendas, there will be failures and setbacks and we will not always balance our separate agendas. But this is no different than respectable negotiations or grievances where everyone rarely gains all they set out to accomplish. We have approached our involvement as an opportunity to learn and develop our union's resources, so that as an organization CWA will be able to proactively respond to the needs of the membership, regardless of the relationship the union may have with its employers. The Communications Workers of America has begun to develop the knowledge and resources necessary to mobilize members to address the complexity of issues they confront in their communities, at work and where they live, reaffirming the union's role as an organization for social justice and progress.

*Chapter Eight*

# Graphic Communications International Union
## *A National TQM Approach*

**Herald Grandstaff**
*Managing Editor, GraphiCommunicator*
*Graphic Communications International Union*

Cooperation between a printing union and management to attain quality, productivity, and competitiveness is hardly a new concept. Sometimes, there is a misperception that labor and management are archenemies and that the natural course of each is to try to take advantage of the other. The Graphic Communications International Union (GCIU) has for nearly 30 years been striving with employers to develop and implement ways to advance mutual interests. Today's printing/publishing industry is fiercely competitive. It has significant overcapacity and a large number of nonunion companies. Cooperation that is meaningful in the truest sense of the word is a basic requirement for survival for the unionized printing industry.

## THE GRAPHIC COMMUNICATIONS INDUSTRY AND UNIONS TODAY

The graphic communications industry ranks as the sixth-largest industry in the United States and has a wide range of processes. (Figure 1 demonstrates the size of the industry.) The U.S. printing/publishing industry includes commercial printing, book publishing and printing, newspapers and periodicals, business forms and greeting cards, carton manufacturing, and specialty work—such as the production of food wrappers and con-

**FIGURE 1**
*Employment in Manufacturing Industries: 1992*

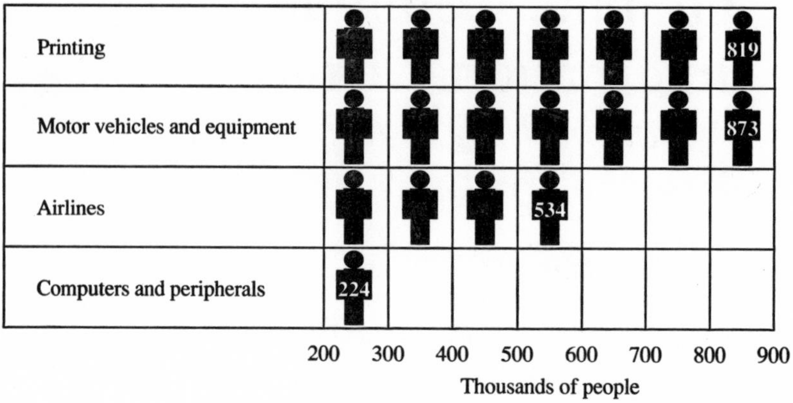

| | 200 | 300 | 400 | 500 | 600 | 700 | 800 | 900 |
|---|---|---|---|---|---|---|---|---|
| Printing | | | | | | | | 819 |
| Motor vehicles and equipment | | | | | | | | 873 |
| Airlines | | | 534 | | | | | |
| Computers and peripherals | 224 | | | | | | | |

Thousands of people

tainer packaging, printing of tickets for sport and entertainment events, circuit boards, and patterns on paneling. (See Figure 2.) The typical commercial printing shop has less than 50 employees, yet shops of this size employ the vast majority of the GCIU's members. Packaging chains like James River or Container Corporation of America employ thousands of GCIU members. Approximately 25,000 GCIU members work in the newspaper segment.

Skills of GCIU members range from running a computer console for a high-speed press and electronic imaging using the latest software on readily available low-cost computers in prepress departments, to labor-intensive bindery equipment in outmoded book press plants, to giant three-story extruders in packaging plants.

Almost all across the United States and Canada there are rapid technological changes, elimination of labor-intensive jobs, more reliance on computers, and tremendous competition among companies with offshore operations.

Times have been basically tough for workers in U.S. and Canadian industries since the mid-1970s. (See Figure 3.) Although its membership has declined, the GCIU is still the largest printing union in North America. While the industry's technological advances are reducing personnel—and creating new challenges—jointly trusteed graphic arts train-

## FIGURE 2
*Printing Industry Sales: $78.8 Billion*

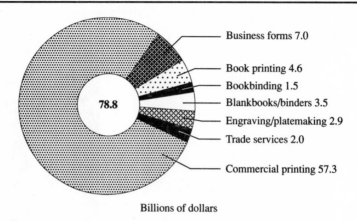

Business forms 7.0
Book printing 4.6
Bookbinding 1.5
Blankbooks/binders 3.5
Engraving/platemaking 2.9
Trade services 2.0
Commercial printing 57.3

Billions of dollars

Source: U.S. Department of Commerce, 1992.

ing institutes still develop highly skilled people who are proud to be part of this industry and proud union members.

The printing/publishing industry is one of rapidly changing technology—particularly regarding printed products. Photoengravers, typesetters, strippers, and stitchers are almost relics of the past as job titles. However, workers whose jobs are becoming obsolete frequently have skills and experience which, with some retraining, can be a valuable asset in a plant with a newer technology. Jointly trusteed schools have been upgraded to focus on retraining for those areas of the industry, such as desktop publishing, where there is job growth and the possibility of adapting the skills and experience of members of the current work force.

## LABOR-MANAGEMENT COMMITMENT TO TOTAL QUALITY MANAGEMENT

In 1993, the GCIU and the Graphic Arts Employers of America (GAE) became the first and only labor-management organizations in North America to have endorsed total quality management (TQM) and mutual-interest bargaining on an industrywide basis. The GCIU is participating in various types of programs that affect the future of the graphic communi-

**FIGURE 3**
*Umemployment Rates in the Printing and Publishing Industry*

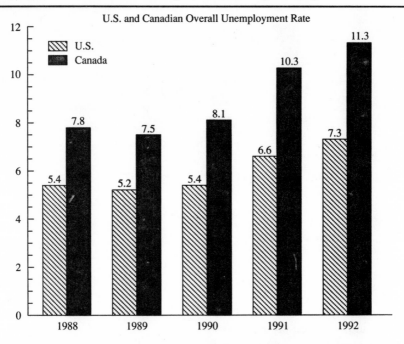

U.S. and Canadian Overall Unemployment Rate

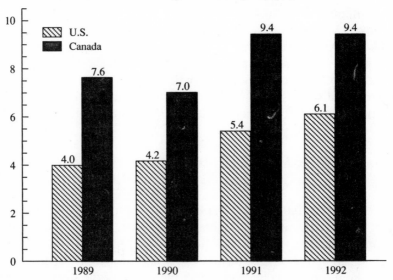

U.S. and Canadian Printing and Publishing Unemployment Rate

Source: BLS and Statistics Canada.

cations industry in Canada and the United States. These programs are jointly endorsed by the board of directors of the GAE. Innovative programs embraced by the GCIU and GAE as mutually beneficial include:

- A continuing, formalized, and effective liaison committee composed of leaders of the GCIU and the GAE meets on a formal basis once every six months and on an informal, continuing basis between the presidents of the GAE and GCIU.
- TQM programs with individual employers and a nationwide packaging company chain.
- The jointly trusteed GCIU technical schools program, with 38 schools throughout Canada and the United States training and retraining GCIU members to keep pace with the printing/publishing industry's rapid technological changes.
- Mutual-interest bargaining, a joint management/labor program to enhance the bargaining process, conducted by the Human Incentive and Resource Education Institute (HIRE) and endorsed by the GAE and the GCIU.

## UNION-MANAGEMENT COOPERATION BENCHMARK

Liaison meetings were established between the Lithographers and Photoengravers International Union and commercial employers in 1966. From that relationship a pact evolved that became known as the *interdependence document*. This document described a series of issues that identified the mutual dependence between employers and employees. It acknowledged the dependence the employees have on their employers for supplying basic needs for themselves and their families. Employers are dependent on skilled and competent workers who can produce high-quality printing that meets stringent customer requirements.

From that agreement on interdependence, further discussions developed on how to keep the momentum alive. There was a joint agreement on the need to retain quality above anything else. Quality, if it became consistent, would be a most attractive and marketable feature. Many clients would gladly pay more to be assured of products that were higher in quality than a competitor's. Quality—and the insistence thereon—thus became the mark of a good shop, a good foreman, or a good superintendent. Joint committees recognized the advantage that this commitment towards quality provided. Then improved contractual relationships began to develop between management and labor.

## JOINT TRAINING

One of the hallmarks of the unionized printing industry has been its long-standing emphasis on excellent education to produce the best skilled workers and, hence, the highest quality. Efficient quality from union employees clearly helped attract employer contributions into educational systems, especially the 38 jointly trusteed graphic arts institutes that eventually developed throughout the United States and Canada. The printing industry's school administrators agreed to work with the kind of equipment that produced a high-quality product. The concept was that if the employees learned on that equipment, they would become better producers for their employers.

The kind of equipment that was installed, and in some cases donated, to the schools was retained in those schools only if the schools felt that the products that were produced with this equipment or particular processes represented high quality. As their products and installations demonstrated new levels of production and quality, word about these new processes quickly spread around the schools that a particular kind of equipment or process was best for producing the best quality. For about a decade, the advancements made in preliminary tests in the schools influenced the purchasing choices of the employers.

Some independent school administrators did not build the best relationship with the union or even with many of the leading employers. Independent school administrators evolved whose sole focus was on quality—not on the people side of the industry. These administrators operated as lone rangers and concerned themselves just with producing what they perceived to be the best-quality products for the industry. When technology began to supplant the experience and the skills of union workers as developed in the printing and publishing industry, the emphasis on quality waned. Technology forced employers into difficult staffing decisions which often led to personnel reductions, which impacted on older (and often more expensive) craftspersons. Due to employment circumstances, many people were urged to avail themselves of early retirement through jointly trusteed funds. These steps were taken in response to competitive pressures caused by technology. With the advent of technology that could supplant union worker skills, it was easier for nonunion investors to enter the printing industry simply by buying the kind of equipment and processes that replaced human skills and experience. This early history of adversarial use of technology chilled joint efforts at quality improvement.

Today, labor and management are looking to take advantage of new technological developments through TQM in ways that benefit both parties. Apprentice programs are still workable, and they do work. Schools, when they get the proper funding, still do the job. The crucial ingredients to producing a competent journeyperson are funding and technology. The entire printing/publishing industry and its end product suffered when labor and management lost sight of the value of education, the value of on-the-job training, and the value of the spirit of cooperation that emanated from these liaison meetings.

## LABOR-MANAGEMENT RELATIONSHIP

From 1965 to 1975, a decent labor-management relationship prevailed in the industry. From 1975 to 1985, there was no further development of the alliance—with probably as rapid a deterioration as there was an acceleration in the period of 1965 to 1975. This was the direct result of an adversarial labor-management relationship within, as well as outside, the industry which existed during that period. In interdependence's place came "quality circles." Quality circles developed rapidly in the printing industry. Some employers who had not yet developed sophisticated labor-management techniques were accused by the union of attempting to circumvent the labor-management agreement. Other employers who had a positive labor-management relationship were able to maximize the influence of the union and make quality circles work.

Many unions—particularly printing and publishing unions—responded to perceived attempts to circumvent the union and the collective bargaining process by becoming very hostile to quality circles. Encouragement for involvement was withdrawn by the union, shop stewards, and local officers. These circles then deteriorated to attracting cliques of antiunion personnel. Sometimes, they embraced members of the bargaining unit who could be persuaded that the position held by the company superintendent or mid-management was the proper way to go. Another circle downside was the kind of narrow thinking that limited union and member roles. Participation became totally unacceptable to organized labor and the GCIU.

## BREATHING NEW LIFE INTO
## PROVEN CONCEPTS

James J. Norton assumed presidency of the GCIU in September 1985. In the latter part of 1986, Norton sought out the employers for a renewal of the liaison meetings that a predecessor union had had from 1965 to 1975. Norton found a willingness from William D. Solomon, president of the Graphic Arts Employers of America, a North American employer trade organization, to renew those discussions in the spirit of the late 1960s and early 1970s. It was agreed that these new liaison meetings would not be used by the union or management for purposes other than to address issues of the day to make companies more competitive in the marketplace and employees more secure and employable. Norton and Solomon began those meetings in the early part of 1987, and they have been going on since. Solomon observes that "this was a major and bold step for the union, which capitalized on management's good faith attempt at introducing a new concept. Graphic Arts Employers then went about informing all of its members that such innovative approaches by the union were a possibility where good faith bargaining continued as the rule of the day."

Norton and Solomon agreed that another objective would be to find a new way of negotiating to eliminate old, adversarial ways and instead bargain based on interests—not positions. Solomon notes that "in today's competitive environment with changing technology and global competition, we don't have time for adversarial collective bargaining. The old way is too time-consuming and very expensive. Both parties are losing in this fast-paced world by playing by rules that are outmoded."

Early in their discussions, Norton and Solomon realized that their efforts must lead to real cooperation—not lip service. Making that commitment of interdependence meant that both parties knew they had a responsibility to deliver, but if successful, the change would have a significant impact on the futures of the union and the employers. It also became clear to the GCIU and GAE that a commitment to TQM was absolutely necessary because printing clients were placing a great deal of emphasis on quality. Employers who could produce according to high-quality standards stood to prosper in a competitive economy. Employers who could prosper could then maintain payrolls and maintain—if not increase—their market shares.

The GCIU General Board (the International union's governing body between quadrennial conventions) has approved the renewal of those liaison meetings. Norton says that "by every measure, they have been productive. Had we been able to spend more time, we would probably be further advanced."

When TQM became prominent in the late 1980s and the early 1990s, Norton "could see the better parts of the old quality circles' goals." A concern was whether the positive parts from the quality circles could be resuscitated as a way to make union-shop products more attractive again. As such, "TQM took on a different meaning" for Norton and the General Board. The General Board supported this type of renewal so long as it did not circumvent the labor agreements and the union could keep its objectives in focus.

## TQM AS A LABOR-MANAGEMENT BOON

Leaders of the GCIU and GAE signed an agreement in June 1993 recognizing that TQM programs are customer-driven, require joint input from labor and management, and are part of a process of ongoing improvement. It was further recognized in that statement that successful TQM programs require change and a commitment to education and employee empowerment. The GCIU and GAE are committed to encouraging local unions and employers to enter into TQM programs. Several successful programs in the United States started as a result of this joint initiative.

By working together, labor and management developed a joint cooperation statement which was published to all union and employer members. That statement is:

> The parties recognize there are various TQM programs related to quality and process measurement used in the United States and Canada. The Graphic Arts Employers of America/PIA (GAE) and the Graphic Communications International Union (GCIU) encourage the company and the union to investigate these programs for the purpose of increasing customer satisfaction and improving quality measurement of our product. The parties recognize these programs are customer-driven, require joint input from management and labor, and are a process of continuous improvement.

Successful programs require change and are characterized by a commitment to education and employee empowerment. GAE and GCIU encourage incorporation of appropriately designed programs as a joint commitment to improve the process and quality of our product and its competitiveness in the market place.

Sometimes, what are considered traditional roles for labor and management leaders may seem to be reversed. For example, Solomon went out to explain to employers a new way of bargaining—and that it was time for labor-management cooperation to exist in a true sense. At the same time, Norton was out advising union leaders that they need to be flexible in making collective bargaining adjustments so that union workers and companies can mutually prosper and grow. Norton said the union's role in a printing industry must change and that, if it did not, the union would lose out. Solomon said the employers' organization intended to push TQM, mutual-gains bargaining, and the joint cooperation statement with "great gusto." Norton, likewise, pledged that the GCIU "would be a full partner" in program planning, as well as placing a priority on bargaining to benefit union employees and management.

## TQM AS A FUNCTIONAL APPROACH

The GCIU reached a TQM agreement with the James River Corporation—the third-largest packaging company in the United States. This agreement has been in force for more than a year. It is too early to quantify the results of the program. Results have not been uniform in every plant. Success of the program depends on the willingness of management and labor to embrace the concepts and make a real effort to meet the goals. In those plants where the program has been implemented with enthusiasm and dedication, management and local unions report major improvements in productivity. This attitude has spilled over into a willingness to deal with other workplace problems in a nonconfrontational manner. This willingness should lead to other improvements in quality, productivity, and competitiveness.

TQM principles are being applied in shops. Some TQM programs are more successful than others. GCIU leaders want to have the successful programs identified in the *GraphiCommunicator* (the union's newspaper) to lend encouragement to other shops that are using this approach. And where these systems are in place, the GCIU emphasizes in a *Graphi-*

*Communicator* technical feature how long the program has been in place, and both management and labor agree that it's fostering the kind of efforts that are valuable to both parties.

Norton maintains that "if you lose sight of the goal of improving quality or set a deadline for this to be accomplished in total, you erode the basis on which the two parties come together." He notes, however, that larger shops can sometimes do this in a variety of ways and show some quick progress in certain departments. Sometimes, the progress is immeasurable. But it does lend a spirit of renewal and cooperation if TQM is carefully nurtured and brought along, Norton points out. Care must be taken so that TQM is not expected to produce miracles. Sometimes, if TQM is not fully deployed in its entirety in the first few months of the program and if the results are not almost immediate, then the enthusiasm of either party can wane. As a consequence, participants might condemn the entire program.

Norton and Solomon observe that it is crucial that the employees understand the joint effort's objectives. It is equally crucial that mid-management understand the goal is not to eliminate particular mid-management positions. In reality, however, if the program is very successful in empowering employees and rethinking how work is done, fewer mid-management services will be needed because the employees will be doing it themselves—and will be performing services with a more gratified sense of purpose.

There is tremendous potential for this program in the printing/publishing industry. The nature of industry facilitates clear identification of quality programs, and the ability to analyze and correct problems is frequently within the grasp of those in the industry. The program has been proven to improve quality. Once a standard of quality is established, the quality of production will also begin to improve. And once quality and productivity are improved, a better product is produced. In turn, the employer becomes more competitive, and the positions of the people who work for that employer become more secure. TQM can be a job security program—if it's managed well.

To implement TQM at an operation, committees must be established to explore what TQM can mean in that shop. There must be agreement on what the goals and objectives are. To improve quality continually and patiently, the committees have to agree as to how quality can be improved. It cannot mean working faster and doing the same things. It can mean that if the job is done correctly the first time, there are no makeovers. That is one way to improve production.

The job can now be done right the first time; it looks better because each individual applies more concentration, and the value of the end product is realized and enhanced. The committees can consider spreading such ideas by asking questions such as, "How would you implement this in, say, the camera department?" Everybody might scale their own copies, for one thing, and read the densitometer tones themselves—with all eyes watching out for quality. If an employee discovers a way that produces a better negative or a better positive, the employee shares this immediately with his or her coworkers. Then constructive critiques are offered. That becomes a contagious practice.

The committees can then inspire separate departmental committees. Those committees can meet—so long as they meet during the workday—to determine solutions to stubborn problems and look at new systems in their own areas. The committees should meet at least an hour a week for a start. This leaves them time for checking their work back in the shop. When they come back to those meetings, they are not starting from scratch.

Many GCIU locals and managers find it best to schedule meetings in the last hour of the workday. Some of these meetings will start to run beyond quitting time because people will gain interest and become more involved. When that happens, the meetings should start a little bit earlier or the agenda be better managed since the track record of successful companies shows that this work can be accomplished during the normal workday.

If a jointly trusteed school exists in the area, then the school can be contacted to see how it can respond and what provisions can be made—especially in the training program. Training programs can be set up to address quality problems that accommodate that shop's requirements. And after that shop's training needs are met, training programs can be set up for another shop, drawing on the experience of that shop.

The measurement and evaluation has to be very broadly conceived by both parties working together to define their measures. Then the measurement process should be strictly followed and due lessons taken from the data labor and management have collected and analyzed. It would be naive to expect instant response to and acceptance of this program. However, labor and management people involved in a TQM effort can be expected to change their attitudes. The essential factor is that the union be involved with management at the outset of the program in its design so that they can jointly assess and share in the results of their efforts.

TQM activities impact such collective bargaining issues as changing starting times. If the change is in violation of the current labor agreement, union members can discuss this at union meetings separate from the TQM meetings to see whether an adjustment is possible. If these changes are coming from the people in the shop, then they're the people who are going to vote on the changes, and it's likely that the changes will be adopted.

At the same time, the employers must be willing to drop one process and go to another—even if the second process may prove to be more expensive than the first initially—if it produces better quality. This is especially necessary if the first process is not going to be workable. Jointly trusteed schools can help there, too, by testing out new approaches before their broader application is made in the shop. The new process can be either bought for the school or installed in the school on some type of cooperative basis with the manufacturer. If it works out, the school will keep it and pay for it. If it doesn't work out, it will be returned. In either case, management and labor in the shop learn about the feasibility and effectiveness of new processes. There must be a sufficient exploration, trial, or enough time testing associated processes so that labor and management are convinced that accepted new processes are workable. Norton suggests that "that is how the TQM program can be related with labor relations in terms of local union policy, local union positions at the regular meetings and executive board meetings, and also the interpretation of the collective bargaining agreement."

Changes in work procedures require agreements at TQM-level meetings and at union meetings and executive board or officers' meetings. The point is they can be done. Labor people cannot undercut something that is going to be good for one shop even though it's eventually going to cost some union membership so that it can maintain the overall health of the unionized printing industry—and thus preserve good jobs for the future.

Union leaders have to be perceptive enough to know that changing procedures is part of the evolution of the industry. It also must be recognized that unions cannot always be looking at processes that eliminate workers in the future—they seek to build an industry and its employment base.

## TQM'S IMPACT ON UNIONS

How does the quality program affect the union as an institution? The union becomes, in a sense, a partner with the employer. Norton maintains that unions should not adopt the TQM concept as the be-all-and-end-all concept and expect that program to work forever. "I think that would be rather foolish on the part of both labor and management," Norton says.

Downturns in the economies of Canada and the United States, in Norton's view, have been caused by the exportation of jobs or merchandise to foreign countries. In many instances, those foreign countries were paying lower wages than those in Canada and the United States. There is an impression that Canada and the United States are losing work because they have become less competitive than some of the countries overseas. Norton says he does not "believe that's true for a minute. But I think labor unions made our people more comfortable than they had a right to expect for a long period of time. Now there are employers who are willing to invest large sums of money overseas because they are convinced that it's not the individual who's producing his profit but the kind of equipment they buy and the kind of processes they adopt. As long as you have employers, however, who think that way—and who go to the least expensive place for producing their work—that theory will work wonders for the employer as long as he's producing an acceptable level of work.

"In a cheap environment, it will not be a long-term successful operation because there's always another country that's coming out of the Third World category of undernourished and underpaid workers."

If an employer is going to constantly produce just that acceptable level in the cheapest environment, the union's membership will decline. The union as an operating, viable institution, able to make a contribution to the industry, is going to be so diluted that it will not be effective in assuring competition based on quality. As a consequence, the union will be unwilling to participate in a program that will ultimately hurt the union. Such efforts will be chilled—particularly with the union that has lost membership. That, Norton says, is "part of the cycle that we're involved in right now. Consequently, if you insist that you're not going to welcome this equipment and processes in your shops or in your unions, we'll go the way of other unions who have resisted technological advancements—and we'll enjoy a very short-lived future. As a result, we will fall short on the pension benefits that we hoped to be able to meet in the long run because of the dearth of replacements coming into the industry."

This grim reality has to be dealt with. Union leaders must be open and straightforward with their members, Norton asserts, and face up to the necessity of leading change rather than be battered by it.

## ORGANIZING FOR RESTORING STRENGTH

Union leaders should not sit on their hands and lament that they are without hope. Members can be added through organizing. Unions, Norton adds, "have to seek a more favorable legislative environment in which to organize, but unions must also stay focused on the conviction that we must seek and promote quality." He adds that unions "must seek improved production, which will bring job security for those people who are involved in the industry. We have simply not done that as well in the recent years as we had done in the past in recruiting members. If we do better, we bring more people into the industry," he says. "We will be lessening these standards as these people come into the industry but must provide them with the training, skills, and support in the shops that will make them top quality employees."

So long as contracts can be negotiated, grievance procedures will be retained in those contracts. Norton thinks that eventually fewer grievances will arise "because the emphasis of these TQM programs will be more of cooperation and coordination than of confrontation and suppression. And the aggressive positions that some of our locals had—and even the GCIU at times has had—will be more moderated in the collective bargaining approach." Norton says that so long as improvements in the cooperative spirit occur, "there will be less of the type of grievances that we used to have associated with discharges. And management could feel less need to discipline its employees. I think that will vastly improve the grievance procedures in the contract—there will be less of them, and there will be more of a 'shopper' approach on the part of both labor and management to the processing of these grievances."

## NOT POLITICS AS USUAL

How will the union be affected as a political institution? Norton predicts "it will be a positive one for both the union as a political institution and the country, as well. If quality has its full impact in the industry and the economy, it will improve the ability of the consumers to develop more disposable dollars because of the quality process, organizing process, and the collective bargaining process. If we remain competitive, some of the work that used to go overseas may well stay in the United States and Canada. And if employers see profits returning to their American shops, they will not be as quick to send these investment dollars overseas." A stable and growing union has a more favorable internal political environment.

To communicate inside the union, Norton suggests assigning a local union officer to make periodic reports on TQM at the union meeting. The frequency of reports depends on how many shops are involved and how much they have to report. "I think these reports, if they're positive, can lend a more responsive pick up from the membership attending those regular union meetings. If you don't have good attendance at the regular union meetings, you have to use some kind of informational pamphlet, periodical, or newsletter from the local unions to bring a focus and attention on the progress of the programs in the various shops."

Norton and Solomon believe that a more favorable atmosphere for workers and unions may now be evolving. They know that many printing and publishing establishments would not have initiated TQM programs had it not been for the endorsement by the two international organizations. The foundation for joint progress for the industry and everyone who works in it has been laid. That foundation can now be built upon for everybody's benefit, Norton and Solomon agree.

## Chapter Nine

# National Treasury Employees Union and the Internal Revenue Service
## Creating a Total Quality Organization

**Robert Tobias**
President
National Treasury Employees Union

Federal employees and federal employee unions, particularly the National Treasury Employees Union (NTEU), recognize the world is changing and evolving at an ever faster rate. We see it; we feel it; we know it.

We are conscious of the budget deficit and its impact on federal employee work life. We see more women, African-Americans, Hispanics, Asians, and other minorities in the workplace. Technology confronts us, particularly in the Internal Revenue Service (IRS) which is about to spend $8 billion to put a taxpayer's total tax record on the computer screen, changing the way every IRS employee does work.

In this changing world, the question is whether the federal government in general, and the IRS in particular, will respond in the traditional manner by exhorting employees to work harder while managers unilaterally design the new work systems; or whether managers will recognize the value of collaborating with the representatives of employees who perform the work—their union. The gurus of the quality movement—Juran, Crosby and Deming—all assert that 80 percent of an employee's productivity is determined by the work system and 20 percent by employee effort. It accomplishes little to exhort an IRS employee to eliminate those cases in his/her inventory of cases which are defined as "old" when the rules mandate an inventory of 50 cases and every case is classified as overage when assigned. Exhortation to invest sweat equity is not a viable substitute for creating a partnership with employees and their unions to improve the work processes and work product.

The IRS and the NTEU initially met in 1987 to jointly create a strategy to address these types of issues. But the groundwork for the effort began many years before. In 1979, the NTEU and the IRS had just completed two years of term bargaining. The negotiations had been hostile and left the parties feeling bitter. In retrospect, the clash was inevitable.

## THE IRS CULTURE

The IRS operated within a highly centralized, multilayered, quasimilitary, hierarchical structure designed to collect taxes uniformly, efficiently, and without political intervention. The IRS management viewed itself as the ideal rational organization: well-managed, task driven, and insulated from the political swirl driving many federal agencies.

Employees in the workplace felt like cogs in the grinding productivity wheel. No value was ascribed to employee knowledge about work systems; little attention was paid to quality; the decisions of highly trained lawyers and accountants were subjected to four or five levels of review; suggested changes in work processes could not be made because "we've always done it this way" or "nobody in Washington will listen"; and teamwork or cross-department sharing of information was discouraged in the assumed interest of preventing the development of conspiracies among employees to "fix" tax returns for bribes. The focus on maintaining a clean work force led the IRS to investigate employees frequently and aggressively, creating an overpowering climate of intimidation. IRS employees felt diminished, demeaned, and powerless.

In that culture, it is not surprising that IRS management considered NTEU as an interloper, analogous to a prying Congress or the inquisitive public, and equally to be resisted. IRS management violently and adamantly resisted the intrusion of any force between itself and its work force.

## NTEU'S AGGRESSIVE REPRESENTATION

In response, NTEU developed a strategy during the late 1960s and early 1970s for empowering its members by challenging the powerful. The NTEU national president staffed the union primarily with attorneys whose function was to focus on the adversarial processes—bargaining, administrative hearings, and courts—and to win. If victory was elusive, the goal was to use the administrative hearing as an adversarial bludgeon to make the manager look like a buffoon and to extract embarrassing information for later use. IRS management was always cast as the enemy.

The strategy led to successful internal and external organizing. NTEU grew from representing 20,000 IRS employees in the mid-1960s to currently representing 155,000 employees in 18 different agencies. Successful lawsuits against President Nixon in 1972—resulting in a total of one-half billion dollars in back pay—and President Reagan in 1980—rewarding back pay to those whose job offers were unlawfully canceled in President Reagan's grand inauguration-day slap at federal employees —NTEU captured the attention of federal workers. With successful individual and class action lawsuits, NTEU had become a force to be reckoned with. At the same time, NTEU had been aggressively litigating grievances and unfair labor practice charges in the growing list of agencies in which it was winning exclusive recognition rights. As a result of our successes, NTEU had acquired a reputation as the leader in creating much of the constitutional, labor, and administrative case law in the federal sector.

Given the institutional direction of NTEU and IRS, it is not surprising that the 1977–79 IRS/NTEU negotiations constituted a showdown. The IRS was bargaining for take-backs, and NTEU for significant improvements in working conditions. NTEU was winning and the IRS seemed to see the bargaining as a "last stand." When the IRS said *no*, NTEU used all of its resources and skills—negotiation, organizing (picketing, leafleting, membership building), litigation, and lobbying the administration and Congress. NTEU achieved its stated bargaining goals and declared victory. But the contract had come at a very high organizational price for both parties. Both organizations had expended significant energy; yet, not much had changed in day-to-day work processes or relationships.

## SEEKING INVOLVEMENT AND COOPERATION

We wanted to do more than win—we wanted involvement. NTEU, however, was excluded by law and IRS hostility from negotiation over many fundamental issues: design and implementation of work processes, work review systems, rewards, production standards, and so on. IRS determined the fundamental issues, and NTEU fought a rear-guard action to ameliorate the adverse impact.

Shortly after bargaining ended in 1979, NTEU urged Congress to investigate the cost of conducting labor relations in the IRS. NTEU argued it had experience and expertise to offer which would benefit IRS operations. NTEU made similar suggestions to the IRS. We hoped the IRS would discover it was in its own interest to conduct labor relations less adversarially and take advantage of NTEU's expertise.

The IRS responded by conducting an internal study. The IRS asked itself whether it should have a different relationship with NTEU, one that was less adversarial, less costly, and provided some operating benefits. As part of its process, the IRS asked NTEU for the first time for its suggestions for change. The study ultimately recommended a significant shift in policy: that the IRS accept the fact that NTEU was indeed the employees' elected representative and could not be ignored; that the IRS strive to create a relationship with NTEU leaders at all levels outside of the formal bargaining process; and that the IRS and NTEU engage in a cooperative effort.

The IRS defined a *cooperative effort* as problem resolution outside the formal bargaining process. In short, the IRS wanted discussions/bargaining without the legal obligation of interest arbitration after reaching impasse and without being subjected to the unfair labor practice process. Most importantly, the IRS said it would agree to discuss subjects and NTEU proposals which might otherwise have been declared as nonnegotiable; that is, beyond the limited scope of bargaining in the federal sector.

The recommendations were greeted as heretical by many IRS managers. The "management knows best/I know best" culture left no room for NTEU's involvement. The IRS did, however, adopt the recommendation that it engage with NTEU in a cooperative effort. The IRS internal dissenters were mollified because the cooperative effort was only a limited experiment that could be controlled, and most IRS managers thought NTEU would reject the overture.

Within NTEU, the IRS suggestion struck a responsive chord. Although we won the 1979 war, we also wanted to win the peace of day-to-day labor-management relations. We wanted to discuss issues heretofore forbidden. NTEU leaders had begun to recognize that its members could not be empowered solely by winning grievances, unfair labor practices, and lawsuits. *Empowerment* meant experiencing and feeling power. It came from involvement and participation; it resulted from members taking an active role in creating work processes and procedures. We were beginning to realize that providing service does not create the feeling of power in members. Rather, power must be personally felt as the result of personal involvement in group action. In short, *empowerment* is being powerful. NTEU was ready to trade its right to file unfair labor practice charges, or to engage in impasse arbitration, for a broader bilateral role in identifying and determining work processes and procedures.

## FIRST COOPERATIVE EFFORTS

Appropriately, the impetus for the first cooperative effort was an out-growth of the adversarial process. In 1979, the IRS unilaterally implemented 10 different incentive pay systems in 10 work locations covering approximately 2,000 data transcribers at each location. These incentive pay systems were designed to reward data entry operators for production rates exceeding a base standard. NTEU filed an unfair labor practice charge arguing the IRS was obligated to negotiate before implementing such a system and seeking a *status quo ante* remedy that would require millions of dollars in back pay. NTEU's right to bargain was not clear; but, once again, we were seeking to create the law in this area.

During the course of settlement discussions, the IRS admitted the incentive pay formulas it had developed were costly and failed to stimulate high performance from anyone except those who were already high performers. NTEU was leery of winning back pay but losing the right to negotiate the incentive system. Eager to set pay (an issue banned from bargaining), NTEU proposed to hold the unfair labor practice charge in abeyance while the parties discussed the incentive pay system as a cooperative effort. The IRS, freed from the pressure of the ULP charge, and searching for ideas related to increasing production, agreed.

NTEU and IRS spent three months creating a process before any substantive discussions began. We hired a consultant who served not only as a subject matter expert, but also as a facilitator who possessed group dynamics skills.

The first critical step suggested by the facilitator required each party to identify its interests, the reasons it was participating, what it expected to obtain by its involvement, its expectations of the other party, the types of information it would be willing to share with the other party, and its standards for measuring success. The exercise indicated that each party wanted to be present because it had something to gain. For NTEU, that goal was creating an incentive pay system that was credible and rewarded performance. For the IRS, the goal was to increase productivity.

That exercise was the first step in the very difficult and fragile process associated with building and creating trust. It provided the basis for struggling jointly to create guiding principles (e.g., 50 percent of all savings will be returned to employees, increased productivity will not be the basis for increasing standards, standards may change only with a change in the hardware or work process) and criteria for evaluating outcomes rather than using the traditional labor-management practice of submitting proposals.

As trust between the parties developed, information was freely exchanged; both parties learned to focus on issues, not personalities; trust of the new process developed and the eventual agreement was satisfactory to both sides. Neither side felt pressured to make an uncomfortable compromise.

The NTEU and the IRS implemented their national agreement by conducting joint training of the local incentive pay committees at each of the 10 work locations. Locally, each committee, one-half management and one-half NTEU appointees, chose facilitators, adopted ground rules, operated by consensus, and set the incentive pay standards for each job. As a result of NTEU's participation, the process of creating incentive pay formulas was demystified and accepted in the workplace, productivity increased, and NTEU received credit from its members for expanding their involvement in workplace systems.

Between 1981 and 1987, NTEU and the IRS initiated several additional cooperative efforts intended to solve specific problems. For example, in 1982 the IRS announced it wanted to consolidate its taxpayer service operation by reducing the facilities in which it was offered from 1,200 posts of duty to only several hundred locations. Approximately 8,000 employees were affected. To ameliorate the negative effects of this project, NTEU and the IRS created a process of voluntary transfers, paid moving costs, additional training, and other incentives. The process was so successful that neither involuntary transfers nor grievances resulted.

## A CRISIS IN QUALITY

NTEU-IRS collaboration on a broad national issue was born of a 1985 disaster. That spring, the IRS tax processing system broke down. Tax returns were lost, refunds were not processed timely, employees burdened with unattainable production standards destroyed tax returns, computers broke down, and the American public watched the story unfold on television every night. IRS could no longer ignore Congress or the public outcry. Its reputation as an efficient collector of revenue was in tatters. The previously confident management hierarchy began to question its ability. And NTEU heightened the national spotlight with press releases, press conferences, and appearances before Congress where NTEU was able to demonstrate that many of the IRS's problems resulted from an emphasis on quantity over quality.

IRS predictably circled its wagons. It consulted widely and attempted to identify the reasons for failure. The IRS concluded that its work processes were in disarray, there was little focus on taxpayer satisfaction, the quality of the work product was unacceptable, and root-cause analysis coupled with data-driven decisions didn't exist. The IRS solution was to train its management cadre on quality improvement as practiced in Japan. NTEU and its members were specifically excluded because, it was argued, management must learn these techniques before involving the union, and many stated there was no need for union involvement.

Although the IRS invested more than a year training its executive cadre, little improvement in the quality of the external work product had occurred. Cynicism within the work force, and continued public pressure by NTEU, finally focused a critical mass of IRS managers. In 1987, led by the new commissioner, Larry Gibbs, the IRS began to recognize that in order to fix the problems of 1985 and have a chance at avoiding the same fiasco in the near future, IRS employees and their union had to be involved with managers in improving the IRS work product.

Commissioner Gibbs authorized exploratory discussions with NTEU. NTEU was eager to further expand its role in defining and implementing improved workplace quality. Such an opportunity would allow NTEU's members the opportunity to exercise their knowledge and skills in resolving poorly structured work systems that hindered their efficiency and productivity. The NTEU's members were ready to invest, if given a chance.

## JOINT NATIONAL QUALITY IMPROVEMENT PROCESS

The largest hurdle to a joint undertaking was the one year of unilateral effort. When the IRS agreed that no previously implemented element was beyond modification, total agreement was quickly reached. Because of the trust our previous experience created over the years of working on cooperative efforts, we knew how to identify our respective interests, brainstorm, identify problems, and jointly draft an agreement.

The agreement represented fundamental change in the way the IRS viewed the employees. For the first time, their value as human capital—to be valued, used, and developed—was publicly declared. The Joint Quality Improvement Process (JQIP), created by NTEU and the IRS, recognized what social scientists had been saying for years: that people want to work and excel; to produce a good product; and to be given a chance to exercise responsibility. The agreement provided that opportunity. It stated:

> There is a recognition that the primary resource of the Internal Revenue Service is the knowledge, skill, and versatility of its employees, and that it is necessary to encourage the active, involved participation and collaboration between NTEU, bargaining unit employees, supervisors, and managers in order to improve the quality of the internal and external work product in IRS.

We jointly declared that an involved employee becomes a committed employee, one who looks forward to coming to work, and one who looks at problems as challenges. We also jointly declared that we wanted employees who were actively involved in the workplace, not passively waiting to be told what to do; we wanted curious employees, who weren't counting the years, months, days, and hours until retirement. We began the process of creating a new partnership in the public service, one that recognized the value and contribution to public service of bargaining unit employees and their union.

Recognizing that symbols of change are important, we wanted to announce the new agreement in a way that emphasized its significance. The announcement of the creation of the Joint Quality Improvement Process was made in October 1987 in a Washington, D.C., auditorium by Commissioner Gibbs and the NTEU national president. Present to witness this first joint appearance of an NTEU national president and an IRS commissioner were all local and national IRS managers and all national and local union leaders. Many of the IRS managers and union leaders knew each other only by sight. For the first time, an IRS Commissioner, with words and actions, publicly acknowledged NTEU's existence and declared that the goals the IRS was striving to achieve could not be reached without the joint effort of the NTEU and the IRS.

The national agreement created a Joint National Quality Council and a Joint Quality Council in each IRS region and district office. The Council consisted of the local union president and one other union leader appointed by the local union, and an unlimited number of management officials, including the highest management official in the jurisdiction (e.g., district director, regional commissioner). The Councils operated by consensus and were assigned the following tasks:

1. Make all decisions necessary to establish, support, and nurture quality improvement initiatives . . . (e.g., determine the method for soliciting quality problems from employees; determine which quality problems will be addressed through the use of quality improvement projects; create and appoint teams and team leaders to study quality problems and to make suggestions for resolution; appoint facilitators for each team; establish methods for reporting the disposition of recommendations made by teams; provide for the training of facilitators and team leaders; promote the existence of and encourage participation in the process).
2. Create an understanding and acceptance that quality improvement is a permanent, never-ending process.
3. Select a facilitator to attend all meetings to assist the council in carrying out its tasks.

The agreement was an attempt to change the IRS culture by making NTEU and employees jointly responsible for quality improvement efforts; recognizing that cross-functional teams, using facilitators, were the primary source for new ideas and improvements; using data as the primary resource for making decisions; and acknowledging that 80 percent of improved quality and quantity was associated with improving work systems.

## JOINT QUALITY IMPLEMENTATION

The first phase of the process was implemented in 1988 with the conducting of a series of jointly designed and presented training sessions for each joint council. Representatives of the IRS and NTEU jointly served as members of two-person training teams. The interactive training sessions addressed the goals of the process, the reason it was adopted, details of the agreement, the reasons consensus had been adopted as the decision-making process, and the role of facilitators. In addition, the participants engaged in exercises that allowed them to discuss their fears and doubts and to begin to build the trust and commitment so critical to creating a successful collaborative effort. Additionally, each local Quality Council conducted awareness training for all employees.

These were heady days. Goals seemed clear and expectations of achievement were high. No surveys or readiness analyses had been conducted, so ignorance was truly bliss. We expected transformation to occur because an enlightened plan had been created and made known. Reality followed shortly.

The parties quickly realized that the execution of an agreement coupled with energetic training does not automatically change culture. The resistance to involvement can take many forms and be clothed in multiple justifications.

The critical question regarding which issues were to be referred to the Quality Councils for joint investigation and consensus decision making, and which issues were to be retained by management for unilateral decision making, soon surfaced. According to the national agreement, quality improvement initiatives, which included improving "the quality of the internal and external work product" and "the quality of work life" were subject to the jurisdiction of Joint Quality Councils. By narrowly construing the agreement language, however, local management officials who wished to continue resisting NTEU's involvement and the collaborative process were able to circumvent the Councils, and to conduct business as usual. Other managers ignored the joint process because, they argued, it took too long and required unnecessary research and testing before implementation.

## RECOGNIZING AND CONFRONTING RESISTANCE

Early in the process it became clear that NTEU and the IRS had failed to focus on the root of the problem: strong managerial resistance to collaborative joint decision making and data-driven decision-making processes. We had failed to anticipate the strength of the resistance and to confront it. Instead, the parties tried to address the problem through written word from the top. Consequently, 14 months after signing the initial agreement, the parties signed an addendum which further defined a *quality improve-*

*ment effort* as "an organized activity, such as a task force or study group, that is brought together for the purpose of improving work processes or issues affecting quality of work life and which affects bargaining unit employees." The addendum also stated that management could decide, on the basis of "time constraints or the size/scope of the effort" to exclude the issue from the Joint Council process. The oral assurances given to NTEU at the time the addendum was executed promised that few issues would bypass the local Joint Councils. Unfortunately, the IRS failed to make good on its promise.

As time went on, it became easy to measure the success of the joint quality improvement process by comparing the number and scope of the quality improvement issues discussed by the various Joint Councils, as opposed to those issues management excluded from the process because of time constraints. The scope issue was a continuing source of discussion and dissonance.

Not surprisingly, the first- and second-level managers often mirrored the resistance at the top. A frequent refrain was that NTEU should not be allowed to intrude into management's role. From setting agendas in group meetings, to addressing intra-group relationship issues, to solving complex tax cases, the supervisors saw themselves as responsible and in charge. The history and culture of the IRS neither supported nor rewarded those who promoted team efforts; rather, those who were able to distinguish themselves through independent action—often at the expense of others—were promoted and rewarded. Management control continued to be the operative formula for many IRS managers.

Another form of resistance we frequently experienced was the evaluation and promotion of employees based on quantity rather than a combination of quantity and quality. IRS managers knew how to evaluate on quantity. But they did not trust their organization's announced shift to measuring quantity *and* quality.

In addition, in many locations, managers distinguished working on quality improvement from performing the "real work" of the IRS. Supervisors criticized employees for loafing on quality improvement teams; many managers considered *quality* as something separate and apart from their work processes or systems. *Real work* was defined as accomplishing measured tasks, as distinguished from such abstract concepts as *continuous improvement*.

It is important to note, however, that resistance lay not only with management. Many local NTEU leaders had become involved in NTEU after suffering injury and/or enjoying success as local leaders because they were "winners." They were not interested in forming a cooperative or collaborative relationship with management officials. Arm's-length fighting was the preferred form of combat. There was little interest in changing the terms of engagement.

Initially, NTEU and the IRS also had erred in assuming that it is possible to create collaborative relationships and to work on quality improvement, while all other aspects of the traditional labor-management relationship remained adversarial. We erroneously believed that the excitement and challenge of working together to change the work processes and procedures would provide sufficient incentive for local managers and union leaders to check their guns at the door while they worked on quality.

Not true. We learned that the quality improvement process was an inherent part of the labor-management relationship, that it could not operate independently. The existence of a good labor-management relationship is a condition precedent to a successful quality improvement effort. We came to realize that such factors as trust, problem-solving skills, and the desire for change must be developed in the context of an improving labor-management relationship. Then, and only then, would it be possible for the quality improvement effort to succeed.

We also learned that the parties frequently failed to articulate their expectations of each other. Managers assumed that they would be immune from NTEU's public criticism because the union now had the facts related to specific problems and had heard the IRS state its interest in solving them. NTEU leaders had entered the process assuming that their arguments and interests had not been adopted over the years because of malevolence. They expected their ideas would be adopted in this new era of good feeling. Not only were the expectations unrealistic, they were also not shared. There was, therefore, little chance they would be fulfilled. Consequently, considerable alienation resulted and many of the gains that had been made were lost.

Another problem that arose concerned the fact that only about 15 percent of the IRS employee population participated in the quality improvement process as facilitators, team leaders, or team members. Therefore, 85 percent of the work force did not have an active role and consequently, in their eyes, the quality improvement process was just another grand strategy gone awry.

## ROLE OF THE JOINT NATIONAL QUALITY COUNCIL

During this period, the Joint National Quality Council (JNQC)—composed of IRS headquarters, regional and local management officials and the NTEU national president, executive vice president, and local union officials—was attempting to provide leadership and direction to the national effort. Essentially, the JNQC's role was similar to a steering committee for the IRS/NTEU quality improvement effort. Its responsibilities were many: (*a*) to champion the quality process by sponsoring national conferences to highlight and reward accomplishments and learn from the experience of the private-sector organizations which had undertaken quality initiatives; (*b*) to provide information to local councils by creating a national database of Quality Improvement Teams chartered, issues under study, and results in the form of savings achieved; (*c*) to develop and continuously refine training modules for facilitators, teams, team leaders, and Quality Councils; and (*d*) to encourage dysfunctional local Quality Councils to request facilitation assistance from internal and external facilitators who were funded at the national level.

The JNQC was limited in its programmatic impact, however, because it had no line authority over the local managers who, in conjunction with the local NTEU presidents, were responsible for implementing the process. The JNQC only had the power of exhortation; it was not vested with the authority to evaluate individuals or program features, or to compel either participation or collaboration.

NTEU regularly raised these problems and failures in the JNQC and in private meetings with the commissioner and deputy commissioner. The JNQC could not and IRS officials did not act to correct these problems or counsel recalcitrant managers. There was understanding at the top executive levels in the IRS that NTEU's role must change, but an unwillingness to drive that change down through the management structure.

## SUCCESSES OF THE JOINT QUALITY PROCESS

In spite of the problems and limitations, there were some successes. Almost all who participated on teams or as team leaders or facilitators became converts and wanted to participate again. They reported feeling the empowerment that flowed from the successful implementation of improvements resulting from their ideas, creativity, and involvement. Skills learned in the quality improvement teams—process analysis, brainstorming, multivoting, working toward consensus, data-based decisions—leaked into the everyday work environment. At a number of work sites, the use of the new processes led to a more involved work force and better decisions. Participants were energized.

The IRS work product has substantially increased, and efficiencies implemented as a result of quality improvement team recommendations now amount to more than $1 billion. For example, the accuracy rate in response to taxpayer questions has increased from 65 percent in 1987 to 88 percent in 1993. And a recent cross-functional team recommendation has been projected to yield an estimated $7 billion per year in additional revenue from taxpayers who previously failed to file tax returns.

The experience of NTEU leaders and IRS managers talking to each other on a regular basis in an effort to solve work-related problems helped to build trust and understanding in the labor-management relationship. Union officials were being asked by managers for the first time to use their energy and effort to solve a management problem. A union's traditional role of asking for more and management saying *no* had changed. Managers were now asking for help to achieve their goals. The parties' relationship was moving toward a level of equality, resulting in the strengthening of the foundation critical to building trust.

## THE SHIFT TO A TOTAL QUALITY ORGANIZATION

Between 1987 and 1989, NTEU's efforts to reduce the obstacles to its full participation coincided with the IRS's realization that it needed NTEU's lobbying assistance to obtain funds from Congress in order to purchase computer hardware and software priced at $8 billion. In addition, several high-level IRS managers, responsible for the tax system modernization effort, recognized NTEU's argument and concluded that the IRS could not successfully leverage the increased computer capacity into increased productivity without NTEU's full participation. There was a dawning recognition that the introduction of hardware simply offered the opportunity to change work processes. The design and successful implementation of those processes must, as NTEU had long stated, come in large part from the minds of those employees currently doing the work. Some IRS officials began to comprehend the significance of NTEU's assertion that (*a*) the quality improvement effort had to be integrated with the business strategy of improving productivity, and (*b*) the present hierarchical, layered-management structure ambushed policy implementation, creative problem solving, and the sharing of power with NTEU.

While the IRS was moving, though tardily, toward a higher degree of commitment to the joint effort, NTEU was assessing whether it should withdraw from the joint quality improvement effort. NTEU's credibility with its members had suffered because the IRS's promise of work restructuring based on employee involvement and the promise to focus on quality as equal to quantity had not occurred. The unwillingness of local managers to engage in a process that would significantly improve local conditions continued unabated.

In addition, local leaders were concerned the service/benefit rationale had been lost as a reason for new members to join and become involved in NTEU. In its open shop environment, NTEU had pursued potential members by promising protection from management. We had now become less adversarial but at the same time the expected empowerment of employees as a result of NTEU activity had not occurred as fast as anticipated. As a result, many nonmembers felt they no longer needed to join NTEU for protection, and saw no need to join to stimulate change.

Finally, there was a growing anti-quality political movement in NTEU seeking to get NTEU out of bed with management. These "anti" members sought a return to the labor-management model associated with a totally adversarial relationship. They believed that labor and management should not collaborate because of the potential for corrupting union officials at the expense of members.

But NTEU had experienced the success of involvement at the national level and at a number of local offices. Some NTEU leaders and members had felt the power of influencing positive, productive change in the workplace. And many NTEU leaders and members experienced prompt grievance resolution without arbitration and less time consumed negotiating term and mid-term contracts as a result of the trust developed in the quality process. The majority of NTEU leaders wanted more of these successes.

By the fall of 1989, IRS top-level managers concluded Congress would support the $8 billion hardware/software acquisitions only if IRS not only automated preexisting processes, but also leveraged the automation to significant quality and quantity increases. And, the managers concluded, this could not happen without NTEU's total involvement.

These managers came to NTEU and stated that the IRS wanted to become a Total Quality Organization (TQO) by 1996. The IRS said it wanted to negotiate a cooperative agreement to implement TQO. Specifically, the IRS said it wanted to include NTEU representatives in the strategic business decision-making process, in the creation of quality measurements and all other business measurements, and in all aspects of the quality improvement effort. It was a significant change in direction by the IRS. NTEU agreed to explore the IRS proposal because we recognized we could influence Congress to disallow the purchase of the automation equipment if the IRS ultimately was unwilling to do what it said it would do.

Discussions continued for three years. Each party had formed a group it used for gathering information about the existing effort, and testing suggestions for going forward with TQO. The parties recognized that if they agreed to go forward, a broader understanding of the goals, objectives, and potential pitfalls was needed, in contrast to the limited exploration in which we had engaged in 1987.

In January 1993, NTEU and the IRS signed an agreement with the specificity of purpose and guarantees for NTEU that were lacking in 1987. The new document recognized the equal partnership between NTEU and the IRS. The agreement represents a clear understanding by both parties of their own interests. The IRS recognized that a TQO was a fantasy without the equal participation of NTEU and employees, and NTEU decided to continue involving itself in determining the direction of the agency. The agreement states in part:

> The Internal Revenue Service and the National Treasury Employees Union agree that the accomplishment of the mission of the Service, improving the quality of employee work life and enhancing our labor-management relationship are of primary importance to both organizations and are the common focal points, as we continue with our joint improvement efforts. In order to increase voluntary compliance, reduce taxpayer burden, and improve quality and productivity to achieve customer satisfaction, we will jointly continually pursue innovative approaches which maximize the contributions of individual employees, managers and the Union to work together to achieve those objectives. To be a Total Quality Organization, the Service must integrate and involve employees and NTEU at the early stages of the formulation of those decisions and processes that are the basis for the redesign and continual improvement of the IRS organization.

The parties agreed that a TQO consistently meets or exceeds internal and external customer needs and continuously improves organizational performance. Implementing TQO concepts changes our focus from problem-solving activities to improving the quality of work life, bettering the labor-management relationship, and empowering the work force by engaging executives, managers, NTEU, and employees in managing and improving work systems.

Implementing systems management into the IRS represents a sea change. It will require the IRS to organize its work around its several work products rather than an outdated management structure that has insulated the various compartments of the IRS from each other, Congress, and the public. Managers and NTEU will be responsible for determining how the processes actually will work and who will be responsible for each part of the process. Systems will then be selected for improvement. In contrast, presently no one is clearly responsible for any work process. The managerial responsibilities are often overlapping and so muddled that no one is assigned real accountability and, therefore, change cannot be effectively implemented.

The parties believe that improving the quality of work life (QWL) is important, because satisfied employees produce more, have higher morale, are more loyal, and are eager to take on responsibility. There is a recognition that work locations must be safe, easily accessible, clean, comfortable in temperature, and have good air quality. In addition, the office equipment and furniture must be safe and in good working condition.

QWL also extends to a recognition that an employee's personal life has an impact on his or her work life. Therefore, the parties pledge to explore alternative work schedules, flexiplace, flexitours, and other nontraditional work arrangements.

## GROUNDING IN THE LABOR-MANAGEMENT RELATIONSHIP

In contrast to the 1987 agreement, NTEU and the IRS specifically identified the labor-management relationship as a critical condition to success in the 1993 agreement. The parties recognize that a working labor-management relationship must exist in order to maximize employee involvement. The parties also recognize that their interests are both separate and partially overlapping. We cannot expect or be expected to merge ourselves into the

IRS or they into us. Improvement in the labor-management relationship can be maximized only when managers, employees, and the union all value one another as resources, recognize and respect one another's legitimate needs, focus attention on common goals, and work together to meet those goals. This relationship is dependent on developing lasting, open, and honest communications and mutual respect among the parties. This does not suggest a move toward *comanagement*, in which the interests and responsibilities of all parties are the same. It recognizes that while management, employees, and NTEU have many interests which overlap, they also have some which differ. The parties recognize that the words alone will not create the understanding, acceptance, and changed behavior necessary. It will take planning, training, inducement, and enforcement.

## EMPOWERMENT

*Empowerment* is an often-used word which must be specifically defined in order to have meaning. The parties have attempted to define the term to make clear that employees must be included in every step of a system's redesign. Managers will:

- Assist in enhancing employees' knowledge, skills, and abilities.
- Minimize managerial post-review of work products.
- Nurture the acceptance of responsibility, authority, and accountability in employees by believing in them, encouraging them, and looking for ways to build on their potential.
- Describe the expectations, latitude, and discretion employees have in the job, especially as it relates to making improvements and satisfying customers' needs.

## CONSTRUCTING THE TOTAL QUALITY ORGANIZATION

To implement the IRS TQO, NTEU will become part of the strategic decision-making process, participate in designing all quality measures, and be involved in all systems redesign efforts. The parties have created a structure to guarantee the NTEU role:

1. The NTEU national president will join the IRS executive committee, which currently consists of the IRS commissioner, deputy commissioner, and six core systems business owners, to participate in all discussions and decisions concerning the efforts to achieve a TQO.

2. NTEU will appoint representatives to all permanent and ad-hoc groups at the national, regional, and local levels that have responsibility for trying to improve quality by changing work systems, processes, and procedures.

3. NTEU will participate in the strategic planning efforts to achieve a TQO and in designing the measures to chart the progress.

Rather than implement the 1993 agreement nationwide, the parties assumed that the mutual advantages of an enhanced partnership may not be clear at every location or, even if clear, the local parties may not have the skills to take advantage of a partnership. Therefore, the parties at the national level agreed that the pre-1993 process, although limited, would remain in place until the JNQC certified the eligibility of each local council to proceed under the new partnership agreement. To achieve certification, the local parties must jointly conduct a self-assessment and rate themselves on the four TQO elements (systems management, empowerment, labor-management relations, and quality of work life), each of which is extensively defined. The information from the self-assessment is then used to create a joint five-year plan for moving from where they find themselves to a level of behavior that "consistently demonstrates the behavior which achieves the desired TQO level of performance." Finally, an agreement must be negotiated between NTEU and the IRS in each locale, specifically identifying NTEU's role consistent with the national agreement. We expect most applications for certification to be received by January 1995.

The local parties will have a wide array of resources to choose from, including written material, training, and facilitators. The real incentive, however, is a declaration by the commissioner of the IRS that the subject office will become a Total Quality Organization by 1996, and managerial promotions and bonuses will depend in part on how well the partnership agreement is managed. For NTEU leaders, the incentive is to increase the union's role far beyond that which exists today, to involve its members in changing oppressive work processes, and to appoint one of its members as a quality coordinator. This person, under the direction of the local chapter president, and given release time, will be entitled to coordinate the local union quality effort, talk to employees and work on teams. This appointment will help ensure that NTEU has the resources to effectively participate as a true partner in the process.

## NTEU'S FUTURE AGENDA

The impact of the 1993 agreement on NTEU will be great. As a result of our intense adversarial posture, NTEU developed a service-based union structure. When members were injured by IRS actions, they were provided skilled service by stewards, officers, and NTEU staff. We trained our officials to respond aggressively, quickly, and effectively.

We now need more of an organizing approach. We must go into the workplace and identify the issues of concern, gather information from all affected members, communicate to them that a particular issue has been placed on the joint problem-solving agenda, communicate the progress of the effort, ask the members to take action—form committees to gather information, participate on union/management committees, provide an analysis of the problem—regularly communicate and celebrate progress, and celebrate success.

An organizing approach requires broad-based local chapters. Proactive contact with members requires planning and a large cadre of stewards in constant contact with the workplace. This approach gives us a real opportunity to address problems before they produce pain, but it requires union leaders to identify issues, set priorities, and plan for resolution. A few aggressive chapter leaders responding to aggrieved members cannot survive in an organizing model.

As more members become actively involved, change occurs. Hope and skills—ingredients for additional larger change—are created. Union leaders must be more inclusive, manage their time more effectively, learn the skills associated with brainstorming, multivoting, and consensus decision making. Union leaders are faced with a membership demanding more energy and effort. At the same time, these leaders are often challenged by a substantial group of voters who like the old way and don't want any change in dealing with management. The political stress on union leaders is substantial.

NTEU must provide training and support to its leaders and staff to prepare them for their challenges. The new skills needed are many: managing a large cadre of volunteers as well as a strong representation system, becoming familiar with the intricacies of the federal budget process, dealing with the public and the press, and developing other group dynamics skills. Some of the training can be joint with the IRS, but some must be provided solely by NTEU to its leaders. Leaders, and in turn, members, must constantly be educated and reminded that their collective voice is responsible for shifting power from supervisors to employees—democratizing the workplace. It is their union which is responsible for negotiating agreements which guarantee employee participation and involvement. There must be constant repetition of the themes and skill building.

## LESSONS OF NTEU'S QUALITY QUEST

NTEU has learned lessons about the process during its six years of participation:

1. Identify the union's interests before participation, reassess them regularly, and pursue them relentlessly.
2. A service-based model of assistance to members must be changed to an organizing model. Union leaders, members, and staff must change to reflect the changes which will occur in the workplace.
3. Plan for resistance—anticipate it in advance, confront it when it occurs, help create solutions. If it persists, it must be neutralized.
4. Fear of the unknown is an inherent part of the process.
5. Successful implementation of involvement unionism democratizes the workplace and infuses new energy into local unions. Changing from a service-based, adversarial process to one based more on organizing requires training union leaders for their new role.
6. Changes in organizational structures, power relationships and measured accomplishments almost always take longer and are more difficult than anticipated. Plan for that reality.

Although NTEU and the IRS have come far, much remains to be done. The irony of this process is that the longer you are in it, the harder it becomes. Each success yields more satisfaction to member/participants and requires more union leaders to expend more effort involving more members who, in turn, will identify more problems and work processes to be resolved. The options available to a union leader to resolve disputes increases, while the certainty of the "correct" decision diminishes.

At some point in the future, we will reach a point where the process has a momentum of its own. NTEU looks forward to the day when NTEU members will see both their union and their workplace as total quality organizations.

## Chapter Ten

# Employee Involvement and Quality Improvement
## American Federation of Government Employees/U.S. Department of Labor

**Bruce A. Waltuck**
National Coordinator for Employee Involvement and Quality Improvement
National Council of Field Labor Locals (AFGE)

**Jim Armshaw**
Department Coordinator, Office of Quality of Work Life and Total Quality
Management
U.S. Department of Labor

## INTRODUCTION

Since August of 1990, the U.S. Department of Labor (DOL) and the National Council of Field Labor Locals (NCFLL), an affiliate of the American Federation of Government Employees (AFGE, AFL-CIO), have forged a system for employee involvement and quality improvement (EIQI).[1] Addressing the operations of the field locations of the U.S. Department of Labor, EIQI covers more than 9,000 employees at nearly 900 individual work sites.

This initiative has fostered a number of approaches to quality improvement and participation in a unionized workplace. Starting with basic

---

[1]The opinions expressed herein are those of the authors and not necessarily those of the U.S. Department of Labor. An earlier article by Jim Armshaw, David Carnevale, and Bruce Waltuck, "Cooperating for Quality: Union-Management Partnership in the U.S. Department of Labor," appeared in *Review of Public Personnel Administration*, Summer, 1993, pp. 94–107.

assumptions about labor-management cooperation, the DOL and NCFLL have crafted a working partnership which has met the tests of a highly diverse organization, geographic dispersion, and significant political change. In its brief life, EIQI has addressed the difficult issues of developing and implementing a nationwide, multiorganization quality improvement initiative, frequently finding unique solutions to common problems. Throughout, this union-management endeavor has remained employee-oriented and has relied upon the core values of cooperation, commitment, communication, and consensus.

The story of EIQI is also the story of dynamic agendas. Both the NCFLL and the DOL have undergone significant changes in their underlying interests since the inception of EIQI. They have experienced a major shift away from traditional models of labor-management relations to collaborative, interest-based practices. They have responded to changes in the administration and concurrent changes in the leadership of the department. Both organizations have struggled to maintain perceived prerogatives and extend influence, while seeking to expand areas of mutual interest.

## THE PLAYERS

### U.S. Department of Labor

The U.S. Department of Labor is organized into more than one dozen agencies nationwide. The missions of these organizations vary considerably, from the data collection and analysis of the Bureau of Labor Statistics, to the inspection of underground coal mines by the Mine Safety and Health Administration, to the protection of migrant and seasonal agricultural workers by the Wage-Hour division. The majority of the DOL's field employees are engaged in some form of regulatory enforcement such as minimum wage and child labor laws; occupational safety and health; and federal contract compliance. Many others work in support of very different public services including job training; worker's compensation claims processing; and alien certification for work. The common element is a focus on the interests of the American worker.

Most DOL agencies have offices in major cities such as New York, Atlanta, Chicago, and San Francisco. Some agencies have all of their employees centrally located at their regional offices. Those engaged in regulatory enforcement have networks of area and district offices throughout the country. The department is organized along a traditional hierarchical model. The secretary and deputy secretary lead an organization of assistant secretaries—program heads who direct and administer the various agencies within the department. The agency heads are political appointees who serve at the pleasure of the president, and require the confirmation of the U.S. Senate. At the regional level, agencies are typically managed by a regional administrator. These are career bureaucrats, the majority being members of the Federal Senior Executive Service.

Within this diversity of organizations and functions, five principal agencies account for the overwhelming majority of field employees. These are:

- Bureau of Labor Statistics (BLS).
- Employment Standards Administration (ESA; includes Wage-Hour, Federal Contract Compliance, and Worker's Compensation components).
- Employment Training Administration (ETA; includes Apprenticeship and Training, Job Corps, and Unemployment Insurance components).
- Mine Safety and Health Administration (MSHA).
- Occupational Safety and Health Administration (OSHA).
- A sixth agency, the Office of the Assistant Secretary for Administration and Management (OASAM), administers personnel, financial, and other administrative activities throughout the department. Consequently, it plays a significant role in daily interaction with employees and other agencies.

### National Council of Field Labor Locals (AFGE-AFL-CIO)

The National Council of Field Labor Locals is the exclusive representative of the Department of Labor's bargaining unit employees outside the metropolitan Washington, D.C. area. The NCFLL consists of 24 local unions located throughout the United States. Delegates from these locals elect the 11 officers of the NCFLL Executive Board to four-year terms of office. As a council, the NCFLL negotiates a single labor-management agreement directly with the Department of Labor rather than having each local union negotiate separately. The department recognizes the NCFLL, and not its constituent local unions, as the exclusive representative of the employees.

Local NCFLL unions also maintain elected presidents and other officials for the conduct of their business. In addition, the local unions also appoint varying numbers of stewards, typically representing employees in particular agencies and work sites. Under the terms of the current DOL-NCFLL agreement (also referred to as the *contract*), the NCFLL also appoints representatives to Regional Collective Bargaining Committees (RCBCs). These groups typically consist of local union presidents within a region, as well as other senior union leaders. The chairperson of each RCBC serves as the ranking NCFLL official in each DOL region, and is consequently the liaison between the council and the department at the regional level. In a sense, the NCFLL has its own bureaucracy—a hierarchy not unlike that of the department's management.

Principal NCFLL activities include the negotiation of the master agreement, interim negotiations on novel issues or changes in working conditions, the filing and resolution of employee grievances, arbitration, and other third-party processes. There are two principal forums for dialogue between the DOL and the NCFLL. Four times a year the Executive Board of the NCFLL meets in Washington with department and key DOL agency officials. These meetings address issues of national scope and interest such as reductions in force or employee drug testing. At the regional level, the NCFLL RCBCs meet three times a year with regional labor-management and agency officials. These meetings deal with issues of regional scope or interest, such as office relocations or unit performance awards. The NCFLL is an affiliate of the American Federation of Government Employees (AFGE, AFL-CIO), the largest federal government employee union in the United States.


## THE STATUS QUO ANTE


### Traditional Labor-Management Relations

Collective bargaining in the federal sector is governed by the Federal Service Labor-Management Relations Statute (5 U.S.C. §§7101–7135). This statute establishes the basic representational rights and obligations of employees, federal agencies, and labor organizations. The law reserves to management the rights to assign work; determine means, methods, and technologies of work; establish necessary security measures; and so on. Unions are entitled to be notified of any proposed changes in working conditions and to bargain over the impact and implementation of any changes. While some rights are specifically reserved (management's right to assign work; the union's right to organize) or are otherwise nonnegotiable, others are permissive areas of bargaining. In these, one side or the other may elect to negotiate, at its own discretion. From such straightforward origins, federal agencies and unions have crafted contracts dealing with a broad range of topics. Some are fundamental to any collective bargaining agreement. These include procedures for filing grievances and other third-party rights of appeal. Also included are provisions governing merit promotions and other personnel actions. These likely include language on disciplinary and adverse actions. More recently, other areas of interest have been addressed, such as wellness and elder care.

Typically, labor-management relations is thought of as an adversarial process. The underlying interests of the union and management are frequently depicted as being mutually exclusive, or of having little commonality. The process of negotiation is historically adversarial. Both union and management take positions on an issue. The adversarial model has the parties making demands, exchanging proposals, and offering concessions back and forth across the table until some agreement is reached. In this way, both labor and management protect their perceived prerogatives, and simultaneously pursue their respective agendas.

### *Labor-Management Relations between the DOL and NCFLL*

Since at least the mid-1980s, the NCFLL has enjoyed a good working relationship with Department of Labor management. Since the tenure of William Brock, each secretary of labor has met personally with NCFLL leadership, frequently consulting on issues of mutual interest. The collective bargaining agreement between the parties had been largely unchanged since 1978. Repeatedly, the parties had agreed to extensions on the life of the agreement. At the institutional and national levels, working relationships between DOL and NCFLL officials were good. Even when the parties vigorously disagreed on an issue under negotiation, such as employee drug testing, participants maintained a professional, even cordial tone.

Nevertheless, both sides perceived that their experience in crafting and administering agreements was not keeping pace with the social, political, and technological changes impacting DOL employees. Rarely was the guard let down and underlying interests discussed. Information was frequently kept secret, as if complete disclosure might weaken one or the other party's position. It was the common practice of federal managers to refuse to negotiate in so-called permissive areas, such as methods and technologies of work. For example, as personal computers and their attendant ergonomic problems spread through the workplace, the union increasingly sought to negotiate employee safeguards. Local unions within the council were often free to initiate bargaining themselves, sometimes resulting in a patchwork quilt of supplemental agreements. These memoranda of understanding became part of the agreement, and in some cases appeared to contradict one another from region to region. It was clear that new approaches to supplement traditional collective bargaining ought to be examined. This was particularly the case where uniform interpretation and application was not a principle criterion.

## THE GENESIS OF EIQI

### The Winds of Change

The climate of labor-management relations in the DOL suggested the need for change through the late 1980s, reflecting trends in the society at large. Both human and fiscal resources were becoming more scarce. The restrictive budgets of the post–Gramm-Rudman era challenged federal managers to do more with less. As the gap between federal and private sector pay widened, agencies noted an increased brain drain of skilled employees leaving government jobs. Recruiting and retention problems led agencies to offer incentives such as hiring bonuses and special pay rates in certain occupational and geographic areas. Where private sector firms like General Motors and Xerox saw market share erode in the face of diminished productivity and increased foreign competition, the Department of Labor and its agencies struggled to retain "market share" in the face of increased competition for Congressional budget dollars.

Through the 1980s, American businesses increasingly sought alternative management models which would increase quality and productivity.
As the Japanese had done before them, firms like Xerox, Ford, and
Motorola turned to proponents of the total quality philosophy, such as
Deming, Juran, and Crosby. In 1987, the federal government took its first
steps toward total quality. President Reagan signed an executive order
mandating governmentwide productivity increases over a five-year
period. The Federal Quality Institute was created to encourage new
approaches to government management. These organizations served to
foster and promote improved methods of management.

At the Department of Labor, the mandate for productivity gains was
met with a variety of responses. Some agencies formed regional and
national productivity improvement committees. These groups met to draft
improvement goals and establish performance measures. In a few cases,
teams considered the difficult issue of defining quality in a regulatory and
service environment. In other agencies, officials believed that productivity improvement was simply a matter of more closely enforcing existing
management policies. Some agencies felt that they were already improving productivity and needed no change.

In the summer of 1989, the NCFLL was not focusing closely on the
issues of productivity and quality improvement. Although the council had
representatives on national and regional improvement committees, there
were few recommendations coming from these groups which impacted
either the contract or working conditions generally. By chance, one
NCFLL official, Bruce Waltuck, had been invited that May to attend the
Federal Quality Conference, sponsored by the Federal Quality Institute
and the PCMI. Waltuck was then a vice president of the council, and
served on a regional productivity improvement committee. The conference experience provided a wealth of information on total quality management, which was reported back to the union.

November 1989 saw the NCFLL celebrating its 25th anniversary of collective bargaining with the DOL. As the union planned a dinner event in
Washington, they considered a special joint event which would bring union
and management officials together for the occasion. On Waltuck's recommendation, Council President Jesse Rios met with DOL Assistant Secretary
for Administration and Management Tom Komarek. The NCFLL proposed
a one-day orientation on employee involvement and operational improvement, to coincide with the union's 25th anniversary celebration. The

Department welcomed the proposal since one of its stated objectives that year was to extend quality of work life and total quality management to the field organizations.

Jim Armshaw, then the newly appointed coordinator for quality of work life (QWL) initiatives in the Washington area, was asked to develop this orientation seminar. Armshaw knew that the NCFLL had rejected earlier DOL proposals for quality of work life initiatives. These earlier proposals called for involvement by both the national office and field labor organizations. They proposed various cooperative program structures, and led eventually to a departmentwide QWL initiative in the Washington metropolitan area with the headquarters' union, AFGE Local 12. The NCFLL had listened to these proposals, but declined to participate at that time. Based on their limited experiences with small QWL initiatives, the council felt that employee and union interests were not being well served through this structure.

In planning the orientation seminar, Armshaw recognized the need for neutral third-party presenters. These experts had to have strong backgrounds in both organizational change and labor-management cooperation. Two professional consultants who had impeccable reputations and were highly regarded by the AFL-CIO and AFGE were chosen. Both Ed Cohen-Rosenthal and Sue Clark had worked with DOL agencies on the headquarters' QWL initiative. From its inception, the orientation was designed around the "mutual gains" philosophy. These principles recognize both the individual prerogatives of the parties, and their common areas of interest.[2]

That orientation marked the real beginning of the DOL-NCFLL employee involvement-quality improvement effort. The session was attended by Labor Secretary Elizabeth Dole and AFGE President John Sturdivant, both of whom expressed strong support. The NCFLL leadership attended, along with nearly 80 union and management representatives from the field agencies of the department. Together and in breakout sessions, the participants were introduced to the concepts of quality improvement and participation through labor-management cooperation.

---

[2]Edward Cohen-Rosenthal and Cynthia Burton, *Mutual Gains: A Guide to Union-Management Cooperation*, 2nd ed. (Ithaca, NY: ILR Press, 1993).

Simple brainstorming and consensus techniques generated lists of opportunities for improvement, elements of success, and barriers to achieving the goals.

As plans for the initial orientation seminar progressed, the NCFLL made no commitment other than to attend and listen. They understood however, that the department hoped to use the seminar as a starting point for a journey towards quality and cooperation. As a follow-up to the orientation, NCFLL President Rios named Bruce Waltuck as the NCFLL representative to work with Armshaw. Together, this two-person team would jointly research, develop, and present options for a new cooperative effort. The intent was for this union-management team to reach agreement on a proposal and then obtain the support of the NCFLL and DOL leadership communities. While this approach committed neither the Department nor the NCFLL to a specific course of action, it provided the opportunity to begin working together. Both parties were free to withdraw at any time. This approach also gave a great deal of freedom to consider options for a cooperative initiative.

## EIQI DEVELOPMENT

### *Examining Options*

Both the Department of Labor and the National Council of Field Labor Locals wanted a comprehensive system for employee involvement and quality improvement. Given the diversity of the field activities of the DOL, any quality initiative would have to be flexible and not totally prescriptive. Given the diversity of organizational cultures among the field agencies of the DOL, there had to be an opportunity for each agency to craft the particular approach to empowerment and improvement best suited to its interests.

The NCFLL had very little experience with joint labor-management initiatives prior to the development of EIQI. The majority of council officers at the time had risen to leadership under the adversarial model of labor-management relations. Their paradigm, often validated by experience, suggested that management officials could not be relied upon to negotiate openly or share information fully. In January of 1990, the notion of cooperating with management, of building mutual commitment and trust for quality improvement, was foreign to most NCFLL leaders.

At the regional or local level, there were exceptions to this experience. The San Francisco region of the Wage-Hour division had successfully negotiated a prototype employee involvement effort with the NCFLL local affiliate. In the early 1980s, Waltuck had worked in a Wage-Hour office which promoted such quality improvement concepts as teamwork, brainstorming, root-cause analysis, and consensus.

During January 1990, the DOL and NCFLL representatives, Armshaw and Waltuck, began meeting regularly in Washington. They examined a wide array of existing models for employee involvement and quality improvement. They studied union-management efforts in both public and private sectors. They wanted to learn from those that failed as well as those that were succeeding. To bring extensive knowledge of change processes within a context of labor-management cooperation, the representatives engaged Ed Cohen-Rosenthal. Ed was also at that time an assistant to the president of the International Union of Bricklayers and Allied Craftsmen, and a noted author and consultant in labor-management cooperation.

Throughout the process of evaluation and development, Armshaw and Waltuck were mindful of their organizations' concerns. The Department of Labor was motivated by the objective of enhancing its relationship with the NCFLL and improving the quality of departmental operations. At the same time, the DOL was concerned about the utilization of its resources. Given the far-flung organization of the department's field activities, both geographic and cost considerations had to be accounted for.

The NCFLL had its share of concerns as well. Chief among these was the fear that an initiative which might directly involve bargaining unit employees in problem solving with managers might undercut the necessity for the union. Or worse, that the union's legal entitlement to be informed of changes in working conditions (and the attendant right to negotiate impact and implementation) might be eroded or ignored. Some union leaders expressed a more subtle concern. They argued that a cooperative, rather than arm's-length, relationship with management could co-opt the union's sovereignty. The NCFLL could be perceived by its constituents as part of the problem, rather than part of the solution. Perhaps the most serious concern among union leaders was that bargaining unit jobs could be cut as a result of quality improvement. While there was little empirical evidence to support this, union officials did not want management's "more with less" philosophy to mean less NCFLL membership.

There was one area which represented both a fear and an interest. Management and union leaders hoped to find the means to jointly address issues which might otherwise be prohibited topics of collective bargaining. Management recognized the union's legitimate interests in the impact of new work technologies and security measures, for example. A cooperative labor-management initiative might provide the means to address these issues in a new and meaningful way, without establishing negotiation precedent.

## Elements of Success

In addition to examining various approaches to employee participation and quality improvement, the union and management representatives had to consider the task of actually implementing the new system. After receiving recommendations from others in their organizations, they brainstormed a list of what it would take to make this new effort succeed. The first element of success was top-level commitment. Both union and management agreed that supervisors and rank-and-file employees had excellent "bull barometers." People would know in short order if their leaders meant what they said, or were just paying lip service to the fad of the week. The second key element of success was the commitment of adequate resources. Starting a wide-scale quality initiative clearly required considerable time and money for training and travel. Measurable benefits might take a long time to appear.

There were two other significant elements of success listed to address union concerns. If employees were going to get involved in quality improvement teams, they would have to take time away from regular job duties. This might lead to a short-term reduction in productivity. Consequently, no employees could suffer any adverse impact as a result of participating in the new quality effort. In addition, the union wanted an assurance that jobs would not be lost as a result of any quality improvements. This was considered critical to the rank-and-file acceptance of any cooperative effort.

# THE EIQI MODEL

## Overview

As previously stated, the EIQI system had to be flexible enough to accommodate the varied interests of the department's agencies and local NCFLL affiliates. Rather than being singularly prescriptive, EIQI was designed to provide a "toolbox" of component concepts. In this way, an agency would be free to implement a highly structured TQM approach, based on statistical analysis and structured problem solving. Another agency might implement a more loosely structured initiative, focused on broad employee participation, with few ground rules. So long as the basic precepts were included, EIQI could assume a variety of forms.

At its core, EIQI is built around a lean and unique system of governance. It has no policy manual, but it relies on a set of clearly-defined normative behaviors. The architecture of EIQI rests on a foundation of principles, values, and intentions.

## Agency Union-Management Pairs

Any system of employee involvement and quality improvement had to have a *governance*, or administrative component—people representing the respective institutions of union and management who would have the responsibility to oversee day-to-day developments. In some cases, these individuals might also have policy-making responsibilities, in concert with their union and management constituencies. The most common approach to governing a cooperative labor-management endeavor is some form of steering committee. Indeed, the Department of Labor was involved with quality of work life steering committees in its national office partnership with AFGE Local 12. Committees there have equal numbers of union and management representatives. Neither the DOL nor NCFLL wanted the field employee involvement and quality improvement initiative to be burdened with unwieldy committees. They did not want to adopt the steering committee model at the agency level. Such large groups often made consensus difficult to achieve, and the geographic dispersion of NCFLL representatives made frequent meetings both difficult and costly.

> The NCFLL and the Department recognize the need to build cooperative and participative work relationships among employees, union officials, and managers. Together, we share the goals of improving employee morale and motivation, enhancing Department operations, work processes, and service to the public, by making continuous improvements in our products, services, and work environment. . . . Both labor and management can benefit from this joint initiative, and it is in their mutual interest to support it.
>
> Source: EIQI Joint Statement of Purpose, August 6, 1990.

Instead, the DOL and NCFLL representatives agreed on a model that stripped the steering committee concept to its absolute minimum. Every aspect of governance, from initial development through implementation and day-to-day administration issues, would be handled by a union-management pair (UMP) within each agency. These partners would typically be senior management and senior union officials. The union partner in the pair would carry the backing of the NCFLL president, and represent the interests of the union in all EIQI matters. The management partner in the pair would be empowered by the assistant secretary of their agency to speak for the agency in developing and implementing EIQI. Together, the partners of a union-management pair would effectively function as a two-person steering committee for their agency. Communicating broadly with their respective constituencies, the union-management pair would operate by consensus. This helped achieve the overall EIQI goal of minimal bureaucracy.

In addition to the national union-management pairs, agencies could also designate regional union-management pairs. These pairs would work in concert with their national counterparts. The designation of regional pairs reflected the sometimes significant differences in organizational and operational cultures from region to region within each DOL agency. It also accounted for the significant distances between regional office cities, which a single union-management pair could not administer alone.

In its design, EIQI recommended the designation of union-management pair partners in each major agency, with nationwide responsibility. While it was not required, it was hoped that union-management pairs would be appointed at each organizational level in the field agencies as well. This included regional and area offices, as well as the national agency level.

## National Executive Committee

Initially, union-management pairs were named in the DOL agencies listed earlier in this chapter. Management designees were sought who had senior status and were knowledgeable of their agency's field organization. Similarly, the union sought representatives with comparable knowledge and experience. These 12 people were brought together to form EIQI's top governing body, the National Executive Committee (NEC). The NEC would work to achieve department-level coordination and administration of EIQI. This committee would also serve as a forum for general policy questions, and the resolution of common problems. It was also intended to be a clearinghouse for exchanging information on EIQI between agencies. The NEC would meet three to four times per year, rotating the meetings among cities where DOL regional offices were located. In this way, the union-management pairs could also spend time with local agency managers and union officials.

Cochairing the EIQI National Executive Committee were the NCFLL president and the Deputy Secretary of Labor. In the absence of the Deputy Secretary, another appropriate designee of the secretary could serve as a substitute (as had Tom Komared, Assistant Secretary for Administration and Management, on several occasions). The EIQI model also provided for two full-time coordinators, who would serve as staff to the NEC during the committee's meetings, and support its other activities as needed. On a day-to-day basis, the coordinators would handle departmentwide EIQI administration and coordination. At the direction of the NCFLL president, the union's NEC members would work with their EIQI coordinator. The coordinators would provide expertise in such areas as organizational development for EIQI, training design and delivery, facilitation, and team building.

## Linkage to Labor-Management Relations

Early in the development of EIQI, a fundamental question had to be answered: would this new cooperative venture be in or out of the collective bargaining agreement? Reviewing the scarce literature at the time gave no clear-cut answer. Neither did the review of existing total quality efforts. Some quality efforts, like the quality improvement partnership between the Internal Revenue Service and the National Treasury Employees' Union, were written into their organizations' labor-management contracts. Others, like the total quality agreement between the Bakery, Confectionary, and Tobacco Workers Union and RJR Nabisco, were excluded from the contract. The DOL quality of work life agreement with AFGE Local 12 was articulated in a negotiated memorandum of understanding.

The DOL and NCFLL wanted their employee involvement/quality improvement system to encourage cooperative, consensus behavior. A quality improvement system placed within the confines of a collective bargaining agreement would immediately attach rights and responsibilities to both union and management. Consequently, disputes under such a system may be entitled to the statutory rights of third-party problem resolution (grievance, arbitration, unfair labor practice charge, etc.). The exercise of such rights of grievance and appeal were not consistent with the emerging philosophy of EIQI. Consequently, the DOL and NCFLL decided to create EIQI outside the framework of their contract. By building a system predicated solely on the commitment and trust of the parties, it was hoped that issues would be resolved collaboratively. This represented a change in the dynamic of third-party problem resolution and would further enhance the cooperative relationship.

It should be clear then that EIQI stands in contrast to traditional labor-management relations. By its very definition, EIQI seeks to supplement, not replace, the DOL-NCFLL collective bargaining agreement. But where the union contract is based on rights and positions, EIQI is based on trust and commitment. In traditional labor-management relations, law, regulation, and contract language provide the criteria to evaluate issues. Under EIQI, however, the parties spend much of their time addressing issues which are outside the scope of the contract or the federal collective bargaining statute.

Essentially, EIQI is a relational system. Union and management partners must learn to build trust and mutual respect together. They must learn the intricacies of their organizations' interests, and the techniques of effective communication. The union-management pairs must develop both personal and professional relationships. It is within the context of these relationships, or partnerships, that issues under the EIQI system are raised, tested, and resolved.

With the EIQI system squarely outside the contract, linkages between the two systems had to be defined. If the DOL and NCFLL wanted to try the new cooperative process to reach a consensus, there had to be a clear way to suspend legal bargaining rights while an EIQI team worked on the issue. Decisions of EIQI teams would have to be reviewed by appropriate union and management officials prior to implementation in case either side felt their contractual rights might be adversely impacted. In that event, the EIQI process would have to yield to traditional bargaining. The

**FIGURE 1**
*NCFLL-USDOL EIQI System*
*Labor-Management Relations (LRM) and Employee Involvement/Quality Improvement (EIQI)*

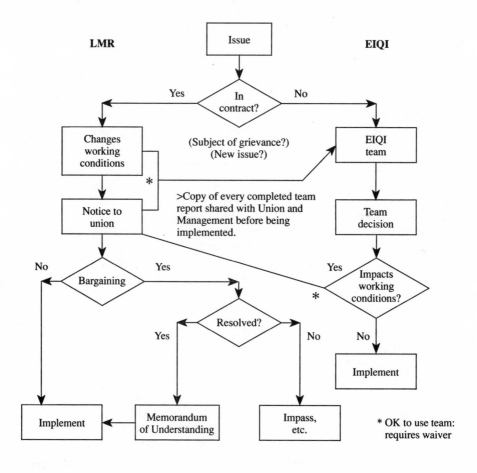

Source: Flowchart by Bruce A. Waltuck, 1991.

linkages between EIQI and the labor-management relations process at the Department of Labor are graphically illustrated in the flow chart shown in Figure 1.

## *Cornerstones of EIQI*

The evaluation of various quality efforts by the NCFLL and DOL coordinators suggested that there were a number of factors common to successful quality systems. These became the foundation of EIQI. They were:

- *Decisions by consensus.* This was absolutely necessary to empower employees and move away from the hierarchical model of management behavior. More than a mere decision-making technique, the use of consensus was an essential EIQI value.
- *Problem solving/process improvement teams.* It was envisioned that most work under EIQI would be accomplished by teams. These teams would include both managers and bargaining unit employees. It was envisioned that team issues could be initiated in a number of ways. Issues could flow top down, that is, from agency or higher leadership down to the level of the team, or bottom up, where issues would be self-initiated by the teams and directed to higher-level authority.
- *Structured approach to decision making.* As EIQI evolved, there was a concern that team members would have a tendency to substitute their perceived wisdom about a process, rather than seek fundamental knowledge of the process. There was also a desire to maximize the efficiency of the team approach. Consequently, EIQI would encourage the use of a structured technique to reach a decision. In various forms, these are all variations on the "plan-do-check-act" cycle fundamental to total quality efforts.
- *Union-management partnership.* Building this partnership lies at the very heart of EIQI. If the DOL and NCFLL were going to cooperate at all, it had to be on an equal footing. Where there were areas of mutual interest between the parties, those interests had to be in balance.[3] Practically speaking, union-management partnership meant that consensus had to be obtained on every decision. Every EIQI development, from training courses, to consultant selection, to meeting agendas would have to be jointly supported.

---

[3]Ibid.

- *Voluntary participation.* Some experts on employee involvement and quality improvement argue that one can not achieve "total" quality unless every employee in the organization is involved.[4] The NCFLL and DOL were both concerned about mandating participation in a system that was not included in their contract. Consequently, the parties agreed to make individual participation in EIQI voluntary. This would not limit the ability of any agency to craft employee performance standards which encouraged contributions to quality improvement.

- *Customer focus.* Much of the field activity of the Department of Labor is investigatory. In many cases, penalties or violations are assessed. Prior to EIQI, the notion of customer service in this context was not well understood by the parties. Under EIQI, the concepts of internal and external customer relationships—everyone from coworkers to Congress to the general public—became essential. Enhanced service to the department and the union's customers was part of EIQI's overall improvement strategy.

## EIQI RESULTS

### Agency Examples

Following are brief descriptions of EIQI implementation in several DOL agencies to date:

**Wage-Hour Division.** At the same time that the DOL and NCFLL coordinators were developing EIQI, the wage-hour division of the Employment Standards Administration was preparing its own quality management journey. The Assistant Secretary for Employment Standards had come to the DOL from General Motors, where he had worked in their joint-venture plant with Toyota. Together with the designated Wage-Hour administrator, they formulated a plan to make Wage-Hour world-class. Working with union leaders and private consultants Sarah Evanoff and

---

[4]Patrick Townsend and Joan Gebhardt, *Commit to Quality* (New York: John Wiley and Sons, 1990), pp. 19–20.

Dave Leslie, a quality management curriculum was developed under the EIQI framework which introduced TQ concepts, team building, problem solving, and union-management partnership. The NCFLL was fully included in the development and delivery of the training course, which cascaded top-down throughout the organization. In less than a year, Wage-Hour trained every one of its 1,600 employees for a full week on quality management. Regional union-management pairs were designated, and quality management teams formed throughout the agency. Within six months of implementation, more than 250 teams were functioning.

The majority of these self-managing teams chose to focus on issues of work process improvement. Significant results were achieved in many areas. One excellent example involved a plan to reduce the inventory of complaints pending investigation. As an enforcement agency, Wage-Hour frequently receives complaints from the public alleging violations of its laws. If the complaints have to wait too long for resolution, the interests of many people may suffer. A quality management team working on this issue reengineered the work process. They decided to move away from the traditional individual investigative approach, and use a peer assistance committee to expedite the resolution of certain investigations. The cycle time for complaint resolution was improved significantly. The result was a savings of investigator time, which equates to fiscal resources.

Unfortunately, the top-level drive to quality diminished in Wage-Hour when the politically appointed progenitors of the movement left. Although successors state their ongoing support for quality management, resources for training have dried up. Agency budget constraints have curtailed employee travel to attend team meetings. Moreover, some managers refused to acknowledge consensus or implement otherwise appropriate team decisions. In a number of regions, supervisors have pressured employees (subtly and otherwise) to forego quality management and return to the "business" of Wage-Hour. In some cases, the union has formed regional EIQI councils, or committees, to work on these problems. In other cases, issues have been addressed by the union-management pair at the national level. These methods have met with varying success at resolving the problems.

The consequence of these behaviors should be obvious. Where supervisors continue to encourage quality management, and promptly implement the changes decided by teams, Wage-Hour's EIQI effort is flourishing. The San Francisco region of Wage-Hour received a Federal Quality Improvement Prototype award in 1992. The application for the award spoke about the agency's partnership with the NCFLL. In those areas where commitment has not been strong, morale and support for quality management have suffered.

***Mine Safety and Health Administration.*** Union-management pairs were named in 16 MSHA districts, for two divisions, and at technical support and administrative centers outside Washington. An EIQI training curriculum was developed with assistance from the EIQI coordinators and agency training staff. The training included segments on group dynamics and team building, problem solving, quality analysis tools, and labor-management partnership. Union-management pairs were provided with training, both on EIQI concepts, and on replicating the training in their home districts. The pairs were asked to cascade this training downward in their own organizations. In addition to this training experience, the group of union-management pairs was put to work as a project team to tackle one of the most troublesome processes in the agency. This particular work process, part of the mine inspection reporting procedures, had been the subject of labor-management controversy for several years, but the agency and the NCFLL had been unsuccessful in resolving the matter through the traditional labor-management process. In a series of meetings which were conducted as part of MSHA's EIQI training, the agency's EIQI team had redesigned the process in a way that was appealing to both management and the union. Field testing of the procedure was approved with NCFLL concurrence, and evaluation done. The results were overwhelmingly positive, and national implementation is underway.

The Mine Safety and Health example illustrates EIQI functioning as intended. Issues can be moved from traditional labor-management relations processes to EIQI, or from EIQI back to labor-management relations (LMR). An issue under the contract was handed over to an EIQI team, which crafted a successful consensus. Both union and management reviewed the procedure before implementation, and endorsed further implementation and development. The underlying interests of the parties, which had never been fully explored in the traditional adversarial process, were expressed and addressed. This process constituted a rather special case, since the majority of EIQI issues were then beyond the scope of traditional collective bargaining.[5]

---

[5]The scope of bargaining in the federal sector was expanded by Presidential Executive 12871 dated October 1, 1993, which directed federal managers to bargain on so-called permissive subjects of bargaining.

*Occupational Safety and Health Administration.* The union-management pair in this agency selected an EIQI initiative based more on employee involvement than strict TQM. To achieve this aim, most regions designated not only regional union-management pairs for EIQI, but pairs at the local office level. Union-management-approved training in EIQIwas delivered to all regional union-management pairs first. Then each region developed its own training. In some cases, the initial training was cascaded down through a region. In other cases, regional training was developed with consultant input. As this implementation is spreading through the agency, teams are forming and deciding on initial improvement opportunities.

Some bold initiatives have already been implemented through OSHA's EIQI efforts. In one region, the agency has adopted an initiative which flattens many aspects of organizational structure. Traditional systems of assigning, performing, and reviewing work have been delegated from supervisors to the employees who do the work. This downward delegation of responsibility to front-line employees has included management performance planning, resource allocation, budget, and procurement. The Kansas City region, for example, used EIQI to develop its annual regional performance plan, modify inspection procedures, and implement streamlined case management and file process computer applications. All of these decisions were made by consensus teams under the EIQI system. Virtually every regional and area office has experienced a dramatic move toward employee involvement and participation. The extensive EIQI pair network within OSHA has enabled the agency to become a highly participative organization within a relatively short period of time.

*Employment Training Administration.* This agency recognized a need to align the sometimes disparate interests of their field and national office operations. To address this issue in the context of EIQI, a quality coordinating committee was formed. This small group brought the union-management pair together with national management representatives to discuss strategic initiatives. Union-management pairs were named in all regions and provided training in group dynamics, team building, and so on, comparable to the MSHA pairs. Some regions adopted a TQM approach, while others used less structured approaches. The Seattle region's TQM effort has achieved significant results. Their regional pair chartered teams on mission, work schedules, technical assistance, and peer and subordinate appraisals of supervisors. An in-house training team, working with state representatives from Montana, conducted a training needs survey. They then worked together on course design and delivery. The Boston and Denver regions have also used EIQI processes in networking with state and local government officials on job training, employment service, and other common-interest programs.

*Bureau of Labor Statistics.* The bureau initially named union-management pairs in its Kansas City and San Francisco regions. Pairs have recently been named in all remaining regions. The majority of the bureau's field employees are concentrated in regional office locations. Yet the work of conducting wage and price surveys takes these employees through many states, often for weeks at a time. The scheduling of this travel has long been a problem among employees, supervisors, and union officials. The San Francisco region used EIQI to redesign this work process. The Kansas City region subsequently adopted this process and implemented it across its regional area. The result was a new system of travel assignment that everyone supported. This improved morale and efficiency, and actually cost less as well. Both regions also established teams to examine survey response issues. BLS surveys are voluntary, and there appears to be an increase in the employer refusal rate. This issue may have broad implication for government survey efforts generally. Both regions also used EIQI to redesign office space and telephone systems. In this connection, the San Francisco NCFLL affiliate waived its rights to traditional collective bargaining and supported the use of a union-management EIQI team to solve the problem. With members representing all of the various interest groups in the process, this team was able to reach a meaningful consensus.

## SERVING OUR CUSTOMER: AN EIQI DEMONSTRATION

### Background

In late 1991, Labor Secretary Lynn Martin expressed an interest in focusing the entire department on the issue of improving customer service. The coordinators developed a proposal for a customer service improvement exercise that could be implemented nationwide under EIQI. This proposal was based on a similar exercise which had been used successfully in several large private sector firms.[6] Their proposal was adopted by the EIQI National Executive Committee in January 1992 and entitled *Serving Our Customer: an EIQI Demonstration (SOC)*. For agencies already involved in EIQI, this exercise would reinforce employee skills, and generate useful improvements. For those employees not involved in other EIQI activity, the SOC exercise would provide a "quick and dirty" introduction to teamwork, prioritizing, and consensus techniques, as well as the EIQI process.

### SOC Implementation

The Serving Our Customer exercise is designed to generate customer service improvements at the local work site level. Teams of employees with their supervisors would identify service improvement opportunities and agree on decisions to be implemented without further review. Consequently, the exercise would emphasize improvement actions within the group's span of control. In roughly two hours, employees would be introduced to the fundamentals of EIQI, customer service, brainstorming, and consensus techniques.

The greatest challenge in implementing the SOC exercise concerned the delivery of a balanced union-management message. Both the NCFLL and the DOL wanted to be perceived as taking the lead in implementing a positive EIQI customer service initiative. But the hundreds of DOL work sites across the country made it virtually impossible to have an SOC-trained NCFLL official at every SOC session.

The solution was to produce an SOC videotape. This tape would instruct participants in the SOC exercise and deliver personal messages from the NCFLL president and the Secretary of Labor. In this way, the positive and encouraging messages of SOC and EIQI could be delivered equally to all employees.

The EIQI coordinators produced the tape themselves, using DOL facilities. Union and management employees were selected to appear in the video, simulating an SOC session. A nationwide "talent search" found a

---

[6]SOC was based on the Participatory Customer Service Program developed by ECR Associates. For more detail, see Jim Armshaw, Ed Cohen-Rosenthal, and Bruce Waltuck, "Serving Our Customer," *Journal for Quality and Participation*, July, 1994.

bargaining unit employee to appear as the on-camera narrator, leading participants through the exercise. The opening and closing sequences were delivered by the Secretary of Labor and the NCFLL president. In just a few months, the SOC videotape went from planning to completion. Several hundred copies were made for distribution across the country during October 1992—National Quality Month.

### SOC Results

In about six weeks, the Serving Our Customer exercise generated overwhelming results. Of the nearly 9,000 employees in the field locations of the DOL, over 7,000 voluntarily participated with their supervisors in the SOC exercise. Some 750 individual SOC sessions were conducted using the videotape, and in a few instances, conference calling. Checklist summaries reported over *5,000* decisions for internal customer service improvement, and another *4,000* decisions for improving service to external customers. Aside from a few sessions where local union officials had not received proper advance briefing materials, the implementation went smoothly. Several agencies decided to adopt SOC techniques and decisions as a basis for further EIQI process improvement work. The NCFLL and DOL could justifiably take great pride in being the first federal organization to ever focus on improving customer service in this way.

### EIQI LESSONS LEARNED

After four years, EIQI has produced some outstanding results. In several agencies, implementation has spread to all levels of employees. Still, in other agencies, training and teamwork have barely taken hold. As noted, some agencies have seen the initial euphoria of TQM empowerment choked by harsh realities. However, the overall experience has been extremely positive. The labor-management relationship between the NCFLL and the Department of Labor has never been better. In the wake of EIQI, the council agreed to renegotiate the contract with the department using a nonadversarial, interest-based process, emphasizing areas of mutual interest. The resulting contract was the first fully consensus-driven agreement of its kind in the federal sector.

It was negotiated in the shortest time ever, and was ratified with a very high positive vote.

The years of EIQI experience have also validated the strength of the system's design. As questions and controversies arose, EIQI's definitions and expectations settled every one. Each agency was satisfied with the flexibility afforded them by the EIQI architecture. In addition, the parties' experience with EIQI has validated the importance of the original Elements of Success list.[7] The original Elements of Success were as follows:

- Commitment of top union and management officials.
- Set goals and objectives that are important and attainable.
- Involve employees, supervisors, and union representatives.
- Open communications and shared decision-making.
- Build trust and commitment.
- Provide sufficient training and other resources.
- Though not collective bargaining, union is full partner.
- Recognize and reward achievement.
- Expect to make mistakes.

However, in areas where the top leaders of the NCFLL and DOL have not truly bought in to EIQI values and behavior, support for the effort has suffered.

Where EIQI has failed to effect desired outcomes, the failure has largely been a function of the system's lack of adequate enforcement provisions. The inherent risk in relying on good faith and commitment for changed behavior has sometimes backfired. Resistant managers or union officials have been able to undermine the strong currents of grass-roots support for EIQI.

## CONCLUSION

EIQI has proven itself to be an exemplary system for implementing employee involvement and quality improvement in a large-scale federal organization. Building on sound concepts for union-management partnership, EIQI has made significant improvements in the labor-management relationship at the Department of Labor. Employees throughout the orga-

---

[7]This list is from the initial EIQI briefing package of May 1990, by Jim Armshaw and Bruce Waltuck.

nization have been able to have direct input into improving the processes of the work they do. Real cost savings and efficiencies of operation have been achieved. These achievements would not have been possible without the dedication and hard work of many union and management leaders.[8]

The future of EIQI is being written every day. It serves as a vital part of the department's present efforts to reinvent government with the NCFLL. The energy unleashed by Vice President Gore's National Performance Review and Secretary Reich's initiative to reinvent the Department of Labor have greatly accelerated the pace of EIQI activities. The department and the NCFLL agreed early in 1993 to use EIQI as a principal means of bringing reinvention to the field organization of the department. In remarks presented at the 1993 Federal Quality Conference, both the Vice President and the Secretary of Labor defined a clear path for existing quality efforts to work in support of reinvention. As National Performance Review team member Tina Sung has said, "the movement to reinvent government must be built on the foundation of quality management."[9]

Through much of 1993, the Department of Labor forged new partnerships for reinvention with both the NCFLL and AFGE local 12. Reinvention leadership teams at the departmental and agency levels focused on opportunities for organizational change and improvement as they never had before. Issues of administration and governance were addressed along with the impact on collective bargaining agreements.

In early summer 1993, the EIQI National Executive Committee discussed options for integrating EIQI with the department's ongoing reinvention efforts. This model was proposed, which was predicated on the continuing use of

---

[8]The authors would especially like to acknowledge the following individuals for their singular contributions to the success of EIQI. Tom Komarek was the DOL Assistant Secretary for Administration and Management throughout the period described in this chapter. From the genesis of EIQI, Tom provided legitimacy and support to the effort. He was especially helpful in presenting proposals for change to Secretary Elizabeth Dole, and working with her executive staff to obtain acceptance and support for EIQI. Jesse Rios is the president of the National Council of Field Labor Locals. Jesse worked hard to rally the support of the NCFLL Executive Board for EIQI and overcome traditional union concerns. We also want to thank the members of the EIQI National Executive Committee, who have championed the initiative in their respective agencies: BLS—Mike Powers (Union) and Gunnar Engen (Management); ESA—Jim Greene (U), Scott Gear (U), Sue Herren (U), Jim Valin (M), and Helene Haase, (M); ETA—Sue Peet (U), Dick Makela (U), and Louis Sepulveda (M); MSHA—Hugh Smith (U), Bill Henson (U), and Ken Howard (M); OASAM— Caroline Neal (U), and Darlene Lorman (M); OSHA—Ken Maglicic (U) and Leo Carey (M).

[9]Tina Sung, senior quality executive, and national performance review member. Remarks to seminar audience on "How Transforming Government and Quality Management Fit Together" at the July 1993 National Conference on Federal Quality. Videotape distributed by DOL audio-visual services.

union-management pairs. The pairs would continue to function as leaders on the newly constituted reinvention leadership teams. In fact, this approach was successfully deployed throughout the department, and the results continue to demonstrate the inherent strength of the EIQI/UMP system. The alignment and integration of EIQI with reinventing DOL has become a reality.

Today, EIQI supports a broad range of reinvention, quality improvement, and organizational development activities. The Occupational Safety and Health Administration (OSHA) is using the EIQI infrastructure and process to address its major restructuring objectives. The NCFLL has celebrated these efforts by writing about them in its national newsletter. Other DOL agencies have similarly carried on the use of the EIQI system.

The cover of a booklet describing the reinventing DOL initiative contains a diamond-shaped logo of many words woven together. On close inspection, you can see that this "fabric" of reinvention is also the fabric of EIQI: consensus, involvement, brainstorming, partnership, and so on. EIQI is essentially teams of empowered people using a structured approach to make better decisions together. Whatever the future may bring, the National Council of Field Labor Locals and the U.S. Department of Labor can take great pride in having built a marvelous engine of change—one that truly involved employees in decision making, and measurably improved the quality of government service.

# PERSPECTIVES ON QUALITY AND UNIONS

## Chapter Eleven

# Alignment of Quality and Labor Relations

**Cynthia Burton**
President
ECR Associates

## INTRODUCTION

Applying quality principles to the labor relations system presents powerful opportunities. Often when union and management leaders decide that they will work together to pursue total quality or continuous improvement of their operation, they bypass the improvement opportunities at hand within labor relations. In their zeal to build internal customer relationships within the work force and external customer relationships within their marketplace, they initially ignore the internal customers of the labor relations system. When looking for processes to analyze and improve or systems to realign, these same leaders skip over the labor relations systems and its two core processes: contract administration and collective bargaining. Both union and management leaders apparently don't see labor relations as central to the overall operation in the same way as production- or service-related parts of the operation.

Unfortunately, a negative dynamic can develop between a joint quality effort and the labor relations system when they are not linked. Maintaining the traditional labor relations system can and will eventually become a barrier to truly developing an empowered work force and to becoming an organization continuously improving. Usually this occurs because employees perceive a real value conflict between the traditional labor relations system, in which they are too often approached as untrustworthy employees and the total quality or continuous improvement arena, in which they are positioned as valued stakeholders. One of the most familiar, most longstanding joint arenas, the labor relations arena, becomes isolated from the customer/quality effort underway. The labor relations professionals within the union and management also become isolated from the quality effort. If the quality effort is successful, it eventually pursues work redesign and new work systems. At that point, the expertise of labor relations professionals is critically needed to insure that standards of fairness, equity, and lawfulness are maintained in the new work system.

Six quality principles which management and union leaders almost universally incorporate into their quality visions are the same quality principles which can be applied to the labor relations system. When this is done, they transform that system into a powerful force for workplace change and improvement. These principles are:

1. *Customer satisfaction.* A primary focus is placed on satisfying and exceeding the needs, expectations, and requirements of both internal and external customers. There is recognition that external customer satisfaction can only be achieved when internal customer satisfaction is achieved.

2. *Employee empowerment.* Employees are empowered in new ways to be able to deliver high-quality services and products to both internal and external customers in ways that not only satisfy them but delight them. For most union-management quality partners, this means pushing day-to-day problem solving and decision making down to the lowest practical level. This principle is based on the belief that employees who perform the work know best how to improve it. The second requirement of this principle is that employees must be enabled through education, training, and ongoing development. Continuous learning supports and advances continuous improvement.

3. *Systems or process orientation.* To bring about the large-scale change desired requires that entire systems and subsystems be tackled simultaneously and in a coordinated fashion. It also means examining entire processes rather than isolated problems within them. Holistic approaches for doing this are at the heart of this principle. These holistic approaches emphasize the synergy, cooperation, and collaboration needed among all the players and all the parts within the workplace.

4. *Structured problem solving.* Truly solving problems and eventually preventing problems are key to success in a quality effort. This principle means defining and analyzing a problem before ever developing solutions. This is far different than the "ready, fire, aim" approach often taken in more informal problem solving. This principle also means developing multiple possible solutions and using some kind of analytical approach such as criteria screening to assess their value.

5. *Data-based decision making.* Data-based decision making has three elements to it: all decisions grow out of a complete set of data used to make the decision; employees are directly involved in developing and using that data; and data is used to evaluate the impact and results of the decision and it will be modified on that basis. This principle is the opposite of more traditional "decision making in the dark" and the more tactical approach to decision making of decision first, and then data to support the decision. This principle is the foundation for broad-based, continuous, open communication and information sharing that characterizes true total quality organizations.

6. *Continuous improvement.* The overarching principle of continuous improvement reflects an organizational commitment to routinely and constantly search for better ways of doing everything within the workplace. In the long term it means improving customer service and satisfaction, improving the production and service delivery processes, and improving the daily work life, job security, and financial well-being of all employees.

When these six principles are applied to the labor relations system, many opportunities to change individual and organizational behaviors and to transform key workplace relationships through the labor relations systems are discovered and pursued. Accomplishing these kinds of changes contributes immeasurably to building the work culture necessary to achieving continuous improvement or total quality. This chapter examines five key areas of opportunity resident in the labor relations system:

1. Developing a customer focus as a means for rethinking traditional attitudes toward and approaches with the labor relations systems.
2. Benchmarking labor relations practices.
3. Applying quality principles to contract administration.
4. Applying quality principles to improve the collective bargaining process.
5. Developing a new labor relations model.

## DEVELOPING A CUSTOMER FOCUS AS A MEANS FOR RETHINKING TRADITIONAL ATTITUDES AND APPROACHES

Developing a customer focus within the labor relations system forces both management and the union to rethink their traditional attitudes and approaches to labor relations. This rethinking prepares both parties to change the ways they administer the contract.

Developing a customer focus anywhere in the workplace means doing the following:

- Knowing who your customers are and what services and/or products you deliver to them.
- Being clear about the current level of customer satisfaction with the services or products and knowing the customer requirements and desired level of customer satisfaction.
- Having a means to continuously measure service or product performance and customer satisfaction and using that data to continuously improve performance and satisfaction.

When work units develop a customer focus they do all three of these things. By doing these things within the labor relations area or function, the parties begin to rethink traditional attitudes and approaches to labor relations.

The point to start is by defining the supplier/customer relationships within labor relations. Both bargaining unit and nonbargaining unit employees are the true internal customers of the labor relations system. The union and the labor relations function are the service providers. Bargaining unit employees look to the union to represent them, their rights, and their interests. Managers and supervisors look to the labor relations function to advise and guide them as they fulfill their responsibilities to employees and the organization within the labor relations context. When the labor relations professionals from both the union and management begin to examine these fundamental supplier/customer relationships, they cannot help but begin to rethink their approaches to labor relations.

This rethinking continues when the labor relations professionals try to determine the current levels of customer satisfaction and true customer requirements. Lucky is the workplace which achieves a labor contract relatively easily and with a lower-than-average grievance load in which most customers of the labor relations systems are basically satisfied. Many workplaces routinely have difficulty reaching a labor agreement, an above-average grievance load, and mediocre customer satisfaction with labor relations.

Both sets of customers—bargaining unit employees and supervisors and managers—want problems solved quickly, effectively, and completely so that these problems are prevented in the future. Most employees won't ever and don't want to have to file a formal grievance. They want resolution of their own and other's grievances. Most supervisors and managers don't want to have to deal with an endless stream of problems arising from the labor contract in force. Everyone wants to be able to address a concern or issue before it becomes a full-blown problem that makes its way into the grievance handling system. Both bargaining unit and nonbargaining unit employees want to work within a labor contract which enables everyone to do their best, have a high quality of working life, and have job security by being part of an organization successful in the marketplace. No one values the periodic stress of the bargaining process which too often leaves the overwhelming majority of employees, both bargaining unit and nonbargaining unit, in the dark as to the dialogue and progress within the bargaining process. To meet these customer expectations and requirements, both union and management labor relations professionals need to rethink their attitudes and approaches to their traditional responsibilities within the labor relations system.

Too often common supplier attitudes are in marked contrast to these customer expectations. Often union representatives made their reputations by a "shootout at the OK Corral" approach for dealing with management. This dramatic approach often obscured the reality and importance of a more pragmatic day-to-day approach to problem solving between the two parties. Similarly, labor relations specialists employed by management frequently approach their work in the expert mode—adopting a highly procedural approach. They spare the supervisors and managers from becoming too involved in labor relations by taking responsibility for them. Supervisors and managers seem only too glad to have one less responsibility—especially one surrounded by conflict.

Both parties often view bargaining with great trepidation because their traditional experiences with it have been wearying at best and destructive at worst. Alternatively, negotiators can and do approach the bargaining table as if it is some final contest at which they will seek redress for all of the wrongs committed during the term of the expiring contract.

Finally, in most labor relations systems, measurements count only the number of grievances, arbitrations, days spent in bargaining, and pages in the agreement. If and when cost figures are attached to these statistics, it is primarily for budgeting purposes so that both parties will be able to project how much money they will be spending within the labor relations system. The labor relations measurement systems are not investigating operational effectiveness, customer satisfaction, cost-effectiveness, or the true organizational impact of continuing to operate in the traditional mode. The labor relations measurement system, such as it is, measures labor relations activity. There is little basis for continuously improving the labor relations system here.

Clearly this is a system ripe with opportunity for improvement. Customers of the labor relations system expect something different and better than the suppliers have been traditionally delivering. Suppliers— the labor relations professionals of both management and the union—may not even recognize the customer/supplier relationships they have with employees or the customer expectations and requirements. The labor relations players on both sides have defined their roles and responsibilities fairly narrowly and act out their roles in a rote fashion. As a result, the labor relations service as traditionally delivered disappoints, dismays, and in some cases demoralizes the entire work force. While there is some information about what is occurring within the labor relations system available to the parties who own this system, it is difficult to determine what this information really means. It is a system in which it is all too easy to blame the other side rather than reexamine one's own systems and behaviors.

Rethinking the attitudes and approaches to labor relations can be as simple as asking yourselves several important questions:

- How can we strive to achieve 100 percent compliance with the contract?
- How can we build a good, working union-management relationship throughout the work force for the term of the contract?
- How can we resolve disputes in the most effective and timely manner at the lowest organizational level closest to the origin of the dispute?
- What information do we need to routinely share and discuss with each other to insure that we both have the information we need to be effective labor relations service providers?

- What data do we need to develop to give us a clearer sense of what is actually occurring within the system and allow us to continuously improve that system so that our customers—managers and employees—see labor relations as a high-value system which facilitates needed workplace improvement?

Some management and union leaders will feel uncomfortable thinking about employees and the labor relations system in terms of customers and service suppliers. Before rejecting this rethinking process, these parties need to examine exactly why they feel uncomfortable and ask whether they are being open-minded about strengthening the labor relations system. It may be helpful to return to the six quality principles and assess the extent to which they are and are not applied with the labor relations system at this time—and the consequences of not applying them.

## BENCHMARKING LABOR RELATIONS PRACTICES

After both parties have begun to rethink their attitudes and approaches to labor relations, it can be useful to benchmark the labor relations practices of workplaces recognized for the quality of their union-management relationship, their contract administration system, and their collective bargaining process. By learning about these best-in-class labor relations processes, the union and management can compare their own labor relations processes and practices. They not only gain additional insights into their own labor relations system but also will identify superior processes and practices which they may adopt to strengthen their own labor relations system.

This is an opportunity for learning and collaboration. The parties can brainstorm together which practices to review, use their sources of information (managerial or other labor relations managers or the union), agree on the criteria for assessing the information collected, and then engage in in-depth analysis of the data gathered. This honest appraisal of current labor relations practices, willingness to learn from pacesetters in the area, and development of action strategies to improve current practice can help organizations improve and relationships mature. While benchmarking can be done unilaterally, joint benchmarking on labor relations can not only generate a broader data set on what can be improved but can in and of itself lead to higher-quality labor relations.

# APPLYING QUALITY TO CONTRACT ADMINISTRATION

The effectiveness of the contract administration process has a major impact on the effectiveness of the operation overall. Research conducted over a three-year period at Xerox's primary manufacturing facility in Rochester, New York demonstrated a direct connection between key patterns of interaction within each work unit and the economic performance of that unit (i.e., between cost, quality, and schedule performance, and productivity). To conduct this research, the company and the union, Amalgamated Clothing and Textile Workers Union, identified 10 key patterns of interaction which capture the true functioning of the work unit. It is interesting to note that of these 10 indicators, four are directly involved with contract administration: frequency of conflicts; speed of conflict resolution; informal resolution of grievances; and the number of 3rd- and 4th-step grievances.[1] For these quality partners, the effectiveness of contract administration is central to the economic performance which led to them receiving the Baldrige Award.

Unions and management can examine the effectiveness of the contract administration process. Applying quality principles to that process is a powerful vehicle for improving effectiveness for all concerned. This examination starts with how a new contract is initiated and administered. The mutually agreed to contract provides a standard for organizational behavior. When there are reported variances from the standard resulting in grievances or discipline, then the root cause must be identified and corrected. Traditionally, the two parties have oriented and trained their first-level representatives who handle contract administration within the work units separately. Little, if any, attempt is made to design quality in by ensuring that both parties learn the same information and develop the same understanding of the agreement. A clear and common understanding of the labor contract is the first step toward designing quality into the contract administration process. The best way to achieve that is by jointly training the first-level supervisors, managers, and union representatives who administer the contract on a daily basis together.

---

[1] Joel Cutcher-Gershenfeld, " The Impact on Economic Performance of a Transformation in Workplace Relations," *Industrial and Labor Relations Review* 44, no. 2 (January, 1991), pp. 241–60.

Contract administration training needs to have at least two parts: training in the substance of the contract itself, and training in key skills that enable management and union representatives to be effective in administering the contract. The contract training is best delivered jointly by negotiators from both sides. In this way, the people who have to administer the contract hear what it means from those who developed it. Furthermore, they hear the same thing at the same time. Even when there are already different or potentially conflicting interpretations of the contract, at least stewards and supervisors know that up front. They also understand the portions of the contract for which the intent and meaning are clear and commonly agreed. If both parties understand the contract differently—or don't really know what is in it—the probability for violations—or variations from standard—are greatly increased.

Knowing the contract won't be enough, however. First-level union representatives, supervisors, and managers will probably need training in communications, problem solving, conflict resolution, and group development to really be able to deal effectively with employees' concerns and issues when they arise. These key leaders have a common customer base—the employees—whom they need to satisfy. Building common knowledge and skills in these areas is necessary for them to be able to satisfy their customers.

Finally, top management and union leaders need to set clear expectations of these first-level contract administrators. They should explicitly say that first-line managers and union stewards will effectively administer the contract themselves, involving others only when it is absolutely essential. In other words, once the first level is empowered to administer the contract through education and training, then they are expected to do so to the best of their ability. Unfortunately, some top union and management leaders have traditionally set the opposite expectation. They not only don't *expect* the first level to truly administer the contract and handle grievances, they don't *want* or *allow* them to do so. This de-powering of the first-level union and management leaders flies in the face of the empowerment principle, of the idea that the people closest to the problem should solve it. High percentages of grievances going beyond the first level for resolution often indicate that stewards and supervisors are not empowered to resolve the grievances they are handling. Apparently as workplaces and contracts have become more complex, unions and management decided formally or informally that stewards and supervisors cannot and should not resolve grievances without intervention and involvement from higher organizational levels. Over time, little if anything is resolved at the first level. The first step in the grievance process becomes little more than a notification that the grievance is moving on to the next step. However, positions often become solidified and entrenched at this stage, especially if there is little real communication about the grievance at the first level. This fact makes it even harder to resolve the grievance at higher levels, even though management and the union are bringing more organizational power to bear at those levels. It turns from problem solving to face saving. Posture, blame, and scorecards make situations worse than they need to be.

A reempowerment of the first level in the contract administration process is necessary for effective contract administration process. At least four actions begin the process of reempowerment:

1. Both parties need to address the issues and concerns which led them to de-power the first level. In most cases, the primary concern by both parties is one of precedence setting. The easiest approach is to specify that resolutions at the first level are not precedence setting. This approach can benefit both stewards and supervisors by freeing them to address the specific situation at hand and truly resolve it. When higher-level parties are worried about an allegedly poor decision, both parties can discuss it and try to resolve it before it becomes an issue again or they can educate their own representatives about how to handle future similar situations and why.

2. Both parties can sponsor ongoing training and development for first-level supervisors, managers, and union representatives. The training and development should focus initially on making them effective in their contract administration roles and responsibilities. Then it should extend to focus on making them leaders who foster employee empowerment and help employees become high-skill performers within high-performance groups.

3. First-level labor representatives, supervisors, and managers need to have a common understanding of not only the labor contract but also company and union interests and policies. They should have the opportunity to work with leaders from other levels to shape the labor contract and workplace interests and policies to reflect the needs of the operating level of the organization. By doing this, the principle of empowerment is demonstrated. A broader awareness of interests provides important measuring rods for dealing with new situations.

4. Both parties at all levels ought to agree to continuously analyze the grievance-handling process to measure its effectiveness and determine the true impact of the reempowerment of the first-level leaders. Does it result in more effective contract administration and higher levels of customer satisfaction?

After the new labor contract has been properly launched and the first-level leaders have been reempowered to resolve problems and grievances, the two parties can apply various quality techniques to analyze what has been happening within the grievance handling process. As menioned earlier, grievances can be viewed as variances within the system, with compliance to the agreement being the standard. By analyzing past and current grievances, the parties can learn how to design quality into the grievance-handling system and how to do it right the first time. There are four common ways to analyze the grievances generated by the system:

1. *By topic.* Grievances can be sorted by the clauses in the contract to which they relate. Then a pareto analysis can determine the significant few clauses or topics that generate the greatest number of grievances. Finally, a cause-and-effect analysis can be done to determine the true cause of these grievances.

2. *By the work unit or work area generating the grievances.* Usually certain work units or areas generate more than their fair share of the grievances. Pareto analysis helps to uncover such work areas. Then the union and management can do a root-cause analysis to try to determine why a certain work area or unit is generating so many grievances. At a minimum, such a work unit is less able to resolve issues and conflicts before they become formal grievances than other work units or areas. Grievance contributors may be work situations, particular contractual mismatches, or personalities.

3. *By the time it takes for resolution to be achieved.* An analysis of the cycle time for resolution of grievances in general or of particular kinds of grievances provides additional insights into what is happening within the grievance-handling process. Opportunities to reduce the cycle time and to make the grievance-handling process both more efficient and more effective will usually result from such an analysis.

4. *By the percentage of grievances resolved at each step of the grievance-handling process.* Resolution at the lowest possible level of the grievance-handling system is the goal of both the union and

management when they apply quality principles to the labor relations system. Determining what percentage of grievances overall or particular kinds of grievances are resolved at the different steps in the grievance-handling process provides another view of the performance of the labor relations system. It identifies chronic or systemic problems. In a labor relations systems with quality designed in, few grievances should travel to the third or fourth step for resolution. Sadly, when the grievance-handling process is out of control, many grievances travel to the third and fourth steps and there is a common perception that true resolution can only occur at these levels.

All of these analyses may lead management and the union to conclude that an in-depth process analysis of the grievance-handling process is in order. Such a process analysis should involve a cross section of stakeholders who have a strong interest in understanding and improving the grievance-handling process. Sometimes labor relations professionals on both sides are so close to the process and have so much invested in it that they have lost their perspective and their ability to analyze it objectively. By involving customers of the process directly, everyone can be confident that all perspectives will be included and that a valid process analysis will be conducted. An analysis of the grievance-handling process often reveals systemic or chronic problems such as: limited and/or distorted up-front and ongoing communications; narrow or flawed decision making associated with grievance handling; the failure to apply a structured problem-solving process; and the failure to truly resolve the conflict. Such an analysis can also reveal a process fraught with redundancies characterized by muddled decision making and/or decision making pushed not lower and lower into the organization but higher and higher. Process analysis of a grievance-handling process out of control is characterized by:

- An absence or de-emphasis of day-to-day problem solving by first-level supervisors, managers, and union representatives.
- Customer (employee and organizational) interests lost in endless, ritualized, procedural battles rather than focusing on the problem that prompted the grievance and the substance of the dispute at hand. Examples of such procedural battles are fighting over whether the union can have the data it requested from management or flooding management with so many information requests that it is impossible to fulfill them.

- Grievances pushed to higher and higher levels, taking longer, and having poorer and more narrow resolutions.
- Decisions based on limited and often biased data and information, with forced, not open, communications and tactically driven information sharing.
- Trade-offs of grievances prior to a negotiation or horse-trading of grievances to resolve particular cases.

Situations characterized by these circumstances mock the very quality principles the parties are pursuing. While this might seem like a worst-case scenario, any workplace can begin to drift into a situation in which the grievance-handling system is out of control.

## APPLYING QUALITY PRINCIPLES TO COLLECTIVE BARGAINING

As with contract administration, benchmarking the best collective bargaining processes and practices of union and management partners is one starting point. Rethinking the attitudes and approaches the parties bring to collective bargaining is also necessary. Too often, the union and management negotiators have adopted a kind of tunnel vision when it comes to reexamining the bargaining process. They frame this tunnel vision by a strong sense of the way it has always been as well as their recognition that certain aspects of the process are dictated by the agreement itself, by company and union policies, and by labor law.

Bringing a customer focus to the bargaining process itself is one way to design quality into the bargaining process. Clearly, bargaining unit employees indicate their satisfaction or dissatisfaction with the agreement via the ratification vote. Both bargaining unit and nonbargaining unit employees have many opinions about the process used to arrive at an agreement. Usually they have no organized way to express their opinions as the customers of that process. There are a variety of ways to obtain customer feedback about the bargaining process—not the bargaining product—such as surveying, structured interviews, and focus groups. Such customer feedback should particularly focus on how employee input is obtained and utilized in the bargaining process and how employees are communicated with during the bargaining process. This is especially important if collective bargaining is to support and facilitate employee empowerment within the workplace.

Developing a shared database for bargaining is another way to apply quality principles to bargaining. Data-based decision making should be at the heart of the bargaining process. Traditionally, both parties develop their own data for use in bargaining. Very often, the development and use of that data serves primarily tactical purposes in the bargaining process. Less often, such data informs and enriches the bargaining process. Strategic scanning is a technique which unions and management have used to develop a comprehensive present and future database for use in bargaining. Such a database includes the problems, challenges, and opportunities of the present and the future in seven key areas: products and services; market and competition; operations and technology; natural and energy resources; financial resources; human resources; and economic, social, and governmental trends.[2] Having such a comprehensive database facilitates the use of data-based decision making. Some partners also will develop a set of questions relating to each bargaining topic for which they need information and answers. Then together they build that topic-specific database. The use of a common set of questions for which answers are sought makes the data-collection process in preparation for bargaining more systematic. When quality principles are applied to the bargaining process, it becomes a shared data-driven process rather than one in which data is withheld and used selectively to gain a bargaining advantage. Also, having this common database makes it much easier for the partners to develop one or more sets of criteria to use later in bargaining to evaluate options or proposals under consideration. This use of common criteria within the bargaining process represents another way in which the bargaining process is made more systematic.

Applying a structured problem-solving process within bargaining is another way to build quality into the bargaining process. Integrative bargaining is exactly that kind of process. In integrative bargaining, the parties identify and analyze the critical problems they face and seek solutions that can be incorporated into their agreement. At its simplest, integrative bargaining is the joint search for better solutions. It also includes the creation of a free flow of information and ongoing attempts to understand the other party's needs and objectives. This is in marked contrast to more traditional distributive bargaining where the parties want to maximize their share of the available resources regardless of the needs and objectives of the other party.

---

[2] Cynthia Burton and Edward Cohen-Rosenthal, "Collective Bargaining for the Future," *The Futurist,* March–April, 1987, pp. 34–37.

Continuous improvement of the bargaining process requires continuous education of the direct negotiators. Enabling negotiators through education and training is yet another application of quality principles to bargaining Traditionally, both parties have trained their own negotiators separately. Sometimes, the parties have come together once before bargaining for a basic orientation and some team building. Very often, both negotiating committees are essentially new groups. Experience with group development shows that it will be difficult for either committee— let alone the entire group—to develop into a high-performing group without some developmental group-building activities. Some union and management negotiating committees have jointly pursued just such developmental activities prior to the opening of bargaining. These activities concentrate on the following:

1. Negotiating behaviors, including both individual and group behaviors.
2. Communications skills, with particular emphasis on practicing active listening and giving and using constructive feedback.
3. The union-management relationship among members of the negotiating committees.
4. Development of the bargaining principles used to guide the bargaining process throughout.
5. Decisions about the focus, approaches, and techniques to be used in the bargaining process.

Lastly, an analysis of the bargaining process conducted by key stakeholders in that process can yield useful results. At a minimum both parties will obtain additional insights into exactly how bargaining really works, not the sometimes obscuring mythology of bargaining. Hopefully, both parties will recognize and accept opportunities for improvement in the bargaining process, especially as they bring a stronger customer focus to the bargaining process, lead to pursuing data-based decision making, and stimulate the use of the bargaining process to solve key organizational problems.

For some parties, it will be difficult to apply quality to the bargaining process because that process has become a kind of sacred cow within their workplace. It is fed and maintained and can roam wherever and whenever it desires. These unions and management need to take control of the bargaining process in a constructive and collaborative manner that brings the customers of the process (i.e., bargaining unit and nonbargaining unit employees) more into the process. Collective bargaining has been and will continue to be one of the most powerful forces within the unionized workplace. Top union and management leaders need to ensure that that force is used to promote the success and well-being of the workers and the workplace. Applying quality principles can be a means for refocusing collective bargaining to support that kind of future. It can bring the process of collective bargaining into alignment with other organizational change strategies and result in agreements that maximally mesh organizational and contractual practices.

## BUILDING A NEW LABOR RELATIONS MODEL

As unions and management apply quality principles to the labor relations system, the roles and responsibilities of both parties at all levels undergo significant change. They broaden to include representation in the nontraditional employee empowerment arenas. Improvements growing out of process analyses of the contract administration process and the collective bargaining process begin to reshape the labor relations system, making it more customer focused, more effective, more problem-prevention-oriented, and more decentralized.

Outside of the labor relations systems, there are other powerful forces at work as well. As the overall quality effort evolves, two new complementary paths begin to run side by side: the path moving toward new work systems and the path moving toward alternative compensation systems. The redefinition of work and work relationships and the restructuring of compensation raise important questions about the roles, responsibilities, and contribution to be made by the labor relations system and the union and management professionals within it. As work and work relationships are redefined through the new work systems, the labor relations services of both parties are needed. As employee compensation becomes more like a layer cake, with base compensation as the first layer and multiple layers of alternative compensation such as performance-based pay and pay for skill on top, the labor relations services of both parties are in great demand. The labor relations professionals have a store of experience and expertise relating to making jobs, work relationships, and compensation fairly, equitably, and lawfully structured. At the same time, traditional labor relations approaches are not aligned with nor are they adequate to the challenge presented by the redefinition of work and the restructuring of compensation.

These strong forces within labor relations and in the larger workplace raise an important question, what model of labor relations would properly support the new direction of the work organization? Answers to that question are being developed as union and management partners move down the paths of new work systems and alternative compensation in a framework of continuous improvement or total quality. No doubt the specific answers will vary from workplace to workplace. Long before a new model of labor relations is fully developed, however, labor relations and human resources professionals from both sides have important transition roles to play.

Labor relations professionals, like all employees in a high-performance workplace, need to be able to make a value-adding contribution to the operation. They need to direct their services to supporting changes being driven by others elsewhere within the organization. Their key role is as change agents. At the same time, they have to rethink the attitudes and approaches they bring with them from their more traditional experiences in labor relations. They have to change themselves while functioning as change agents. They will be joining forces with other change agents, especially from human resources. The experiences and expertise of the human resources professionals are no less necessary to redefine work and restructure compensation.

To begin this journey, union and management leaders need to do three things, all of which initially are focused on supporting labor relations and human resource professionals in their transition role as change agents:

1. Create a preliminary description of the roles which labor relations and human resources should play and of the responsibilities associated with those roles. To do this well probably means examining the strengths, weaknesses, and implications of the old or traditional roles as well as contemplating new roles. Then they have to define what roles will be truly value-adding as the organization moves toward the organizational vision of the future. Ideally, a cross section of the labor relations and human resource professionals from both parties would be actively involved with union and management leaders in defining their new roles and responsibilities.

2. Create a development process for the labor relations and human resource professionals to enable them to successfully assume their

new roles. That process would lay out the knowledge and skills needed for the new roles and responsibilities. It would also provide concrete feedback on the current knowledge and skill levels of labor relations and human resource professionals. Lastly, it would provide education and training to help them close any gaps they have between their current knowledge and skills and the knowledge and skills they need for their new roles.

3. Align the performance appraisal process by which labor relations and human resource professionals are assessed and rewarded to support their new roles and responsibilities rather than their more traditional roles and responsibilities. By this action, management and union leaders would send the strongest signal and provide the strongest motivation to labor relations and human resource professionals to make the necessary changes and to pursue their change agent roles.

Eventually, workplaces in which the union and management have pursued continuous improvement or total quality will evolve a new model of labor relations, one which is prevention-oriented and a system that serves as a vital communication link with the organization. A step that can be taken immediately is to revamp the roles and responsibilities of labor relations professionals so that they can act as effective change agents in the organizational transition already occurring. Such change will provide a renewed sense of purpose and positive contribution from those familiar with labor relations.

## SUMMARY

Fifty years ago the collective bargaining process was one of the most powerful forces operating in American workplaces. The initiation of the union-management relationship in much of heavy manufacturing transformed those workplaces. That transformation played a major role in those workplaces becoming the productivity and economic powerhouses for the next 30–40 years. Unfortunately, the processes of contract administration and collective bargaining have become rigid and resistant to change and adaptation. Applying quality principles to both of these processes can have immediate, powerful, positive results that benefit both parties. At a minimum, unions and management should explore the opportunities which lie within the labor relations system: the opportunity to develop a customer focus within the labor relations system as a means for rethinking traditional attitudes and approaches; the opportunity to bench-mark labor relations practices to learn about the state of the art; the opportunity to apply quality principles to contract administration to make it a premier problem-solving and conflict-resolving process; the opportunity to apply quality principles to collective bargaining to make it a more effective, high-value force for change in the workplace; and the opportunity to develop a new labor relations model reflective of the new work systems and the vision of the workplace of the future which is being pursued. Not all of these opportunities are for every set of union-management partners. Yet for union and management leaders to effectively lead their workplaces into the 21st century, they must align the labor relations system with their new direction. Pursuing opportunities such as these is the means for bringing the labor relations system into that quality alignment.

## Chapter Twelve

# Challenges for Unions in Quality Programs

**Sally Klingel**
*Programs for Employment and Workplace Systems*
*Cornell University*

The battery of terms used by organizations to describe their organizational improvement activities is boggling: an alphabet soup of promising programs that often don't live up to their potential. The quality movement stands out in this as a ray of hope for many unions: at last a concern for the actual product or service, a concern for the consumer, a concern for the way that work is done, a concern for the core daily frustration for many workers. *Quality* is a powerful, potentially unifying and galvanizing concept, one that has been at the base of many union histories and struggles. But unfortunately, creating a quality organization that produces a quality product or service is a daunting, if not impossible, prospect in the eyes of many unions. Although the teachings of quality gurus such as Deming, Juran, and Crosby may appear self-evident and achievable with enough willpower, the realities of organizational change are complex and problematic. The experiences described in previous chapters in this book provide the opportunity to view that change process through the eyes of the union and management leaders who have ventured into the realm of quality improvement. Their progress is admirable, as is their tenacity for finding solutions to the many obstacles they encountered.

The goal of this chapter is to examine the dilemmas and challenges unions may face when they attempt to develop a role for themselves in organizational change processes such as quality improvement, and to suggest strategies for addressing those challenges. The first step at least is clear: unions must develop their own agenda for quality in the workplace, marketplace, community, and the union. The examples provided by the cases in this book show how each union built a strategy and role for itself, based on its own values, to drive change inside the union and with employers in a positive direction for their members. In each case, the union focused on their basic interests and goals, and used their resources in partnership with management to mold the change process in a mutually beneficial manner.

Quality processes promise, and can deliver, much. But total quality management (TQM) is unfortunately not the "magical, infinitely flexible elixir" for success we might wish it to be[1]; like any other systematic philosophy of management, it does not translate neatly into a ready-made solution for every organization. And, it can be used for purposes it was not originally intended, namely to further the gains of some at the expense of others. While unions may recognize and appreciate the potential utility of a quality program for their employer and their members, they must weigh that promise with their responsibility to advance all the interests of their members. When TQM supports or complements union interests, unions should get on board. When it opposes or threatens union interests, unions should vigorously oppose it. But which is it?

A few have argued, with not only conviction but often evidence, that some of the organizational change efforts which occur in the name of quality improvement are potentially damaging to union interests, and in some cases, union survival. The issues raised run the gamut from the dangers of creating speed-up conditions due to suggestions given to management, to working yourself out of a job, to decreased union solidarity and potential decertification. Parker and Slaughter, critics of some of the changes in the auto industry, argue that many of the union-management joint efforts to improve quality and productivity can and probably will lead to speed ups, a weakened union, and other potential problems for workers.[2] In the nonunion arena, Grenier, a sociologist, documented a successful attempt by an employer to use quality circles and other human resource changes as a weapon to keep a union from organizing its employees. The result was a series of workplace changes designed to divide the

---

[1]Tom Peters (as received via electronic mail $$8E1S$##PETER /AD/TPE/083191/09079#) "Beware Politically Correct TQM" 8/31/91.

[2]Mike Parker and Jane Slaughter, *Choosing Sides: Unions and the Team Concept* (Boston: South End Press, 1988).

work force and undermine support for the union.[3] Journalists Fucini and Fucini studied the start-up of the Mazda plant in Flat Rock, Michigan and describe the production process as one designed to produce high quality, but which also produces high injury, overtime, and dissatisfaction for the work force.[4] And Banks and Metzger, after observing the multitude of union-management efforts to jointly create change, encourage unions to participate in management decision making toward organizational improvement. They also recommend a variety of strategies including a parallel union participation structure to protect the union and ensure that union goals are achieved as a result of such participation.[5]

The negative potential for unions in collaborating with management to create quality is always present, but the level of risk a union takes varies from situation to situation, as acknowledged by the authors above. Each union must weigh a complex array of factors in order to arrive at a sound appraisal of its own situation and options. One set of factors is imbedded in the local conditions of the work site (product, market, technology, management competency and past practices, financial health of the firm, work force skill level, labor relations record, etc.). Another set of factors is defined by the nature of the quality program chosen as a philosophy and structure for organizational operation (level of empowerment, rewards, control mechanisms, training strategies, comprehensiveness, etc.). A third set of factors resides in the union itself, in terms of its internal conditions (member involvement and solidarity, leadership structure and stability, past experience with participation processes, resource availability, etc.). Based on these factors, a particular local or international union's approach to fostering quality may thus vary considerably, as evidenced by the experiences described in preceding chapters.

There is no one set of guidelines for local unions to follow in deciding whether or not to participate with management in quality-improvement activities. In each case, the membership must review the situation and decide if conditions are such that the union can responsibly proceed as a partner in improving the organization—with some likelihood of success.

---

[3]Guillermo J. Grenier, *Inhuman Relations: Quality Circles and Anti-Unionism in American Industry* (Philadelphia: Temple University Press, 1988).

[4]Joseph Fucini and Suzy Fucini, *Working for the Japanese* (New York: The Free Press, 1990).

[5]Andy Banks and Jack Metzgar, "Participating in Management: Union Organizing on a New Terrain," *Labor Research Review* VIII, no. 2 (Fall 1989) pp. 5–55.

To make this judgment, unions typically ask themselves a number of questions when they approach the task of initiating, fostering, and institutionalizing quality in the workplaces they represent.

## DOES THE UNION LEAD, FOLLOW, OR GET OUT OF THE WAY?

There are few unions who haven't heard the term *total quality* or something like it in the workplaces they represent. On the face of it, such quality terminology sounds unambiguously good. Most everyone, given the choice, would prefer to do quality work. And most everyone can identify a number of quality problems in their work that they would like to correct. Why, then, do we need quality programs if people are generally willing and able to improve quality? As Juran is fond of saying, 80 percent of the quality problems are due to system problems, not people problems.[6] This is a radical departure from the philosophy of many past management theories, which have focused, sometimes exclusively, on fixing the people so that they work better in the systems, usually highly Taylorized systems.

Many unions have lived through countless such programs, and have fought the effects of attempts to speed up the work, root out the poor performers, get the union out of management's business, and so on. When quality comes along, it can be hard to imagine that it is not simply another flavor-of-the-month organizational improvement tool thought up by management to get more out of workers for less. (And unfortunately in some workplaces, that is what the quality program becomes.) Where there is long experience with management fads, the announcement of a quality initiative is an open invitation for ridicule. Quickly, a TQM program is known as "Try Quality, Maybe that will work." A TQC training is renamed "Total Quality Cult" brainwashing. *Service excellence* is commonly referred to as "servant excellence." Hence, a union leadership interested in working with management to implement a quality initiative may have to face an unwilling membership, made cynical by past bad experiences.

The challenge for these unions is not to convince the membership that management is serious this time and that the union should follow their

---

[6]J. M. Juran, *Juran on Planning for Quality* (New York: The Free Press, 1988).

lead. Arguing that the union should follow management's quality leadership, based on trust that management will do the right thing, is a reactive stance that is likely to create unwinnable battles within the union. Rather, the union's challenge is to develop a shared set of goals among union members that will guide union participation in *any* kind of improvement activities, including quality improvement. A proactive union agenda for organizational improvement allows the union to evaluate management proposals against union standards, and decide on a course of action that best advances the union's goals, independent of management's intentions.

The Communication Workers of America's (CWA) experience with U S WEST illustrates the difficulties of accepting this challenge. In the late 1980s, when CWA and U S WEST began to jointly develop mechanisms to address the changing nature of technology and work in their industry, CWA established basic objectives for the union to use as guiding principles when it entered into any relationship. As local unions tried to apply these principles to their work in joint committees, they realized that simply creating the union objectives on paper was not enough—union members did not always know how to put them into action when working on an organizational improvement project.

The dissension and controversy occurring in locals where "joint work" was making changes in opposition to the labor contract caused some union members to want to discontinue any joint activities. The CWA leadership concluded that if their objectives were to become reality, the union had to be a strong advocate for their interests, and assist locals in fostering and furthering the union's objectives. They began to work proactively with locals through training, education, and technical support to help members create a visible and shared union agenda for use in their joint activities.

It was important for CWA to create a set of objectives to guide their efforts with management at U S WEST, but it was more important for CWA to help members actively utilize those objectives to make decisions about appropriate structures, processes, and outcomes of participating with management. In this case, taking leadership at the onset didn't allow the union to then get out of the way and let the membership carry on. Leadership was necessary on an ongoing basis as a requirement for strong member participation.

Before contemplating any partnership with employers to create organizational change, the first and most important challenge for unions is to create a proactive union agenda based on union values and goals. This requires much internal work on the part of the union on two fronts. First, the leadership of the union must look forward and envision a role for the union that will best advance the needs of its members in the employer organization. Second, the leadership must engage all members of the union in discussion about how to build the best possible jobs in their employer organization—jobs that fill the needs and aspirations of the membership. Out of such discussion can come a set of union objectives for the future on which to base a partnership with employers.

## ARE QUALITY EFFORTS UNION BUSTING OR UNION BUILDING?

Even where unions have had positive experiences with other organizational change activities involving union-management collaboration, the initiation of quality programs can threaten the union. As members experience training and education about quality that ignores or bypasses union issues, they may question whether an attempt is being made to undermine the union. The quality philosophy, as typified by total quality management, has no formal role built into it for union participation. In much of the TQM literature, unions are barely referred to as an institution; rather, the emphasis is on employee participation in quality efforts. The notion here is that all members of an organization must be included in the quality process, regardless of their status or level.

However, because TQM makes no explicit acknowledgment of the role of unions as representatives of the aspirations of the work force, many quality programs deal with employee participation only on an individual basis. Individual members may make suggestions that undercut contractual arrangements in an effort to improve quality. The union is then in the unenviable position of having its membership work on quality improvement teams or councils that the union is not able to adequately oversee or participate in as an institution. This poses problems not just for the union's role as the sole bargaining agent, charged with assuring fair and equitable treatment under the contract, but also for any efforts the union has made in the past to become involved in decision making toward positive organizational change. When quality takes the driver's seat in the organization, and the union does not have an institutional role in its implementation, the status of the union as a force for shaping change in the organization is threatened.

Where there is an open shop, this threat to the union's role and power as a voice for the worker is compounded. Nonunion members and non-bargaining unit employees may participate in quality teams and committees alongside union officials, who have been elected to bargain in the interest of all workers in the bargaining unit. These teams and committees may be involved in problem solving or process improvement—issues that many unions have fought for participation in for years. AFGE's National Council of Field Labor Locals (NCFLL) was concerned when they began their joint activities with the U.S. Department of Labor that encouraging bargaining unit employees to work directly with managers to solve problems might further decrease the need for the union in the minds of non-members. However, the NCFLL and other unions, such as the CWA, have found this to be an opportunity for increasing membership in the union. As nonmembers see firsthand the role and ability of the union to push for positive and equitable change for its members (and frequently also for customers), they become more appreciative of the power and responsibility of a collective voice and more likely to join.

The National Treasury Employees Union (NTEU) found the initiation of a quality process created a stronger role for the union in areas where it had previously had little voice, except through the legal system. The quality process encouraged union and management to talk about workplace changes and issues that have always been management's prerogative to decide; in the past, the union would have tried to change decisions after the fact by challenging them through the grievance process or the legal system. The NTEU believes that it can do a better job of advancing its members' interests by proactively influencing management decision making through a jointly designed union-management quality process. The legal system is always available for those issues that don't lend themselves to joint decision making.

A challenge for unions is to bring quality programs into the fabric of the union-management relationship as a whole. Where there is positive experience with union-management joint decision making on organizational improvement, this task is easier. Quality is at the base of many improvement efforts, and the logic of its inclusion in other activities is compelling. In addition, as many employers have found, it is unions who legitimize employee involvement activities in the eyes of the union work force, not management. If the union does not institutionally encourage and guide members to work for improvement of the work process, it is less likely that such efforts will be successful and ongoing.

Each union must, however, also be prepared to withdraw from quality improvement activities if it believes that they are fundamentally detrimental to the interests of the members. The calculations required to make this decision are, again, dependent on a number of factors that vary from situation to situation. Some calculations are easy to make. When it is clear that organizational change activities are aimed at ultimately decertifying the union, the union knows what to do. But when short-term job loss appears to be one of a number of necessary changes to create long-term job retention or growth, the decisions are not so clear. Knowing when to get out is easier, however, if the union is clear from the start about why they got in. If the union developed a clear set of goals and objectives in the beginning, they can be used as a yardstick against which members can evaluate the quality process as it unfolds.

Another challenge for the union then is to involve members in creating and upholding union goals in joint processes. Where the membership is constantly informed about organizational change activities, and is educated by the union about their intentions and likely effects, decisions about union involvement become easier to make. As eloquently described in a number of the chapters in this book, however, the decisions do not get easier as union-management partnerships mature and develop. In fact, they get more complex, with larger degrees of uncertainty about the outcomes. This phenomenon makes it all the more critical for unions to enter into change activities with clear goals, and return to them at important junctures to keep decisions in perspective.

## IS OUR MANAGEMENT CAPABLE OF MANAGING QUALITY?

Where unions have made the decision to work together with managers to launch quality improvement activities, an immediate question often comes to mind: if management wants to improve quality in order to boost profits, are they truly willing to do what it takes to build quality processes and products? According to Deming, the bane of American management has been its emphasis on the short term and its lack of long-term planning and decision making. Many unions involved in quality initiatives lament that management is unwilling to make the necessary investments in fundamental changes to create quality work systems. They want quick improvements and when those aren't immediately forthcoming, often revert to the old tried-and-true systems that sacrifice quality to production. Conversely, other unions enthusiastically work with a particular management team to jointly plan and begin implementation of a long-term change process, only to see those managers leave after a year or two, replaced by a new management team that quickly dismantles, or forgets, the plans. And virtually all unions have faced the situation where top management assures that a new day has dawned and quality will rule in all decisions, but lower level managers refuse to change their ways—they simply wait it out, hoping for the pressure for change to go away. It often does.

The union faces a dilemma in these situations of what is termed *mismanagement* by some: do we stay out of management attempts to make change given that they have failed in the past, or do we get in and try to fix it despite the odds? The union must ask itself, what are the consequences for our membership of letting mismanagement continue? Are we undercutting potential gains for our members by not taking opportunities to improve the organization?

The experience of the American Flint and Glass Workers Union (AFGWU) at Corning, Inc. amply illustrates these problems. Despite a multiyear effort on the part of the corporate management (without official union involvement) to implement quality work processes, there was insufficient change in the plants, market share continued to decline, and membership in the union continued to dwindle. When the union decided to "put a stake in the ground" and push for substantial action in quality improvement, the real revolution at Corning began. After discussions between the corporation and the union at negotiations in 1986, a series of joint union-management efforts began to push for quality improvements on a variety of fronts; the result is the Partnership where union and management work on every level of the corporation to make quality a reality—a philosophy that extends to labor relations and the contract as well.

On the other hand, the United Auto Workers (UAW) worked with General Motors early in the launch of quality efforts and defined the Quality Network as a joint venture, with language in the national contract defining relationships, goals, and tools. Still, they experienced difficulty in changing the culture of middle and lower management. In addition to massive efforts by GM to change the management culture through reorganization, performance appraisal, product planning, and work procedure documentation, the UAW and GM also continued to push implementation of the Quality Network through every vehicle available, including the collective bargaining arena. One example is a contract clause included in the

1993 national contract known as *Document 40* which creates a mechanism outside of the grievance procedure to allow employees to raise concerns about quality, with redress to the top of the organization, if necessary. This is one of many attempts on the part of union and management to open every possible avenue for overcoming obstacles to quality improvement. The union was clear on the consequences of declining market share on membership in the union and took action.

The challenge for unions here is to determine the level and scope of input into decision making necessary for the union to achieve meaningful change in the entire organization. This may mean pressing for involvement not just at the bottom of the organization, or on a top-level committee, but at every level of organizational life and through every possible means. As the NTEU learned in its experience with the IRS, top-level committees and agreements alone cannot produce the needed change in middle management practices. They found that pushing quality as an organizational concept had to extend beyond their dealings with IRS management at the contractual level. The two parties began to look for opportunities to foster quality at every intersection of union and management interests throughout the organization. They also learned that the transformation of organizations does not occur at one single point in time, no matter how dramatic the moment; ongoing change, and ongoing commitment to change, is required.

Are managers capable of managing quality? As the experience of Corning and the AFGWU illustrates, designing and implementing a structure and process within which managers can manage for quality requires the best thinking and action of *all* players in the organization. The union is one of the most important players, and without its perspective, knowledge, and participation, few management groups can achieve the transformation of systems required to create a quality organization for them to manage. This does not imply that managers are not smart enough to complete the task on their own; it emphasizes that management skill and will is only one necessary component to creating successful organizational change.

## IS TQM SIMPLY A REFINEMENT OF SCIENTIFIC MANAGEMENT?

There is concern by unions that the end result of an effort to redesign work for quality may be a worse situation for workers than what they currently have now. The basis for this concern often lies in the notion of continuous improvement. The continuous improvement philosophy adopted by most organizations utilizing quality tools and principles stresses that there is no end goal for quality achievement; the status quo will never be good enough again. Each and every work process can always be improved, however slightly, ad infinitum, and everyone in a workplace must strive to make those improvements daily.

As a general outlook, continuous improvement can be appealing. Gone are the exhortations to achieve this month's goal, or next year's objectives and the consequent punishments for failure and inadequate rewards for success. In their place is a constant determination to root out problems, and search for better methods and their consistent application. But continuous improvement can also appear to be a method for further controlling the actions of workers, while placing more responsibility on those same workers for constant performance improvement. As some unionists put it, "it sounds like workers time-studying themselves—and liking it."

Statistical process control (SPC), Kaizen processes, just-in-time (JIT) inventory processes, and so on can all help to make continuous improvement a reality. But like any tool for improvement of work processes, these can have a degrading effect on the people who work under them when human needs are not taken into account. SPC documentation can be a punitive tool when it is used to make performance comparisons between workers, instead of as a tool for reducing nonproductive variation. Kaizen can speed up a work process to the pace of the most athletic and able worker, or it can find the least stressful, most productive way to do the job for each individual. JIT processes can reduce a worker's ability to rest or get away from the job for training or meetings, or it can make systemic work problems transparent in order to quickly and completely solve them.

Parker and Slaughter use the term *management by stress* (MBS) to describe those situations where continuous improvement becomes a never-ending speed-up process.[7] An MBS system is not always planned from the start, but can develop over time, sometimes from the overzealousness of well-intentioned participants in improvement processes. Or, an atmosphere of negative peer pressure can be created when work improvement processes are based on fear, rather than mutual gain.

---

[7]Parker and Slaughter, *Choosing Sides.*

The key ingredient that determines whether the design and employment of these tools results in better or worse jobs is criteria for human development—a value that unions have always tried to represent. Historically, unions have tried to protect members from the negative effects of time study and lack of control over work methods, the hallmarks of Taylor's scientific management methods. But unfortunately, in most workplaces using Taylorized work processes there were few avenues for the union to promote the development of its members in the workplace. Continuous improvement can be simply a more refined version of Taylorism, where workers do the job of the industrial engineers of the past by constantly looking for ways to streamline work methods at any cost. Used in that fashion, continuous improvement can lead to deskilling, job fragmentation, stress, and worse, unemployment. Or, SPC, Kaizen, JIT, and other methods can provide for skill enhancement, job improvement, and safer and healthier jobs, with better employment security. It is the job of the union to see that the latter occurs and to protect the membership when the former appears to be the case.

When union and management work together to design and implement the use of these methods, they can build work processes that enhance the human aspect of work. And they can build a healthier organization that provides secure employment with growth opportunities. The challenge for the union is to find out what members want and need out of their jobs, and to build those criteria into the work improvement process as a right due to members who work with their employers to build a better workplace.

The AFGWU is highly concerned about these issues as virtually every plant in Corning, Inc. undergoes fundamental redesign of the way work is done, and is expected to continuously improve over time. In their drive to assure that the criteria of fairness, equity, safety, and skill development are built into the resulting new work processes, they review the work measurement and job evaluation processes in each plant. This means that the union as a whole must have a shared understanding of these criteria, and be willing to constantly search for the best way to fulfill them. The criteria is also applied to compensation, where the union has worked with management to develop a variety of reward systems, including the *Goalsharing* concept which rewards employees for gains made at the plant level, in addition to their regular compensation.

# IS QUALITY ONLY FOR THE EXTERNAL PRODUCT OR SERVICE?

If quality is to become truly the core philosophy of an organization, the question for many unions is, "when do we get quality labor relations, or quality health and safety, or quality employment security provisions?" These systems have a daily impact on the working lives of union members; as eager as a union membership may be to embrace changes that will improve product or service quality, it is difficult to be committed to continuous improvement in one realm of work if others are sorely neglected.

Some employers launch a quality initiative when their labor relations department is up to its ears in grievances, working conditions are borderline safe, and layoffs are a common occurrence. While quality is absolutely necessary to survive in the private or public marketplace, "survival" in the workplace is necessary to produce quality. When basic working conditions are less than stable, workers are likely to participate in making changes only as long as they feel they have no choice, based on fear. They stop participating when it becomes apparent that there is no reciprocity in the arrangement. A positive labor relations climate can motivate involvement in quality improvement activities by providing a reason to believe that contributions by employees to the health of the organization are not solely a one-sided equation. A commitment to retraining, rather than layoffs or downgrading of income, can demonstrate that improvements are to everyone's benefit. Applying quality tools to the health and safety process shows that the well-being of employees is important above and beyond their ability to produce a product or service. "Staying alive" is an internal customer requirement worth putting high on the agenda.

The challenge for unions is to balance the employer's need for their members' contributions to improved quality, productivity, and profit gains with the members' needs for job security and economic and quality-of-working-life goals. These two sides to the equation are not always in conflict. Many unions have found innovative solutions to maximize the gains on both sides. But when there is conflict between the needs of the members and the needs of the employer, unions must represent the members' needs, even if it means setting conditions for their members' contributions to quality. Agreements about retraining, layoffs, or sharing the gains may be necessary to ensure that members' jobs survive the improvement process.

The Graphic Communications International Union (GCIU) has a long history of looking for ways to foster quality in the printing industry as a mutually beneficial strategy. Through an industrywide partnership, they have created quality practices not just in the shop-floor work process, but in training, technology, and labor relations as well. By looking at the industry as a whole, they have found that quality cannot be maintained by focusing solely on each shop's work practices. Quality begins with the training of future employees and the selection of appropriate technology, and continues with the maintenance and development of the technology and the people who use it over time. To make this system work in a world of low wages and nonunion competition, quality extends to the bargaining relationship and to organizing efforts.

To improve the collective bargaining process, the Graphic Arts Employers of America and the GCIU have jointly endorsed a nationwide promotion of training in Mutual Interest Bargaining techniques and principles. But realizing that they cannot afford to devote all of their efforts to current members, the GCIU is actively organizing new members and looking for opportunities to work with unionized employers to grow their businesses.

The challenge for unions is to connect the quality improvement process to all aspects of the organization, not just the external product or service. Improving product and service quality is a common goal that employers and unions can easily agree on. Quality organizational processes to get to that goal should also be a shared concern.

## IF "QUALITY IS FREE," SHOULDN'T WE GET SOMETHING FOR IT?

Crosby helped to explode the myth that it was too expensive to build or provide high-quality products or services by showing that the hidden costs of producing poor quality can often be substantial. This comes as no surprise to many long-time employees in most organizations. What is often surprising is the large amounts of organizational resources spent in launching quality improvement processes. Time spent off the job for training, team meetings, documentation, not to mention consultants and materials, can be substantial.

Unions and management engaged in joint quality efforts usually view these short-term costs of implementing quality processes as an investment in the future. And typically, there are some immediate gains. But the real payoff in terms of reduced costs, higher quality, and market share may be long term. Employees generally value these visible signs of long-term investment in improvement—if the organization's resources are not being overused, or spent in a time of financial uncertainty. In those instances, employees will wonder why wages are held in check while funds are lavished on elaborate quality programs. Unions can help to assure that outlays for quality programs are wise—sufficient to create the needed changes, but not extravagant. The challenge for unions is to evaluate quality investments on the basis of both the future health of the organization and the immediate needs of employees.

Taking a stance that tries to balance the long-term needs of the organization with the desires for tangible improvements for members here and now may be a politically risky adventure for union leaders. A clear *quid pro quo* must be available for the employees who participate in making these training and process investments pay off. Unions generally look for their share of the gains in wages and benefits, but there are other ways to give workers something back for their efforts. Employment security, retraining, skill enhancement, flexible work hours, savings plans, educational plans and other benefits can demonstrate a long-term investment in employees, as well as the business. The challenge for unions who are encouraging their members to make long-term investments in the organization through quality improvements is to create some long-term paybacks for those employees in addition to income and benefit enhancement.

## IS QUALITY ENOUGH?

Improving service or product quality can be the key to an individual organization's survival, and for the sake of their members and consumers, unions should be committed to helping quality occur. But unions also have a broader commitment to the survival of workers in general, which includes the communities in which they live and the industries in which they work. For many unions, simply confining their efforts to helping particular employers build quality into the work process does not satisfy that commitment. They are bound to ask larger questions about quality, to challenge the employer's definitions of quality and customer needs. High-quality products or services can fail in the marketplace because of faulty design or misunderstanding of the customer's needs, and result in the closing of a workplace and consequential negative effects on the community.

According to Deming, companies exist not just to make a high profit margin, but to provide a quality service or product to the customer and job stability in the community. If this is true, unions who want to work with employers to create higher profits, quality, and job stability have a rightful place not just in the determination of quality work practices, but in the determination of quality products or services from inception to delivery. Bluestone and Bluestone, who have written about how union and management might negotiate such partnerships, argue that quality is one of the cornerstones of the union's role in the workplace.[8] Their belief in the importance of quality as a union interest is strong enough to advocate making quality a strikable issue for unions.[9]

The UAW and General Motors recognize that a true partnership for quality cannot afford to focus only at the plant level where union-management opportunities are most visible. They recently redesigned the Quality Network process to include union involvement in decision making from the beginning of the vehicle design process, not just in the manufacturing phase. The joint decision-making process used for the start-up of the Saturn operation is another example of the UAW's involvement in issues far away from the shop floor, in areas such as design, marketing, supplier relationships, and warranties. These areas are not traditional union concerns, but in pursuing the highest possible quality, they are vital. Other unions, like those represented in this book, are thinking long term about the implications of technology on their workplaces and their products. They are looking for opportunities to gain increased involvement in decisions which will affect their members' ability to gain the necessary skills to remain employed, and to build jobs that take advantage of technology and respond to customer needs in a humane and responsible manner. The challenge these and other unions have taken on is to search for quality opportunities in every aspect of the work world, not just in the physical work process.

---

[8]Barry Bluestone and Irving Bluestone, *Negotiating the Future: A Labor Perspective on American Business* (New York: Basic Books, 1992), p. 225.

[9]Ibid., p. 232.

## POSSIBLE UNION STRATEGIES TO CREATE POSITIVE CHANGE

The unions who have described their experiences in this book are representative of many other unions struggling to make positive change happen in their employer organizations. But for every case where union and management have made positive strides toward quality and stability, there are many more cases where little or no change has occurred despite much effort. And there are too many cases where quality improvement of any kind is not even on the agenda for the employer or the union, or where quality improvement is only a tool to get gains that will not be shared with the employees who create them. Each situation is unique, but in those cases that are exemplified by the experiences in this book, the unions have faced a common set of challenges. While there is no one set of union strategies guaranteed to create a positive change process, unions can learn from the strategies described above.

- Create a proactive union agenda for organizational chamge that is based on union values and goals.
- Gain access to the broadest possible level and scope of input into decision making with employers.
- Integrate quality into other organizational change activities aimed at union-management partnership and power sharing. Integrate these activities with contractual obligations.
- Build a shared agreement on union criteria for human development to guide the continuous improvement philosophy. Consider skill development, job improvement, employment stability, or other union interests as union objectives for continuous improvement. Reject refinements of Taylorism.
- Broaden the commitment to quality to include those systems in the workplace that have a daily impact on the lives of the members.
- Encourage individual initiatives toward work improvements but safeguard and promote the interests of the entire membership by developing union involvement at all levels of the improvement process.
- Ensure that the membership receives its fair share of the gains from improvements. Look for investments in the long-term benefit of the membership, not only immediate income gains.
- Work toward gaining a voice in defining quality requirements at the broadest levels.

The actions each union chooses based on its response to these challenges are also unique, but the direction is the same—representation of the interests of its members as working people and members of a community. In any definition of that function, quality should be an interest to which union members feel they have a right in their workplace, as well as a responsibility. The challenge for unions is to make that right a reality, recognizing that the responsibility for quality rests as squarely on the shoulders of the union as it does on management.

*Chapter Thirteen*

# Managements, Unions, and Quality
## *A New Leadership Challenge*

**Ernest J. Savoie**
*Director, Employee Development*
*Ford Motor Company*

One piece of major good news in collective bargaining is the emergence of quality as a legitimate, indeed in some cases an indispensable, subject for mutual activity. Fortunately for our country and for our people, joint labor-management initiatives to improve quality are increasingly recognized as a major new form of progress in American industry.

But with this tidal change in labor-management relationships come new demands on both union and management leaders, and on the members of both organizations as well. These leadership demands have not been sufficiently recognized or attended to, even though they are critical to the success of any joint quality effort.

Giving quality a new status has conferred new power—new authority—on many people who have not previously enjoyed it, and has redirected authority and control from others. But with power, of course, must come its twin sister: obligation. For leaders and members alike, there can be no sustained practice of empowerment without the sustained practice of responsibility. Unless both values are fully grounded, there will be a potential to derail.

In the case of joint efforts, however, there seem to be some particularly sturdy barriers standing in the way of shared responsibility, and thus in the way of true progress. Among these barriers are such factors as the encrusted behaviors of the parties, deep-seated mistrust, bitter past experiences, traditional notions of roles, and the fear that change requires a journey into the unknown which demands too much from us. In such a situation, the factor determining success will be leadership.

## NEW IDEAS DISPLACE THE OLD

Through the 1960s, most industrial corporations probably considered product quality to be exclusively a management function. Quality, after all, is a very complex subject involving numerous critical functions, beginning with the design of the product and ending with its delivery into the hands of the customer. Many of these functions—such as the ability to buy component parts, the establishment of production standards, the determination of work schedules, and the selection and maintenance of technology and equipment—were felt to require managerial expertise not readily available to union leaders in their past experiences or positions. Nor were union leaders deemed to be especially interested in the more technical aspects of quality. Unions, in the eyes of most managements, were regarded as essentially extractive forces, addicted to consuming the economic pie but unwilling to help bake it.

So to conventional managements, the conventional wisdom was clear: do not share any management responsibilities with a union. Planning and control were a management birthright. Quality was a management prerogative.

Consequently, managements and unions had relatively little to say to each other about the subject of quality—inside or outside of the bargaining room. They were ships passing in the night. The topic was off-limits, garbed in a mutual cloak of comfortable indifference. When quality did come up at all, it was usually in a confrontational setting: one party or the other raising its voice to charge the other side with unconscionable behavior that was destroying quality.

Union representatives, for example, might point to quality problems as evidence that assembly lines were running too fast, or that there were too few operators and inspectors on the job, or that management was unfeeling and treated people unfairly. The solution? Slow down the lines, hire more people, and improve the quality of work life, the union argued, and quality will improve dramatically.

Management representatives tended to have an equally predictable perspective. A quality problem was really caused by the union's refusing to address out-of-date restrictive work practices, or by its irresponsibly protecting members who were doing sloppy work, or by the union's indifference to the success of the business. Quality will get better, management said, only when the workers and the union step up to their obligations, agree with management perspectives, and accept the company's objectives.

For a long time, then, a sort of industrial standoff prevailed. When bad quality happened, it was always someone else's fault. The losers in this finger-pointing contest were the American consumers. Far too many of them paid good money for products that were less serviceable and less durable than the buyer had a right to expect.

But as the 1960s gave way to the 1970s the ground began to heave under the feet of both companies and unions. Overseas producers who had been slowly gaining footholds in this country were suddenly capturing larger and larger slices of the U.S. market. A recession and government inaction exacerbated the situation. American manufacturers—many of them long accustomed to being preeminent in their fields—found themselves the leading players in a true American tragedy. From coast to coast plants closed, workers were laid off, families were shattered, industries crumpled, and in some instances entire communities virtually collapsed.

One of the key weapons the foreign competitors used to wage this economic war was quality. Foreign-made radios and television sets, steel, machine tools, motorcycles, bulldozers, automobiles, and countless other products were not only attractively priced, they were made better and lasted longer than comparable items coming from U.S. manufacturers and U.S. workers. Responding as any smart consumer would, Americans bought more and more of the foreign goods.

Many U.S. companies and unions faced the new economic imperative in largely conventional ways: they worked harder at business as usual. In some cases this meant brute-force collective bargaining.

But a few U.S. managements and unions took a different path. They took a searching look at themselves, swallowed hard, and decided incremental improvements in normal activities were not good enough this time. They realized they were engaged in a completely new form of conflict, and yesterday's weapons and strategies would fail. They would have to remake themselves.

Central to this remaking was the need for better labor-management relations. Companies that were prepared to reinvent themselves concluded that to thrive again, they needed to find effective ways of working together with their employees and their unions on matters that are of mutual concern to everyone.

Right at the top of the mutual-concern list was the matter of product quality. In the new environment, both managements and unions began to see that competitive quality was clearly linked to sales, job security, profits, and long-term survival. So the process of collective bargaining shifted onto a new course. Companies and unions found that it made sense to bring workers directly into the quality picture—to give them a defined and important position right in the forefront of the quality quest. What many companies did not realize is that to do this, they would have to lead a revolution in thought, principles, and behavior. This revolution would require supervisors and workers to take on responsibilities that were foreign to them, and that were in many ways the opposite of what the work culture had drummed into them. Supervisors who had been accustomed to deal at arm's length with their employees would have to change. They would have to treat workers as a resource, deal with them with unflinching fairness and respect, actively seek workers' ideas, and enlist worker commitment.

Workers, for their part, would have to overcome their suspicions about their managements, be willing to overlook the past, and pitch in to help their firms provide customers with quality, value, and service. They would have to be given information so they could understand the business and the relentless conditions of global competition. They would have to work better and produce more even as many of them fell victim to an unforgiving marketplace.

Small wonder that many companies, unions, and workers feared this uncharted journey into jointness and quality, even as they knew they had to undertake it. The stakes were too high not to try.

## PARTNERSHIP BARGAINING AND PRODUCT QUALITY

Most of the early forays into the territory of cooperation for quality took place in the first half of the 1980s with principal focus on establishing voluntary problem-solving groups under the sponsorship and guidance of labor-management committees.

For the most part, these first efforts did not have the word *quality* in their program names, but quality was the driving force. These initiatives provided valuable learning experiences, built a small treasury of tentative trust, helped unchain the parties from a restraining past, and provided a platform for expansion, including an enlarged agenda of subject matter (e.g., health and safety, education and training, job security, employee assistance, and work/family balance).

Piece by piece, based on common destiny and shared responsibilities, these forward-looking managements and unions were creating wider avenues for collective bargaining. I call it *partnership bargaining*. In truth, partnership bargaining is a good deal more than just bargaining; it is, more accurately, a total labor-management relationship.

Making the transformation from an adversarial to a partnership relationship is never easy, nor can it ever be accomplished overnight. It cannot be achieved by policy pronouncements or contract language. A partnership relationship can only be achieved over time and with a great degree of interaction at many levels.

Partnership bargaining requires direct leadership attention, constancy of purpose, resource allocation, large doses of employee development and training, and just plain "soak time."

What must management and union leaders do to sustain a large-scale transformation? They must deal in broad terms, align organizational members behind common goals, and leave plenty of room for adjustments and course corrections. They must be willing to periodically recast, redirect, and revitalize even the best cooperative efforts.

Is a partnership relationship an absolute requirement for effective labor-management cooperation on product quality? Probably not—at least not in the strictest sense. But there is no doubt that it does make a difference. Creating a cooperative quality effort is a whole lot easier when a broad partnership relationship is solidly in place and functioning.

A joint quality effort that is entirely freestanding may be under too much pressure—pressure that can result when something not related to the quality effort goes wrong or when an unforeseen turn of events in either organization threatens one side or the other.

Because of its structure and values, a broad partnership relationship offers a much more promising basis for sustaining cooperation on quality issues. When the parties have accepted the concept of cooperative labor relations, they have learned to rely on each other; there is frequent dialogue and feedback; workers are educated about economic forces; information about the company is candidly shared; and the sense that everyone is drawing water from the same well tends to generate a commitment to the relationship.

In other words, because of the wider and deeper interactions that occur in a partnership setting, the parties can create a learning base that is common to both, and can then address the quality challenge in ways which genuinely benefit both and which present serious risks to neither.

This is not to say, of course, that the existence of a partnership relationship will automatically set the stage for an effective joint program to spur quality. Even where the management and the union are solidly committed to the precepts of cooperation, there can be some reluctant players—in both camps—when it comes to a joint quality program. Union representatives, for instance, may feel that if they participate in a joint quality effort they are being manipulated to do management's work. Or they may be fearful the union might have to accept some responsibility for product recalls or in product liability law suits.

Quality is only one element in a complex interacting system and, on the company side, there may be managers who still believe that quality involves just too many sensitive issues to give the union a true voice in it. These management concerns can be magnified when quality takes on a broader agenda, such as in process improvement, service quality, customer satisfaction, total quality management, total quality excellence, and any of a growing number of similar variations (many, unfortunately, representing no more than new garb on established concepts).

## BASICS FOR EXECUTING JOINT QUALITY PROGRAMS

To execute an effective joint quality effort, both partners obviously need to have a common understanding of what they are creating, the methods that will be employed, the goals that will be sought, and the measures that will be used to keep score. It will seldom be easy to achieve this common understanding. Considerable dialogue and initial testing of each side's commitment will be necessary. Both the company and the union representatives may feel strong responsibilities to what they perceive as the welfare of their own constituencies; both probably will want to avoid taking steps that appear especially risky to their interests; and both are certain to have some strong notions about what is really in the best interests of the other side.

Quality is a very large subject, as well as a moving target. As far as partnering goes, what is the agreed-upon domain? Does it encompass more than the obvious on the plant floor? Does it get into schedules, design, procurement, service, vendors, dealers and other such areas? Who will provide the resources and who will judge if they are adequate? How will roles be specified? Who will take the lead? Who will marshall enthusiasm?

In wrestling with these concerns, there may be a temptation to reduce too much to writing. A written understanding of the joint quality program is, of course, necessary—but the document need not provide the wealth of detail that companies and unions customarily put in their collective bargaining agreements. Describing every function and every possible contingency in writing will only tend to generate disputes over the meaning or application of particular provisions. Such a detailed approach could bake in the past and freeze out the future. Continuous improvement in quality requires addressing unexpected events and consciously making change happen. The most important part of a quality initiative is shaping the future and this cannot be done on the basis of detailed prescriptions.

Briefly, here are a few other thoughts on basics for executing joint quality programs:

- For a joint quality program to work, many people who have had almost no contact with each other must, in short order, not only get acquainted, but get to know each other very well. Quality is not an endeavor that can be carried out between labor relations personnel and union personnel. It brings in new players as well as new roles and new subjects: shop people, skilled tradespeople, quality control people, engineers, general management, professionals, and service people—all with different views about work, unions, and management. Key leadership members of both organizations should be prepared to handle competing and sometimes conflicting objectives. Some special trust-building exercises may be needed for the company and union people who must make the joint program work on a daily basis. It is a mistake to begin by focusing exclusively on quality techniques and processes.

- A joint quality initiative requires an extensive commitment to training at all organizational levels. The extent, quality, timing, and delivery of such training is a critical element of quality bargaining and implementation, and is fundamental for success.

- Some of this training will prepare people for techniques that are totally new to them, and some of it will help create entirely new mind-sets. Both management and union representatives, for example, will learn how to function in problem-solving groups; how to use new measurements; how to resolve differences of opinion and judgment; how to analyze and improve processes; how to understand management and union styles and motivations; and how to obtain and interpret information from suppliers, dealers, customers, and competitors.

- The first-line supervisors will usually need special attention so that they know their role in a new joint quality process. Does production ever become more important than quality? What new quality responsibilities do their employees now have? Will supervisors lose some of their authority under the joint program? What will they be judged on? Are they once more caught in the middle?

- Union representatives also may have specific new functions. Some joint quality programs even provide for union representatives who spend their full time on quality issues. Here again, there are always questions. What technical training do the union representatives need to make them proficient on quality issues, and how do they obtain it? How should union representatives deal with workers who are not meeting quality standards? How should they deal with company supervisors or managers who are indifferent to quality?

- Many companies with a labor-management partnership relationship in place are already doing a good job of communicating with the union and the workers. But introducing a joint quality program to the relationship usually means even more attention must be given to communications. It is particularly important to candidly share the data that measures the company's quality against that of its competitors. This is, of course, extremely sensitive information— the kind of data that a company usually likes to keep very close to its vest. But a management that refuses to make its competitive measurements available to its quality partners will be accused of only paying lip service to joint quality. Its refusal will be saying, in a very dramatic way, that it does not trust the union or the workers, and the joint quality program will never accomplish much.

- Even the most carefully designed joint quality program is likely to bump into some organizational barriers and unanticipated developments. Sad to say, managements (and unions, for that matter) still tend to have organizational "chimneys" where people often operate almost exclusively for the perceived good of their immediate group. The suboptimization resulting from such chimney action can stop a joint quality program in its tracks if the management and the union fail to understand what is happening and take steps to handle the situation.

The long-term viability of a joint quality initiative is much more dependent on understanding and effectively managing these basics than it is on the content or structure of the endeavor. Smart managers and smart union leaders quickly grasp this and focus their efforts on getting these basics right.

## ROLE OF LEADERSHIP

In conventional relationships, managements and unions develop their leaders separately, with a heavy, if not exclusive, focus on their own organization's needs and objectives. This approach does not provide "together experiences" and hence is not suited for building partnership relationships, no matter how capable the individual leaders or how good the programs are.

Because leadership is so crucial to the successful conduct of joint quality initiatives, senior leaders will have to give deep continuing personal emphasis to leadership selection and to fostering new forms of joint leadership development and leadership interaction. While some education and development for joint initiatives must take place within each organization, the bulk of it can only occur in together experiences since neither party is now the exclusive owner of the agreed-upon undertaking.

A quality initiative, in particular, requires the parties to take a deep dive into cooperation because it is aimed at a central, ongoing part of the business, and cannot be handled on a once-in-a-while basis. Together experiences can include such matters as: committees and task forces at many levels; joint investigations; joint conferences where participants address problems, evaluate progress, stake out opportunities, share learnings, and celebrate successes; and visits to other locations and to best-in-class exemplars.

During such together experiences, company and union leaders work directly with each other over long periods to solve some unusually vexing or seemingly intractable problems; they learn to network together across both management and union lines; they brainstorm with a strong sense of mutual purpose; they listen to each other with new hearing; they experience critical incidents together without trying to duck responsibility or place blame; and they respond together to sudden new facts or new competitive thrusts.

It is in such encounters that leaders often must come to grips with the new responsibilities that their joint quality efforts request of them. Union leaders must do more than simply protest company actions; they now must be proactive partners who seek to make significant suggestions to improve quality. They must be willing to explore possibilities that they might, in other settings, have tended to reject out-of-hand. And they must look at objectives with a long-term, rather than a short-term, focus. For their part, company leaders must open their information coffers, not play games with hidden agendas, and must avoid sending contradictory or mixed messages. They must inform and align the whole management team, and must fully integrate union leaders into the quality process.

Senior leaders are key to the ultimate success of a joint quality initiative. Senior leaders must charter and finance the necessary "together experiences," but they are responsible for more. Senior leaders must, to the degree they can, personally participate in the interactions and model the right behaviors. Such visible participation will be interpreted as a measure of their sincerity and the organizations will act accordingly.

Today, in all kinds and sizes of American workplaces, the quality chapter is still being written. If American management and union leaders are sufficiently dedicated, they can make it one of the finest chapters in American collective bargaining and American competitiveness.

# Index

## A

A. Nash Co., work with Amalgamated Clothing
Workers Union, 28
Accelerated workshops, 102
Adversarial climate, AFGWU, 130
Adversarial relationship between management
and unions, 88
AFL-CIO
committee on evolution of work, 68
organizing model, 69–70
private asset management, and, 79
Agency union-management pairs, 235–36
Aiken, Richard, 135, 141, 144–45
Alliance for Employee Growth and
Development, 74
Amalgamated Clothing Workers Union, work
with A. Nash Co., 28
American Federation of Government
Employees, case study, 224–50
American Federation of Labor; see also AFL-
CIO
hiring of engineers on staff, 29
meetings with Taylor Society, 29
quality used for recruitment, 33
American Federation of State, County, and
Municipal Employees, constitution of,
61–62
American Federation of Teachers, "Inside Your
Schools," TV series, 77
American Flint Glass Workers Union, 280–81
application of total quality to, 144–45
case study, 129–46
formation of, 130
history of relationship with Corning, Inc.,
129–32
role in early stages of total quality, 135–36
American Transtech, winner of Malcolm
Baldrige Award, 4
Applied futuristics, 69
Apprentice programs, 193
Apprenticeship, 73
Armshaw, Jim, 224, 231, 232

## B

Bahr, Morton, 152
Bankowski, Larry, 135, 136, 140, 142, 144
Banks, Andy, 274
Barrett, F. G., 31
Behavior, desired, descriptions of, 56
Behavioral feedback, 56
Benchmarking, labor relations practices, 259
Benchmarking presentations, 143–44
Best practices, 102
Bluestone, Irving, 89
Boeing, joint administration with International
Association of Machinists, 16
Boston Guild for the Coopers and Shoemakers,
charter of, 21
Boyle, Kevin, 147, 174
Bradshaw, Bill, 132
Bricklayers Union
competency-based model for local
leadership, 73–74
study circles in, 73
Building trades locals, negative image of, 64
Built-Rite, 64
Bureau of Labor Statistics (DOL), EIQI
implementation in, 245
Burton, Cynthia, 253
Business, internationalization of, 65
Business organization, as part of quality
unionism, 61

## C

Cadillac, winner of Malcolm Baldrige Award, 4
Career development, by and for unions, 74–75
Carpenters, union label and, 30
Carroll, John, 149
Case studies
American Federation of Government
Employees and U.S. Department of Labor,
224–50

# PLEASE SEND MORE INFORMATION ABOUT

❏ PARS          ❏ Membership
❏ Education Courses     ❏ Conferences
❏ *The Journal for Quality and Participation*

Name_____ Title_____

Company_____

Address_____

City, State, Zip_____

Phone_____ Fax_____

**AQP**
Association for Quality and Participation
801-B West 8th Street • Cincinnati, Ohio 45203
(513) 381-1959 • Fax (513) 381-0070